I SHOULD HAVE LEFT THE WHISKEY

Cycling Asia with Heavy Baggage and Relative Density

Graham Field

RAMBLING ON: BOOK 1

I Should Have Left The Whiskey

First paperback edition printed 2023 in the United Kingdom

ISBN 978-0-9931993-9-4

Published by Little m Press

littlempress.co.uk

For more copies of this book, please email: graham@grahamfield.co.uk

Copy editing by Ross Dickinson

Cover, illustrations and maps by Amanda Zito

http://blindthistleillustration.squarespace.com

Typeset by Atanas Topalov

https://mind-print.com

Printed in Great Britain

FOR PHOTOS AND A FREE INSTANT AUDIO BOOK DOWNLOAD GO TO

grahamfield.co.uk

For the Field boys before me
I wish you knew

Acknowledgments

Who to acknowledge? Well actually, now I think about it, and this is the very last part of the book to be written, I suppose I have to thank every person who crossed my path during this journey. Because, regardless of how they are represented in the text, they did in one way or another have an influence on my life. Be it a remote Thai mountain community that took me in and fed me or the Muslim gentleman cycling by my side and offering me chai as we rode in a hazy Indian sunrise. Every encounter has redefined my rationale, refined my course and actions, which I suppose got me here, and it happens to be the best place I've inhabited. All the ingredients are currently present, there is contentment, appreciation, general happiness, mountain views, dramatic seasons, cats, whiskey and love.

Every person who has a walk-on part in our lives comes with a sign – some subtle, some mind-bendingly brilliant – but whether it's a direction to destruction or an aspiring alternative route, it seems to me that all encounters affect who we are and help us on our way. We follow, reverse, divert or adapt. So whether you were a happenstance for distraction, infatuation, admiration, inspiration, irritation, enlightenment, exaggeration, deception or aggression, I thank you, to some degree. I've taken something from each experience and that has made me who I am now and it's not too bad, I can live with me and, apparently and more importantly, so can my girlfriend. When I tell her stories of my past she gives a compassionate yet sympathetic smile and says, 'I'm so glad I didn't know you then.' I take it as a compliment, because I've clearly become the person she was looking for, so I must be better than I was before. Also perhaps, as a reader, cringing at my shortcomings and stunned at the occasional triumphs, you too can consider which of my personality traits and behaviours are beneficial and worthy of replicating, and which ones really didn't do me any favours and are probably best avoided.

In other news, I feel the need to personally thank my copy editor, Ross Dickinson, this is the third book we've worked on together and I can almost visualise his comments now as I write: *Were you drinking whiskey or whisky? You can't say Chinaman, it's a Chinese Man. Were the hills literally killing you? Since the distance is written in km, technically it's not a mileage marker* – you'll notice this correction when you get to it and see how I dealt with it. He rips out a paragraph I'd worked on for hours and with it my heart, but the prose flows all the better for the omission. (He hasn't seen the above paragraph). After all those corrections have been made the manuscript is scrutinised by my proof-readers, the speedy Paul Chamberlain, the pedantic Julya Walsh and the meticulous Galena Tsvetkova, to whom I'm eternally grateful as their combined idiosyncratic traits catch all but the sneakiest tyops in the text. While errors are being eradicated, the incredibly talented Amanda Zito was designing this captivating cover, as well as maps, and other illustrations. I feel honoured she agreed to work on this book with me. And when all of the above is complete, Atanas Topalov, the staggeringly patient typesetter, puts everything in order. I'm so indebted to this team of 'producers'. Like a lyricist, your song is only as good as your musicians and I currently have the perfect backing band. Sticking with this analogy, we would have no gigs, I'd be singing alone in the shower were it not for you, my faithful readers. I still attend online seminars for independent writers. The content is mainly aimed at the unknown, the up-and-coming and the daunted 'where the fuck do I even start' types. However, now having been in the writing game for twelve years I'm lucky enough to have a small but hardcore following of readers who have the faith to pre-order and the generosity to review. I get sincere feedback, you share your reading experience and in turn tell of when you've found yourself in a similar circumstance. So yes, you, without you there would not likely be this, the sixth book in the library of journeys through a lifetime. I thank you, genuinely, honestly, gratefully, you've made my dreams of becoming a writer come true. Now, if it's OK with you, I'm going to leave the laptop and go outside for a bit.

Introduction

Whiskey was the name of my first cat, I'm not sure why I gave him that name, I really didn't know then what whiskey was. In fact, at the age of four, I wasn't entirely sure what a cat was. My mum had painted a picture of a kitten on a rug so I knew what to expect when Whiskey arrived. I instantly became a lifelong cat lover, and later I discovered the appeal of the grain-based beverage too. The former is hard to leave behind; the latter is slightly easier to travel with. However, this is not a book about cats. Whiskey does have a walk-on role, but that's the problem, it didn't walk, the bottle had to be carried. Anyway, ultimately, this is a book about life, rambling on through it, and not always with the right baggage, so the title is not deliberately cryptic, simply an insight to the style of travel.

Why would I start this introduction with a cat story when it's not about cats? Well, generally this preamble should set the scene but in this case I feel it's more important to set the pace, to slow you to an anticipation of individual anecdotes and observations as they occur.

As I started to write this book I opened my diary at the departure date, then flicked back a few pages to refresh my memory and give me context. I thought, *Wow, I was drinking a lot back then, perhaps I should put those pages in too*. Travel books that won't begin because the introduction is all about the preparation I find very frustrating, neither am I a fan of the stories that start with the highlight, then go back to the inception. In this case the journey started before the introduction and will continue beyond the final chapter. There is no end, there is no destination. OK, I'm under no illusion, there will be a last diary, a final entry. The point is, this is a story that, like all my books, progresses one day at a time as tomorrow is a blank page.

So I began to think of the first few chapters as a base coat on the canvas, but then, just as I was about to leave, I found the picture I was painting required me to backtrack and fill in some gaps, and what happened next was the background accidentally took dominance. It's a bit like a bikini-clad model draped over a prestigious piece of engineering – initially, you see the flesh, then you realise that what's more interesting is actually what she is *in the way of.*

Anyway, every day is a story, a page in my diary, from cycling in India and Thailand, to stagnating in long term dreadlocked beach communities. Be it relationships, backstory or forward thinking, it's just me rambling on through life, about life, at the speed of life, I'll get there in the end. Every day is a pixel within a picture. Moods, circumstance, company and location are all momentary, micro-chapters worthy of their own identity, which is why I tell myself it's a compliment when readers contact me to say they keep a copy of one of my books by the toilet. And that right there is your insight: this ain't Twitter, I'm not limited by characters, so I can take as long as I like to get to the point, to find the point, that's the point of writing a diary, you don't have to conform to anyone's criteria. The *what page does the journey start?* reader will miss the point: it already has started, slow down, if you're in a hurry, best you go now to whatever is calling you because even when I do start cycling, things don't exactly speed up, I stop, a lot, I have to, those hills are exhausting.

Inevitably, en route there are moments of serendipitous luck and, more frequently, the times I fucked up. Travel is not about instant gratification but the reward of finding that elusive awareness of the moment that is being travelled through. Those rare and valuable occurrences that generate an all-consuming satisfaction, because there is no time like the present.

In other published diaries I've written of years previous to the time this book covers, and I've told of tales that happened after. This is another piece in the jigsaw that slowly reveals the big picture of a life on the road, on foot, bicycle, motorcycle and just about every other form of transport, public and the ones I'm paid to drive. I still use the maps and guidebooks I bought first time around, which is why I call Mumbai Bombay.

OK, stop thinking about the cosmetically enhanced model on the motor vehicle now and visualise this analogy of the two stories you are about to read. When I sit down to write a book, I generally get up an hour before dawn. I write the previous day's diary entry (which, when I am writing about writing, is somewhat challenging – I don't think that one will get published). Then I go for a 5-kilometre daybreak walk. It gives me time to consider what I wrote yesterday and how that will shape today's chapter. There is a small lake, I stop at the exact same spot every morning, every season, every weather, and take a photo of the tree at the east end of the lake. It is reflected in the water along with lightening sky and coloured clouds, from bare branches to new growth, full-blown foliage and falling leaves, then reflection stops altogether when the water freezes. The scene is backlit, albeit from a slightly different angle every day, and I intend, once this book is complete, to put a year of images into a video depicting the subtle change of seasons. Now, here's the thing, sometimes I go back in the afternoon, to show a friend the scene I've just shared with you – however, the light is now behind us and the photo is very different to the one I took that morning. What would you do, have the video of all the dawn photos, then go back to the start to see it all again? The problem is, the afternoon shots were not taken with the consistency or dedication of the morning ones. It would be a bit *well, we've seen this already and, anyway, it's incomplete*. Better, I think, to gently blend in the occasional afternoon image, to give contrast and help show a bigger picture. That's what I've done with this narrative. This is a story about cycling in India (and Sri Lanka), but the journey began a year earlier in Thailand where I bought the bike, and that storyline, I hope, is gently woven into the tapestry of cycling in Asia with heavy baggage and relative density.

And don't worry about getting lost en route or being left behind. There is a simple key: an elephant image represents a passage about India (as opposed to *A Passage to India*):

And when you see a doodle of some noodles the narrative has gone back to Thailand:

Because, although every chapter has the location and date as a heading, no one ever reads that, not even the copy editor, which is why in one book the header says Tuesday 22st December – see, I bet you still didn't pick up on it, but a bowl of noodles on the page, like an elephant in the room, is harder to ignore.

All I'm really doing is giving you an invitation to share my escapism, it's just a natter with someone you meet on the road, albeit a bit one-sided, although you will get your say at the end if you choose to review what you've read. Come with me, forget about life for a while … your life that is, you're about to get an insight into others'. Right, ready now? No rush, take your time, the first step is a small one anyway, actually you've already taken it. C'mon, let's go.

Maybe I shouldn't have done the second one
The Streets, 'Blinded by the Lights'

Oh boys, would you drink to me now here on the hill,
halfway up halfway down
Fish, 'The Company'

I couldn't pedal a bike as a child, so I had a donkey instead.
I loved the power and freedom it had
Lee Pearson, Paralympian

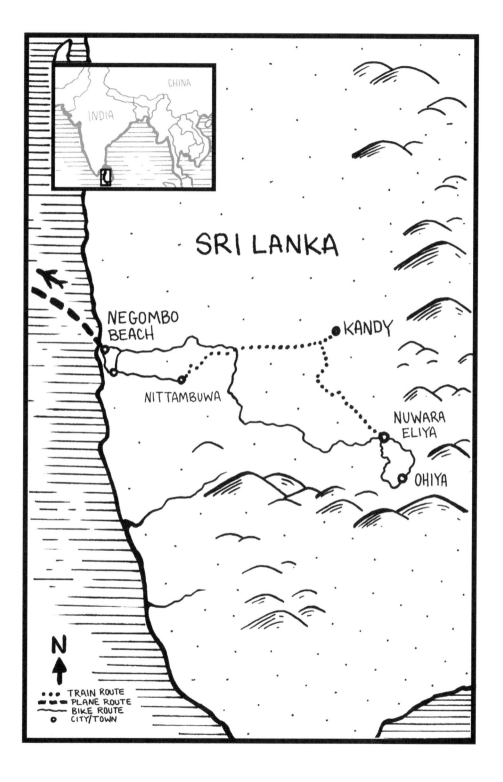

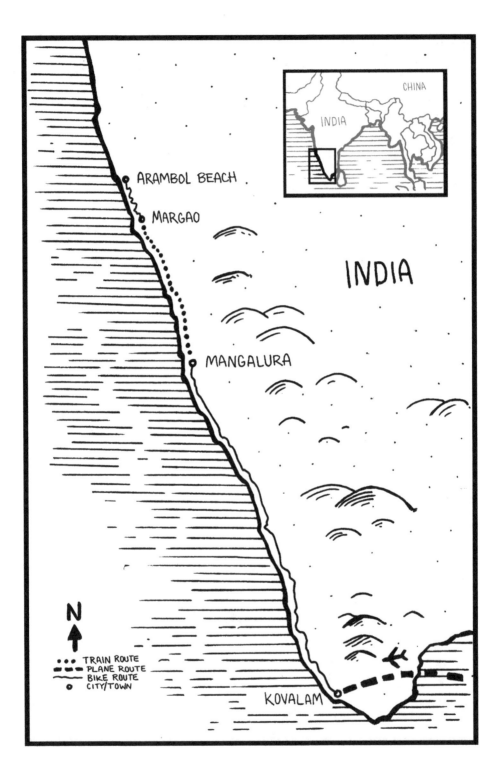

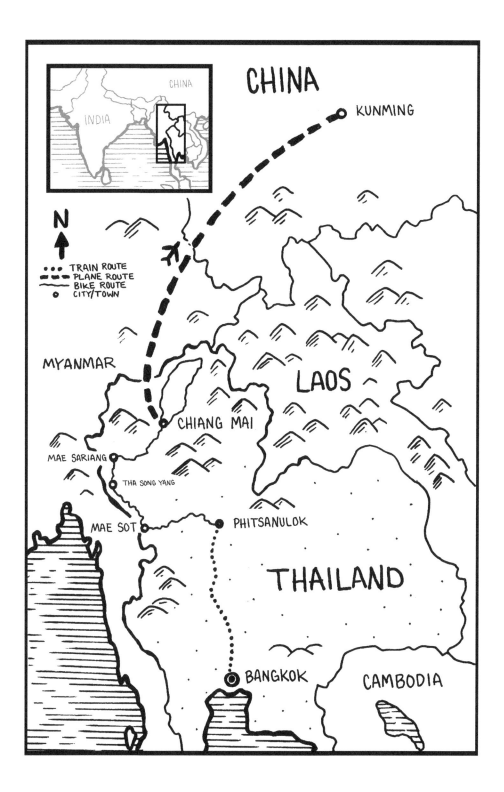

Part 1

Curtains

What's worse than being woken by an alarm? Being woken by someone else's. Sofia's, in this case. Still, I'm glad it's not me who has to get out of bed. She turns over, I caress her back hopefully, maybe I can coax her into staying but I get the cold shoulder. Touch lost on this workday morning; I have to settle for watching her put on her uniform. Damn my conscientious and career-orientated, medically indispensable girlfriend.

My days are numbered – well, all our days are numbered, but perhaps by cycling in India my number will be severely reduced. My father seems to think so, he's insisted I make a will, not so much to clarify what to do with my remains but who gets my leftovers. Anyway, the point is I'll be leaving soon, I need to stock up on carnal satisfaction to keep me going through those long days on the road, on the bicycle, on my own. Last year I cycled around a bit of China. It's a hard quest to quantify, I didn't circumnavigate the vast country, didn't even cross it. I flew into a southern province from northern Thailand with a bicycle I'd bought and ridden from Bangkok, pulled it off the carousel and started cycling. It was exhilarating, exhausting and, when it was over, I was struck with a genuine feeling of achievement. I'll be pulling it off another carousel again soon. I'm left alone in the bed with those near-future thoughts and fading memories: the independence of being self-propelled, cycling with my overfull panniers through tiny bamboo-thatched Chinese villages, the names of which escape me. I hear the front door slam and Wan King comes to mind.

I'd better get up, I have less independence in this hospital accommodation than I did in China and Thailand, I'm reliant on buses and I bloody hate public transport. More specifically, my dislike is reserved for local buses in my native country, where I don't know the route, the fare or the paying procedure. The thing is, despite the common language I seem unable to find out what is common knowledge to every other passenger on said bus. I genuinely think that I felt less anxious gasping in thin high-altitude Himalayan air as I pushed uphill and that I felt more comfortable having my sweat freeze-dried through soaked clothing as I freewheeled down the dark side of a mountain, than I do sitting on a Monday morning commuter bus in Surrey. I'm the apprehensive and attentive passenger, clutching my new phone and scanning through the condensation to spot a train station I've never been to before. Checking if the *Stop requested* alert is a button that needs pushing or a cord to be pulled when I want to get off. However, I needn't have worried – as we approach the level crossing at the station, most of the other passengers rise to disembark here too.

I've got half an hour to wait, so wander to the least populated part of the platform for privacy. The benches glint with morning dew that has clearly deterred every arse so far this morning… until I came along. I put a Led Zeppelin MP3 disc in my Discman, a dodgy copy bought back from Thailand last year. Along with the fake Levi's, the obligatory triangle cushion and a kilo of opium… no, wait, it was just the padded wedge, compressed music files and counterfeit branding. The dampness of the bench begins to penetrate as I immerse myself in the writing of my diary, a ritual I've been doing religiously for fifteen years. A routine that gets a bit sporadic when a new love enters my life, there is more to live for but less time to write about it. Yesterday is recalled and recorded, my scrawl is diminutive but demonstrative. I'm going to either need a bigger diary or a less lurid love life. The angst subsides, my near past is logged, I'm now ready to start my week, a new page in my old diary.

I look around me for the first time today. I mean, really look. It's a misty late-autumn morning, quite dismal really. The leaves have fallen from the tops of the trees and the ones that are left hang in tenacious monochrome. November is a brown month, the colours of autumn have gone and are yet to be replaced with the synthetic enhancement that is Christmas. The moisture of the misty morning cataract to some may say *hunker down*, to me it says *get away*. I'm heading to India today – well, the embassy in London at least.

I have to change trains at Ascot. I'd always wondered where it was, not a place I ever visited with a 40-foot truck, not a name associated with industrial estates and loading ramps. Elusive and exclusive, the antithesis of India, Ascot to me suggests Raj rather than bhaji.

The train is delayed. I'd like to portray myself as the calmest passenger on the platform but the embassy has limited working hours. Annoyingly, my attention is taken by digitally announced deferral. I share the other commuters' tension as we count down the reduction of what will get done today. Although the Indian visa I'm going to apply for today will, for me, represent all I've been working towards, perhaps the other passengers are heading towards work to pay off their visas.

Suburbs turn to city, I see the four iconic chimney stacks before the track ends at Waterloo and it's time to go underground. I emerge from the subterranean maze and engage my efficient and purposeful stride; with sure direction and strong intent I head to the chaos that is the Indian visa application process. It's 11.30 a.m. I take a number, 507; I look at the board, 323. *Hurry up and wait, they do it on purpose, if you can't handle this you are not ready for India. Go to Germany or Switzerland or something, it's for your own good.* Today is clearly going to be dictated by digital displays. Like a dead fish, I will go with the flow.

I'm not a shopper, and I'm certainly not a clothes shopper, other than haggling for fraudulently labelled products in a Bangkok street market. However, there is one style of shop that reduces me to the status of a kid around candy. If only I had a platinum card. Camping, clothing and outdoors equipment; quality, warm, breathable, lightweight, crease-free, high-endurance, need-specific, Western-standard, made-in-China activity wear. I do have a bit of an addiction to performance apparel. Gore-Tex … *oooh.* I look, I touch, feel the fibre of the fabric, I try it on, then look at the price, the security tag, take it off again and leave. An hour has passed, the number now displayed on the digital board is probably 383 (you always have to allow for dud bulbs, and dead LEDs) but they have processed sixty people in an hour which makes it easy to work out how much longer I need to wait. Unless of course the number is actually 888 and a few dodgy connections, or perhaps that's just its default mode after an electricity cut. The mysteries of India start in the queue and continue long after your return, not back to the queue but into your Western culture, with wild eyes and an appreciation for things that previously went unnoticed in your native country. Anyway, I've probably got another two hours to kill.

I go back inside the outdoors shop and buy some quality sandals, reduced, as even worn with socks the demand is low in November. I split my last pair pushing too hard on the pedals, forcing me and my load along an endless road. Four bulging panniers because January in the mountains of Yunnan province is quite literally freezing, which keeps the tourist count low, making guest houses cheaper, the skies cleaner, views further and layers essential. I won't be suffering such hardships this time cycling the west coast of India, I think I can get away with two fewer panniers, light clothing that will dry overnight draped over a mosquito net. Oh yes, this is going to be so much easier than the last trip. Plus, following the coast will generally eliminate those nasty hills. It's gonna be a breeze, a warm coastal Indian breeze. That fantasy of a flat road and a refreshing wind is where inadequate research and optimistic expectations meet: a buoyant crossroads. The trick is to find the freshly flowing route alongside the revisited Kerala backwaters without falling foul to an open sewer.

I spot a Mexican restaurant but decide to go back to see how the numbers are going. 487? Bloody hell, that was fast, probably raced past all the absentees who miscalculated the waiting time and went shopping. I approach the booth, hand over my and Sofia's passports and the money.

Soon I'm drinking a *cerveza* in the capital of England smiling at the India visa stamped in my passport while I wait for a burrito. I'd probably get a chicken tikka masala on my way to Acapulco too.

I feel myself dozing off on an eastbound train home. The difference between me and the homeward-bound city workers is … well, there are loads actually, but the important one this evening is that they appear to have some internal subconscious locator that wakes them at their stop. I could well find myself the wrong side of Colchester. Actually, I'm not sure there is a right side, just a backside.

At this point in the fledgling millennium, phone-staring is still in its infancy. My new Nokia 3510i has infinite functions: not only can I call and send texts, but I can change the on-screen image to a pixilated four-shade rainbow and even play a snake game on it. In addition to that the phone has orange panels on the side. They don't actually light up or do anything

22

but, much like the indicators on a BMW, they certainly give the impression that they might. As I scroll through the menu of multiple polyphonic ringtones, alerts and alarms, the excitement keeps me awake and aware. I think I feel the envy of my fellow commuters – well, it's probably envy, it's hard to say, I'll never know what thoughts go through a head restricted by the confines of a collar-and-tie career.

There's a note on the doormat. My package has arrived, it's at my neighbours'. I don't tell him I'm going away again, don't want him to fret about noisy tenants. Anyway, I'm yet to find anyone to rent my house to while I'm gone and time is running very short now. I've emptied out most of my possessions just in case, it's a well-rehearsed ritual and, with stackable lettuce crates, my cassettes, CDs, vinyl and books are all piled neatly into the shed, which means there's plenty of room in the lounge to upturn the bike and fit the new tyres that have just arrived.

The rental agent calls. He's kind of a friend – well, I wouldn't go out drinking with him, but we have mutual acquaintances, like everyone does in a place they've inhabited for nearly thirty years. He says he sacked his useless and only employee and guarantees he'll find me a tenant before I leave. But then he would say that, he's from the mould of unscrupulous estate agents and if his guarantee came with rental income out of his own pocket his pledge might be worth more than words.

It's a dark, damp evening, designed to be kept behind closed curtains, but I have a glorious plan. So I force myself into the darkness and my dodgy van, where my breath distorts my view through the windscreen as I drive to my creative writing class. I don't want to spend another seventeen years travelling behind the wheel of a truck, I want to tell tales of where I've been. The course is in its second month and all I'm really learning is the reworded and repeated mantra: 'You will never amount to anything, and no publisher will touch you – you'll be lucky if they even bother to send you a rejection letter.' It's inspiring, not the teachers' pessimistic lectures, but to hear the shit the others have written. Except Erica. I'm captivated when Erica is reading out her homework assignment, but that's mainly because I'm captivated by Erica. She's petite, mousey, quiet, thoughtful, deep and intriguing. I bet she lives alone behind dark curtains, where candles flicker over the gothic doom that decorates her dungeon. Or maybe she lives with her mum, who knows? I think fantasy but I write real life.

Sofia calls when I get home, they had royalty in the hospital today, a pregnant princess was having complications, they were sworn to secrecy. 'Don't tell anyone and whatever you do don't write about it.'

'Don't worry, it's cool,' I tell her. Anyway, I've just got home from my prepaid weekly extraction of self-belief, shattered confidence and crushed creativity in my you'll-never-make-it-as-a-writer class. I have been driven to drink, to numb the pain of futility, and dampen my ambitious-author impatience, and her patient today will doubtlessly be eradicated from memory along with that improbable writer's dream. Rather than subject her to those rumblings which have been amplified as the bottle empties, I change the subject. 'Anyway, you now have in your passport a colourful sticker that will allow you entry into India.'

I look at my financial situation, it's a bit grim, it would be a far more comfortable trip if I had rental income, but a far less comfortable winter if I were to stay home to watch the rain. For the freelance self-employed truck driver in the fresh fruit and veg distribution game, even Nokia polyphonic tones will not ring out in autumn. Other than a busy week at Christmas, people, it seems, forget about salad until spring, which is why I don't get much sleep in the summer and choose to relocate rather than hibernate in the winter. I return in March with a tan that fades as I drive through summer nights and close the blackout curtains while attempting to recharge through the day.

My task for tomorrow was to hit the streets and find a new letting agent, now all I can do is wait for my phone to vibrate, indicating Barry has found me a tenant, an unlikely turn of events. There's a higher probability the Nokia's orange plastic side panels will flash.

The butterflies begin

I lie in bed half-asleep, so I'm not sure if wanting the *Lonely Planet* road atlas of India to arrive is a dream or a wish. When I go downstairs an exciting and enticing-looking envelope is on the doormat. If it was a dream, it came true. I look inside, it's shite, I wish my wish had been more specific. I can't navigate by this, it's as vague as an Indian Railways schedule – 'The train will be coming after some time, sir.' It certainly does not have the precision of Ordnance Survey, it's more 'Try that way …'

I wish Barry would call with a tenant, and he does: someone will come and view at 7 p.m. This controlling of events by simply wanting is going quite well this morning, so I wish Tara would bring back the CDs I lent her but she doesn't, so apparently my wishes don't come in threes, my luck has run out. I will continue through the rest of the day like I have most of my life and make my own luck. The bicycle is now completely ready with its new tyres and I take it for a test ride to the post office.

The bike doesn't have a name – well, not one that's stuck. I briefly tried 'Stella 120'. The guy I bought it off in a Bangkok backpacking area was Belgian, selling it on behalf of his Chilean girlfriend: she had ridden from her home country through Australia and then from Singapore north to where I met them, the end of their road but the beginning of mine. Stella is my beer of choice and a product of Belgium, and my favourite red wine when I travelled through Chile three years ago was called 120 – or at least it was by me, as the bottle had those figures on the label. However, the name 'Stella 120' faded with my Thai tan. I'm not one for naming inanimate objects, no matter how much I love them. For example, in the case of any one of my motorbikes I could go into deep descriptions of increased performance, modifications, aftermarket parts and essential accessories, statistics and probable upgrades, but it would still be referred to by its model number as opposed to a pet name. Ultimately, this is just a bicycle, I am the performance. It has more gears than I can count and a little computer that counts everything else: speed, distance, average time and probably the specific gravity of the whiskey in the pannier. I'm not a cyclist, not an aficionado of pedal-propelled transport, I just ride a bicycle, it's got a wheel at each end, a soft bit at the top where I sit, and some sharp bits where my feet are. In fact, if it's not a penny-farthing or a Raleigh Chopper, if it's not got a basket, a bell that rings and things to make it look good, they all look the same to me. So knowing I'm blessed or cursed, depending on your point of view, with eyes that are blind to bicycle refinements, naming it is not really going to give it identity or individuality.

I once worked with a construction guy in the States who had a name for just about all his power tools, they were known by their colour, use or the sound they made. 'You better fetch Buzzy and a long extension cord from the truck.' Based on those criteria I could call my bike 'Blue Quiet Conveyance'. Anyway, today it is post-office-bound transportation, to deliver a letter to the council stating my displeasure at the proposed high-density housing project opposite. Firstly, it will obscure my westerly sunset view across the sprawling inadequate infrastructure that is Colchester. A view that, along with the garage for motorbikes, was the major selling point that persuaded me to take on the debt of a mortgage which would take a quarter of a century to repay. Additionally, with the suggested fewer parking spaces than flats, the overflow will cross to the lay-by on my side of the road, giving my friends fewer parking possibilities unless, like me, they resort to cycling, and that's as likely as a councillor who can't be corrupted. *Dear Sir, I'd like to express my strong objection and utter outrage at this preposterous and ill-planed proposal of ... blah blah blah.* The creative writing class has not been entirely wasted on me.

The next futile task on my list of daunting objectives (after becoming an author) is to continue to clean and empty the house while simultaneously finding what I need for the trip. This involves unpacking what has already been stacked and stored. It's not dissimilar to the way the council resurfaces a road just before a gas main is to be laid, or send a contractor to pick up the excess rubbish after the Christmas backlog. I've watched from the aforementioned westerly-facing window as the carefully divided recyclables were all thrown into the back of one mobile refuse collecting and crushing machine. A vehicle that, if it were given a pet name based on usage, might appropriately be called 'Damns refuse to be given'.

Despite slow progress, the house is tidy, the bicycle has had its first pre-pack, and I even have time to light the fire before the prospective tenant arrives. A very polite Kenyan, I like him instantly and that's important as I'm renting out my home, not just a house. I'm not some capitalist landlord, just a part-time nomad. Anyway, I'm sure he will suit and respect the place. The problem is he only wants it until the end of the year. It's hardly worth the effort of all the paperwork for a six-week tenancy. Anything is better than nothing but nothing is easier than saying no. Still, I'll let him make the call, he says he'll ring tomorrow evening with a decision.

I cycle to a mate's house and we sit in his basement away from the bedlam of his young family and drink Chilean wine listening to the pure reproduction of music. It comes via high-end independent hi-fi modular components, through wires as thick as a baby's arm to speakers with stands on spikes. Several of my mates are admirers of such audio quality and as one of them pointed out to me, 'When we were at school you had the best music system of all of us … and over twenty years later you've still got it.' I do, although perhaps not the acute hearing anymore, thanks to attending numerous metal concerts. As the wine goes down, we talk computers (of which I know little), house prices (of which I'm informed) and sex (of which I want more). This could be conceived as very middle-class company and conversation. We used to be much closer but with my night shifts and his growing family we inevitably drifted apart.

To bring things back to where they first started, we share a joint and walk to the pub. The conversation goes up a notch, not in levels of intellectualism, assets and investments but in interest. No one person can meet all your needs but with Fletch, sex has always been a keen and comfortable topic. Tonight's discussion is a high-volume incrimination of toxic secrets, lustful longings, encounters and teenage kicks. Despite the intoxication, or perhaps because of it, we are both becoming aware the chatter is probably a bit too sordid for the bar. It's cut short and the subject is changed to that of me and Sofia. Fletch and his sister have been discussing us. She, Sofia, was always the spectator, the plus-one at the parties, never really entering into the spirit of the debauched gatherings and therefore never really rattling my radar or entering my diary. Then she went travelling and came back a different girl, hair grown and sun-bleached blond. The wallflower had blossomed, had something to say and the self-confidence to say it. She became noticeable, she became intriguing, she became desirable, she became my girlfriend. Fletch says they think she's come back worldly and wanting excitement and I met the requirements; they think we are a good match, a good catch. Especially when you consider the other disastrous relationships I've had – he doesn't add, and doesn't have to, we both know that. He says he's never seen her as outgoing or happy as she is with me, or drink so much – which he really doesn't need to add, as we both know that too. 'Yeah, it's going pretty well,' is all I offer as I'm not ready to divulge our bedroom activities, not yet. Let him have his fantasies.

Back in the basement we drink whiskey and talk of our previous experiences in India. I think I feel the first stirring of butterflies. There comes a point in the all-consuming preparation when it nears completion and you actually consider what it is you are about to embark on, I think that I've just reached that point.

I cycle home at 1.30 a.m. The night is cold, misty and sobering. I must see Fletch more often when I get back next year, I think to myself, and that's when it hits me. *I'm going to be cycling this bike in India soon.* It's an incredibly exhilarating thought to have as I ride under haloed street lights on silent roads with nothing but signposts and road markings. No stray dogs or roaming cows, no potholes, I'm appreciating how orderly it all is before I even leave. The sewers are underground like secret affairs and nothing lingers long enough to contaminate in this discouraging damp air. These are my thoughts as I re-cycle the road home. Best I get away promptly, unscathed, well behaved, eyes open and aware.

The price of mixing with friends and mixing my drinks

At 7.30 I discover that while I was asleep a hangover was delivered. I'm sure I didn't order that. I manage to doze on and off for another four hours, soothed by the sound of rain on the flat roof, comforted by knowing that I'm not missing anything outside. But the hangover hangs around to accompany me through the rest of my day. Nothing makes me appreciate my house like knowing I'm going to be leaving it soon, and nothing makes living alone as preferable as unapologetic loud wind. It occurs to me that farting with confidence is not a trait generally experienced by the Westerner in India, all the more reason to enjoy it while I can.

The room is cold and the ambiance is stale, personal effects have been packed and there is a toxic taste in the air. When asphyxiation becomes a genuine threat, I drag my abused body downstairs to discover the draft of my will has arrived for me to peruse. I don't spend too long looking over it, this morning I feel like death could arrive at any moment, so best get it signed and sealed. With my pending mortality so prominent upon my mind I decide to go to Tesco and pick out all I'll need for a comprehensive first aid kit for when I'm on the road – or more accurately, if I hit the road, as while I'm upright and riding I'll be running on little more than bottled water.

Tara texts me, she'll come and return my stuff tomorrow, I'm glad it's not today, I'd have to open some windows. I need something entirely more wholesome to occupy my mind and my day, so when the rain stops, I walk to the solicitor's office to submit my will. Walking is my will, due to the risk of someone taking my wheels if I leave my alluring bike out of my sight. I'm invited into the office of an overflowing motherly woman who gushes how intrigued everyone has been to see me: this person who, in the event of his death, has bequeathed a Harley Davidson, waterbed and collection of Pink Floyd memorabilia as well as dictating a specific playlist for his funeral, prior to going off cycling round India. Is that really so strange? What would be a normal will? This is my normal, I don't have much but what I do, I value, and I want the recipient to value it equally, not in a sentimental way but for what it is, the pleasure it gives. I'm told I'm lucky and unique, I would describe it as determined and unswayed by popular culture. Anyway, most of my friends are like-minded, but perhaps I'm the first to have made a will so it's all a bit of a novelty in a life of law and legal responsibility.

The idea for a funeral playlist was conceived as I've heard some horrendous music played to a mourning congregation which in no way was related to, or a reflection of, the deceased. One drunken night I sat with a friend and a sheet of A4 and with great consideration made a list of apt 'inbox' and 'outbox' songs: the music that is played as the coffin comes in and the tune for the final curtain. It wasn't done in a morbid way – in fact, there were tears of laughter as we gave new meaning to well-known lyrics.

Much like my unwavering life philosophy, this is a very tenacious hangover and I'm still feeling a bit fragile. I spontaneously opt for an early bird discount dinner at a local Indian. My phone is perched on the window ledge for reception, the Kenyan guy said he'd call to let me know if he'll take the house. He doesn't honour his promise, so once again I'm without a tenant and the potential income the rent would generate. I go back to a very empty house which looks like it will be staying unoccupied all winter.

Burning the bridge to a feathered nest

After breakfast I write my final invoice of the season and take it to the distribution company I freelanced for all summer. I'd driven twenty-two pallets of lettuce 150 miles through the night to be chopped, cleansed, packed in plastic bags and distributed around the country's supermarkets so that customers didn't suffer the inconvenience of washing a locally grown lettuce from the neighbouring farmer. Five or six nights a week I would contribute to the wasteful efficiency of mass production to feather my nest. One night last summer I got away early and was unloaded before closing time. So I treated myself to a four-pack of Stella as an end-of-shift treat, bought from a West Sussex off-licence with a convenient truck-sized lay-by nearby. In an act of anarchy I decided to run the diesel-powered refrigerator of the empty 40-foot trailer on the three-hour drive back to Colchester, so my beer was at its premium drinking temperature when I got home. It was unlikely my employers would notice the lower fuel level and it was outrageously extravagant and wonderfully decadent to pull into the yard at 2 a.m., take my chilled beers out of the trailer and go home.

Anyway, I don't buy pre-packed lettuce so that's how I can justify my hypocrisy and blatant wastage and today, I'm damn glad too, as not only do I not get an end-of-season bonus with my last cheque but I don't even get a thank you. That's the thankless task of haulage for you, after seventeen years of it, if I never get behind the wheel of a wagon again I really won't be too disappointed. I do manage to photocopy a few choice pages of a seven-year-old *Lonely Planet* while I'm in the office though. I'm not hauling that slab of a book with me. Anyway, Sofia will bring a new one when she joins me next year.

It's time for a trial pack, with my list from last year's Chinese trip and pure determination I manage to get everything that has been accumulating on the couch into the back panniers, meaning the front pannier rack can be removed. I'm going to have such a light load this trip, it's going to be so easy. The lettuce people call, can you do one more south coast run tonight?

'No.' *Treat me like I'm so dispensable, underappreciated, you can shove ya lettuce.* That feels so much better than the £75 I could have earned tonight. That's the greatest advantage of self-employment, when the transport manager calls he doesn't tell me what I'm going to do, he asks if I'm available to do it. I'm not, and hope never to be available for them again, ever. Saying no to lettuce is swiftly followed by a no from the letting agency – the Kenyan guy is not interested. I'd kind of figured that out by his lack of response last night. Apparently, it's easier to leave people hanging than having the consideration to text *No.* Barry, however, says he has someone who wants to view on Saturday. This last-minute letting is a gamble of last-coin desperation followed by a free-spin of hope, it's the slot machine of rental return and I can't hold much longer.

I've brought a bicycle-carrying bag. It's very strong, very big and very heavy, with the wheels and pedals removed the compact and contained bicycle can be carried via a shoulder strap. I discovered from the last trip that, when you are not actually riding your bike, it goes from a physical pain in the arse to a virtual one. Buses, trains, planes and airports are much harder to negotiate when you're wheeling a bicycle beside you. Stashed in this bag the bike just becomes luggage. The problem is, when the bag is not in use, roles are reversed and the rolled-up carrying bag becomes luggage, big bulky and barely used, but invaluable when it is. In a guest house in northern Thailand before I was due to fly to China, I made my own luck: when a fridge got delivered and I commandeered the box to package my bike for the flight, it was discarded without sentiment in a Chinese dosshouse. That was some excellent opportunism but I can't count on it happening again. I've agonised over this purchase and the pitfalls of having to haul the empty bag from one end of the road to the other but I feel it's just about worth its weight. So this afternoon I spray a white image of a bicycle on it in the hope that, now identified, a baggage handler will give it a little more respect than the other anonymous luggage. The argument is that, uncovered, its fragility can be easily seen, but then so can all its bells and whistles. It's a conundrum, there is no right answer. 'Just ride it,' the puritan cyclist might say, but if I did that, setting off through frozen

Europe and across Turkey to traverse Iran and Pakistan, by the time I got to the Indian border, bike, body and budget may well all be exhausted. So travel bag it is.

I really feel like I'm winding things down now, tying up the loose ends. I take my last cheque to the bank and transfer £1,000 into my personal account to cover the costs of flights and other essentials the credit card has been used for. I expect to live very cheaply once on the road, there won't be many camping opportunities in India so I'm spared the weight and bulk of tent and sleeping bag for this trip. Guest houses are inexpensive and plentiful if not very salubrious, but they will only ever be for one night. I'll be back on the road for sunrise to beat the heat. If by chance I do find an idyllic place I'll stick around a while. It's taking full advantage of the pressure-free independence of a solo cyclist, no documents, no deadlines, no petrol, no problem. Staying put, be it through freedom of choice or, as was the case in Thailand, due to food poisoning, your travel experience changes when you transition to the status of semi-permanent residence: the second visit to the vegetable stall provokes a different reaction. I defy any 'adventurer' not to keep going to the same marketeer whenever their ramblings are temporarily paused. Upon becoming stationary, familiarity envelopes you, if only slightly, into the community – you bond with the tribe because you notice daily differences, that you couldn't possibly know of if every moment were in a new location. And it's subtleties like that that embed themselves in memory for recollection years later. A stunning vista has awe but a friendly smile of recognition as you approach the bread seller for the third morning in a row has a value the passing tourists will never know.

When I remind myself of this all the hassles of the daily preparation seem a lot less tiresome, it's all a means to an end now.

Tara turns up. She's one of those visitors with whom I can't help but be aware of my appearance before her arrival. It's been an eight-year crush which never reached a satisfying level of reciprocation. She says she's split with her man, too much hassle, she's just going to opt for casual sex now. I wipe the foam from my mouth. 'Sorry, darlin', I'm spoken for.' Why does this always happen when I get a girlfriend? There's never a ghost of an opportunity when I'm unattached but as soon as my love life stops being single-handed the girls I've lusted after for years suddenly become single. It's a bloody torment. Despite all this she is very upbeat and positive and I'm pleased for her, she's been through a tornado of trauma recently, she's ridden out the storm and now, it seems, is ready to ride whatever else comes her way …

'Err, ya not looking for somewhere to rent, are ya? Special price for you, loved you long time …'

Empty gestures, empty freezer

I really feel quite rough, I put it down to this prolonged leaving party. As a habitual traveller and part-time nomad I've had more than my fair share of leaving and arriving parties. Most departures start with the order of a Bloody Mary at the airport and again on the plane to keep a creeping hangover the other side of passport control. It's a well-practised routine but this time I seem to be stringing out my pre-tour cheerio longer than the proverbial Thomas Cook package holiday. And now the weekend is about to begin, there is no end in sight, the whole summer has been like that.

I cycle to town: Marks & Spencer for champagne and smoked salmon as Sofia will be arriving this evening for our last weekend together this year. The bookshop is a shortcut from the high street to the pedestrian area, and I usually find something to grab my attention on the walk through. Today it's an Indian guidebook and I flick through the pages as if I have a photographic memory, when all I actually have is a liking for photos that stir memories. Images of a low sun over a misty street market, palms silhouetted against an orange sky, I can almost taste it, smell it, sense it, *uh-oh, I think I need a toilet*, increased levels of excitement and anticipation for the imminent trip tend to have that effect on my belly and beyond. With some luxuries for the weekend and an essential for the weeks ahead, namely Canesten, I head home, light the fire and sit on the rug to do my homework for Monday's creative writing class.

An ex calls round. Things have been a bit fraught between us lately, we still move in the same social circles and I'm continuing to let myself be pissed off at her behaviour. She brings a peace offering, the new Robert Plant double CD, it was only released last week, she knows me well and it's a thoughtful gift, certainly a way to my heart, but I'm not quite ready to let her off the hook yet. She's made things very awkward since I hooked up with Sofia and several gatherings have had an atmosphere you could cut into lines and strangle someone with. I've written her out of my will and it's going to take some time before I'm ready to fully forgive her. I don't mind that she doesn't want me anymore, the problem is she doesn't want anyone else to want me either. Forgiveness is not one of my qualities, but on the plus side, my resentments have a limited shelf life, not due to some fabled philosophy that holding a grudge is like letting someone live rent-free in your head. I've just got a shit memory, that's why I keep a diary, and when the allotted amount of wasted sunsets and enlightened rises have passed, all transgressions fade along with the grey matter. Not only that but a foreign foray will inevitably put things into perspective, such distances generally do.

I play the CD as I take my Friday night bath, a ritual which once involved several beers but more recently has required a bit of self-restraint. Sofia, arriving strung out after a Friday evening commute from the other side of London, doesn't like being greeted by a drunk boyfriend, regardless of how clean and enthusiastic I am. It's not a massive compromise and abstaining comes with a few benefits, I'm certainly less likely to cut myself shaving. The CD smacks of marketing and packaging more than quality material, not so much a 'best of' more 'rest of'. When Sofia arrives, she's tired and needs a nap; my sobriety is prolonged further into the evening.

We eat leftovers out of the freezer, much like broken electronics that are put in the loft, I wonder why I ever bothered to keep this stuff. It was shite when it went in the freezer and six months in suspended animation has done nothing to improve its look, consistency or taste. The meal is as disappointing as a bonus CD full of B-sides, but at least I can wash it down with alcohol. We talk of tidying the house for the viewing and that turns into: 'What if we had six months on ice with nowhere to live?' Say the perspective tenants who are coming tomorrow want the place for the more usual minimum term of tenancy. Where to go, come the spring, should we return at all? First-world problems, the rental income could upgrade my status from planet chapatti to a world of oysters.

Champagne and first world problems

Long lie-in, loving this alarm-free lifestyle, although us night workers don't need alarm clocks, not to get up for work anyway. However, there is a more subtle alarm: seven years of night shifts have not only annihilated my summer evening social life but being, or trying to be a day sleeper, is reflecting on my health too. The body is simply not meant to be kept awake through the dark hours, and blocking out the working daylight with thick curtains and earplugs still deprived me of deep, undisturbed, rejuvenating sleep, while simultaneously denying my soul the benefits of natural light. It was a slow awareness that there was a downside to the initially appealing bonus by-product of nocturnal trucking. The precise and prompt scheduling due to avoidance of motorway delays and rush-hour regression comes at a high price. I'd brag at dawn to the bleary-eyed day driver about to take over my hot seat that I'd been in cruise control from Bristol to Brentwood. All I had to do was keep my eyes open; the hard part was keeping them closed after 10 a.m. I want to turn my life around and go back to waking up the day after I went to bed.

When I watch the opening credits of *The Simpsons* I don't think, *I wonder what will happen when they get to the couch*, I see something I've not witnessed myself since I left school. Everyone arriving home at the same time. Normal working hours, and not leaving for a night of solitary work when everyone else is coming together. When I see the Christmas Coca-Cola commercial, I think to myself, *There are the truckers, working during the holidays, away from their loved ones and driving in hazardous conditions for the benefit of delivering joy to others.* Yeah, I've had enough of the job, I want the kind of working hours where I'm part of the rush hour.

I light the fire and we go about making the house look homely and irresistible to any prospective tenant, we even vacuum and everything. I'm perfectly capable of cleaning but Sofia can, without even trying, give the place a woman's touch, and I don't mean putting a pack of tampons in the bathroom. For all my efforts the place will always look like a bachelor pad, albeit a clean one. We work well together, we've never really had 'work obligations' as a couple before, it may only be house cleaning but it's a good omen for what's to come when she joins me in India.

At the arranged time no one comes, no one calls and it would appear we totally wasted our time preparing for the time-wasters. Up and down, it's rented, it's not, there's a viewing, there isn't, pack the panniers prematurely then spread the contents out again on the couch. Fuck this, we have smoked salmon and cream cheese bagels with champagne for breakfast. Fuck the peasant tenants, and Barry and his empty promises. On the plus side I know the house will be instantly available to move back into whenever I choose to return, and it's actually quite clean now too. It's just, without the rental return to pay my way, my return may well be sooner and the way harder. We discuss the possibility of Sofia moving in. Her contract in Surrey expires at the end of this year along with her hospital accommodation, and she may as well apply for jobs round this area when we get back. My internal dialogue kicks in. *You really don't want to go back to the haulage industry next season and there would be more options open if you could accept a reduced income. It would take the pressure off if she was helping with the living costs.* I'm thinking there may still have to be some sacrifices though. 'More champagne, darling?' She proofreads my homework, corrects some errors, again we make a good team, a good couple, and I'm really happy with the story so far, although I'm not quite sure a writer's life will pay the bills, not yet.

We walk over to some grassland that is yet to be built on and fly a kite. A helicopter lands nearby, squad cars turn up and police run around aggressively like wild … err, pigs. A fire engine arrives too. We drink Stella from cans at a safe distance. I have no clue what is going on, which actually stands me in good stead for travelling in India. I never understand how function comes from the seeming chaos of that country. I'm not entirely convinced this force of authority knows what's going on either and the attention-seeking chopper has brought out the spectators, so they have to be seen to do something. My local pub calls out its convenience as we walk back and we stay there until it gets dark. I don't eat there any more.

It used to be a place to go primarily for food but now draught Stella is its only appeal. However, we still sit in the eating area as the place has a pretty rough clientele; once drinks are ordered I'm happy to get away from the bar. Certainly not a place to discuss one's champagne-and-smoked-salmon breakfast. Although I bet they have first-hand knowledge of the kerfuffle with the helicopter and all the uniforms scouting about the land behind, perhaps a tip-off of a serial aerial bender at large. My main-road end-of-terrace backs onto a notorious housing estate. It's not much of a bother, I've resigned myself to coat-hanger reception and puke on the pavement. Other than communal drinking never the twain.

The day ends like it began, by the fire, though not in anticipation of prospective tenants but of the arrival of Thai green curry.

You can't make it up

It's been a month since my 38th birthday and I don't feel like the party has stopped. In fact, in the nine months since I've been back from cycling, life has been hurtling recklessly down the fast lane. Sex and drinks and bacon rolls, everything entering and leaving the body has been pleasurable. With breakfast still on my breath and yet to be digested it's time for the last Sunday lunch. We take mother along for a seafood platter and more champagne. A diary full of decadent days. It reads somewhere between *The Dirt* and *A Year in Provence*. Fresh French bread, prawns, mussels, cockles and crab. Lunch is strung out until 4.30 p.m. which gives us just two hours to kill before honouring a diner invite.

We spend it in bed, entwined in post-coital pillow talk, ignoring the elephant in the room. Sofia's biological clock is ticking louder than an after-sex heart beat and without compromise, and there is no compromise on that one. I may have a daughter, born in America last year, the mother claims she's mine but the dates don't quite comply. I'm told she has my eyes but that would hardly stand up in court. I'm yet to meet her, shit, I'm yet to accept I've got a kid at all. And I certainly don't want any more, none, no way, forget it, it's out of the question.

'I will not purposely impregnate you.' She gets the point. Yep, that's a pretty big elephant, best go to India, they fit right in there.

More food, more beer, more company, more goodbyes, all good distractions. We're the new lovers, more bed than sleep, too infatuated to face facts, too loved-up to listen to reason, too fat to fuck. We are, though, a good couple. When the mood is right, she makes a gesture, putting her hands on her elbows as if holding a newborn, with a *please, just one* look in her eyes. My response is to hold my arms up, fists clenched as if I'm hanging on to the bars of a chopper, which also represents perhaps the tenuous grip I have on my freedom. And to add torment to her longing I've got what she

40

wants, the other side of the Atlantic, but refuse to acknowledge it. It's like telling a twenty-five-year-old Led Zeppelin fan you were at Knebworth for their final gig but drank too much and slept through it.

However, tonight in the company of my least judgemental friends, we can drink and laugh, talking the sincerest of bollocks, with spag bog and wine around the table of the desperately single, the recently divorced, the increasingly broody and my best companion, alcohol denial.

Waiting to go

Sofia too has dark-driving decisions: leave on Sunday evening or before the crack of Monday's dawn for a three-hour commute to start her shift.

The barking of the dog from the house behind starts at 7.30. My choice of disturbances are this obnoxious noise in the morning or sleeping in the front bedroom where I hear the raucous closing-time drunks returning home, bending metal, breaking skin and discarding their kebabs in one of two forms, half-eaten or half-digested. The bed is cold and empty, so is the day outside, there is little consolation that I don't have to leave the former and enter the latter. It takes more than an imminent departure to bring solace to such days. I'm prepared and pre-packed, albeit prematurely to keep the place rental empty. So there's little to do except wait to leave, and telling myself *This time tomorrow* does nothing to relieve the displeasure of waiting and only brings on nerves and a mild stomach-churning panic.

I go into town to collect a completed copy of my will. The Christmas lights are up in the high street, this is as close as I want to get to such festivities. I see some familiar faces, after all this is my town; I listen to an interview with David Bowie on Radio One, this is my country; then Chris Moyles comes on and I'm damn glad I'm leaving it. He used to do an early pre-breakfast show at 4 a.m. For me his voice represented a long night, running late, and I find him as irritating as unpaid overtime. However, I'm not ready to move to cosy and conforming Radio Two, not yet. The day's dismal gloom darkens, meaning it's time for my evening creative writing class. I read my homework aloud, it's not received well, which is disappointing. Everyone's a critic but none are qualified – well, that's what I tell myself in consolation, nobody understands me, what do they know? I won't be seeing any of them again. Not in class and probably not on the shelves of my shortcut through Waterstones either. We have, as a class, systematically had the confidence kicked out of us by our self-appointed judge of creative talent who calls herself a teacher; I no longer feel I'm worthy of writing a text message. Everyone says goodbye and Erica hangs around. I give her a hug and a kiss on the cheek, she gives me her email address. This makes me smile, we both have partners but we clicked and there's something there, the mutual attraction that dare not be spoken of and probably not even mentioned in an email – apparently, we're not good with words, not yet.

This is the last night of the year I'll spend in my house, I have leftover logs in the basket and in the fridge there's a few cans of Stella and the remains of a Thai green curry. It seems obvious what to do.

The delicate art of forgetting some things and remembering others

My mind is on fast repetitive rotation before my eyes open, the inevitable last-minute obligations before I lock up and leave. The tasks are more daunting than the time it will take to perform them so I'm up and running when I could be down and dozing. The last of what I consider valuable and essential is put in the last of the lettuce crates which I gifted to myself as an end-of-season bonus. They won't be missed any more than I will – when next spring's first crop is ready for cutting, I'll be back, unpacked and ready to return their stackable containers. I plug some lights into timer switches, a beacon to say I'm away, because I'd never leave lights on if I was living here.

I fill the van with diesel and drop the house keys through my ex-lodger's letter box on the way to my parents' place, leaving the van down the side of their house with valuables and essentials locked in the back. All that's left to do is give the Harley a pat and cover it up, blankets draped over ape hangers in an attempt to disguise what lies beneath. We go out for a pub lunch; I always get so stressed eating in public in the company of my father, actually taking him out into any public place fills me with anxiety. His deteriorating sight has left him with white-stick blindness, short-fuse intolerance and red-mist anger. Other senses have compensated: he can now hear a child cry across a crowded pub, the smell of cigarette smoke on an outdoor jacket. His heightened senses make him touchy, and tasteless, insensitive remarks are spoken at levels audible to the people in close proximity that he can't see or doesn't care to. Despite my pessimistic predictions no senses are insulted and we leave the pub unscathed, which is as close to a pleasant experience as I can hope for.

To the post office for a road tax refund form and back to mine with mother, who takes away what's left in the fridge and freezer, while I squirt some bleach in the toilet and load my luggage into her car. To the station, music on my mind, do I need new batteries for my MP3 disc player? A brief hug and I drag my excess baggage to the platform. The waiting is over, the journey has begun, or maybe it hasn't, now I'm just anticipating the arrival of a train. There will be a lot of public transport before the wheels of my bicycle are attached and turning. I stand, sweating, it's mild, I collect my thoughts, my attention turns to my appearance, overloaded with luggage and underdressed for mid-November. Wait, where's my fleece? For fuck's, sake I've forgotten my fleece. This would never have happened if my premeditated packing hadn't been disrupted; for over a week the couch had been covered with an accumulation of pre-trip preparation. The problem is, everything got stuffed prematurely into panniers for a potential rental viewing. Those fucking time-wasting, appointment-ignoring prospective tenants, now I've forgotten an intrinsic piece of clothing for the trip. My China-purchased, genuine-copy, maybe factory-second, possibly end-of-season-overrun-but-near-perfect Mountain Hardwear high-quality, breathable, windproof, zippable-armpit-breathing-vents, outdoor-clothing best top I've ever had is still in a house I have no time to get back to or key to get in with.

Now I'm going to have to get my mum to send it to Sofia in the hope she will have the space and weight allowance to bring it, an entirely unnecessary stress. I struggle onto the train, consoling myself with the thought that, unlike returning from the last trip, I'm not trying to carry two additional panniers and all the camping gear and clothing they contained. I was so overweight I had to ship back some excess baggage.

The Chilean girlfriend of Stefan from whom I'd bought my bicycle (Stella 120) had struggled to keep up with her Belgian boyfriend, who had multiple miles behind him. She was resilient but that was no match for his stamina. In Australia the problem needed addressing and an enterprising Aussie came up with a contraption comprising a Honda strimmer engine that sat on the front rack, with a nylon spool press-fitted over the splined shaft. Pivoted and spring-loaded, the engine could be lowered onto the tyre which bump-started it into action, adding motorised assisted power. With a throttle control on the bars she effortlessly rode from Perth to Darwin. It was ingenious and I eventually negotiated its ownership in addition to the purchase of the bike, then promptly paid to leave it in a

Bangkok storage facility. Two months and 3,000 kilometres later I picked it up, packed it up, paid to import it and the engine has been in the shed ever since, never fitted or likely to be. But it was a bargain, I got it thrown in for a paltry sum. There's a lesson there, owning that engine has been like carrying a wheelbarrow, it's never eased anything I've done, only added to the baggage.

I half stash the bike in the end-of-carriage luggage area and choose a seat where it remains in my sight. I put on my MP3 player and continue to consider the annoyance of not getting a tenant. The refreshment trolley trundles by and I order an emergency Stella. Still feels strange to drink on a train. I've been conditioned by my years in America with its restrictive public drinking laws, which of course has kept the country so wholesome, because prohibition worked so well. I just want to be pissed off at something, anything, letting agencies, tenants who didn't turn up or have the courtesy to call, dumb-arse transport managers, forgotten essentials and countries where I might have a daughter. I'm not sure why I should be so angry, I'm on my way, albeit on a train to London. I watch the winter countryside go by and the Stella does what it's been doing for some time now, taking the pain away and, with it, a significant amount of memory too. The train passes the town where Erica lives and I giggle and cringe at how I kissed her last night. London looms, underground, overground, wandering freely through the complex connections that I did last week in reverse but now with three times more baggage than anyone else.

Reliable, punctual, trustworthy, accountable, and of course mustn't forget attractive, Sofia is waiting for me, having the forethought of folding the back seats down to accommodate my baggage. It's little gestures like that which endear her to me. Because that's what I'd do and, if someone thinks like me, I like them, as they must be right. Not subservient, or without opinions, but conscientious and considerate. And as if she knows this, having accommodated my luggage she addresses my baggage and a can is put in my hand upon arrival at her accommodation.

I couldn't live like this, it's way too studenty for my taste. Shared houses come with drama and it's not the kind of entertainment or distraction I need. Dinner on our laps, a beer on one side, me bird on the other, *Eastenders* on the TV in front of us and a buzz from the scooby snack

46

I bought. We go to her room for, I assume, a little last-minute romance, but the evening drifts into nothingness until she brings up the baby thing again. I wish she'd leave it, like I did my fleece – oh, that reminds me, can you bring it with you?

Coming back to me

I always wake up horny when I sleep in her bed, she's got the cure but is off to the hospital and doesn't have time to administer it so I'm left alone with the problem. She'll be back for lunch but no promises. Alone in someone else's bed has limited appeal so I go down to the communal lounge where the TV is on, perhaps it was never turned off. It seems to be a permanent background noise, maybe Sofia's room-mates need distractions too, and this is probably considered more socially acceptable than Stella, certainly at 10 a.m. President Bush is in the UK, which, judging by the coverage his visit is getting, must be of great significance. He was in Australia last month, will be in Iraq next week. I'd be more interested in the news of his tour if he were to have travelled by bicycle, as opposed to a bloody great jumbo jet – *don't worry, George, my pedal power will save the planet for both of us.*

I discover a benefit of house sharing: one room-mate has some quality shampoo and I use a little when I take a shower. I chat on the couch with another inhabitant, he's leaving nursing and going for an interview with the army this afternoon. He's the one who doesn't have the premium haircare products, won't have any hair soon either if he gets the job.

Sofia comes home and it's one more pub lunch. I want something really English as my last meal, the place obliges with bad service with inflated Surrey pricing. Once again, we have stuffed ourselves beyond comfort and sleep it off in her bed. It's dark when we wake and she says there's no time for nookie. I can't believe it, this is our last chance until next year. There was always going to be a six-week hiatus and she's just put three more days on the clock. What she doesn't know is forty-two roses will be delivered to her tomorrow, representing the days until we see each other again. And I don't know what those forty-two days will hold either. So I have ripped those blank pages out of my 2003 diary – there being no point in carrying the 11 months that have already been recorded, and I'd be devastated if I were to lose it. It's hard enough recalling the past day the morning after, and if the diary is lost so will be most the year's events. 2003 has been full on, I don't remember it but I'll never forget it. So I have forty-two days left in the year to find my destiny, follow my dreams and fill the empty parchment until we reunite, and Sofia will have the forty-two roses to fill the void I leave, and although it wasn't written I just assumed that forty-two was how many days I'd have to wait for the next shag, I was wrong – should I order three more?

She takes me to the airport. I don't think there is such a thing as a good departure time for a long-haul flight, only a convenient arrival time. One choice seems to be having to set an alarm to start the dark drive to the airport. The other is to spend the whole day with the underlying knowledge that, regardless of what you are doing, what you are actually doing is waiting until the point comes where you give in and relocate the day's waiting to the airport. Flying is just something that involves occupying yourself for long periods before and while being thrust through time and space in the fastest method available to humans. So I arrive at Heathrow not only uncharacteristically early but without the traditional hangover and not even carnal satisfaction. This is a terrible way to start a trip, no need for a Bloody Mary and no bloody sex.

The last pre-flight niggle was my luggage, but I'm 3 kilograms under. The bike bag is 20 kilograms, the check-in bag is 7 kilograms and my carry-on is 6 kilograms, that's a load off my mind. We go to the bar, both knowing the futility of stringing out this goodbye, delaying the inevitable bitter end. No point in suggesting a quickie in the disabled toilet, I suppose. I'm really going to miss her and I hate this feeling, why am I doing this again?

Why am I doing this?

Well, I suppose the seed was planted in a freezing *refugio* in Patagonia, midway through hiking the W Trek in Torres del Paine National Park. I sat shivering in a shelter of plastic with some random hikers of various nationalities as the rain pissed down outside and condensation dripped on us inside. Some spirit was handed round but it was inadequate in every respect, for drunkenness, warmth or conversation. However, there was a Dutchman there who had cycled from Alaska and this 'little walk' was

49

a break from the bike. He didn't sell the cycling thing – in fact, I don't recall a single experience he had, if he even spoke of any. After three days the hiking ended with a boat that took me from that National Park. I had blistered feet, trench foot, was filthy and malnourished but with an overwhelming feeling of well-being and achievement. As the boat chugged away, the clouds cleared and the full panorama of Torres came into view for the first time, yet I hadn't the energy to reach for my pack and grab my camera. I sat and looked at the three granite pinnacles against the blue sky and felt proud that they hadn't beaten me. I'd gone knowing little and left wondering but somehow I had single-handedly done a very strenuous hike.

I felt that trek had taken me a step beyond the backpacker scene I'd become so tired of: being herded onto tourist buses, coerced into guest houses, blinkered to the Bob Marley bistro for a banana pancake. The well-beaten gap-year path to oblivion was gridlocked with human traffic and it was getting increasingly harder to find the road less travelled. Backpacking lost its appeal after my first lap of the planet, but travel never has, and although I still use the *Lonely Planet*, now it's to avoid what the book enthuses about. Independence has always been my main aim in life. Freedom for me is a feeling most frequently found on a motorcycle but taking something with an engine overland is a costly endeavour. Even a two-stroke strimmer and a backpack was problematic, although I avoided daunting bureaucracy, registration, road taxes, insurance, carnets, vignettes and vehicle compliance. Pushing pedals seemed like an affordable compromise which would inevitably take me through places bypassed by the tourist bus.

From the day I passed my driving test at the age of seventeen, the bicycle took a back seat and was only ever used for a pub run to avoid drinking and driving because my licence instantly became my livelihood. Twenty years later the self-propelled means of transport was upgraded in stature and utilised as a way to see the world, done without the displeasure of the backpacking fraternity disrupting my eternal search for unspoilt tranquillity, isolation and first-hand, first-time experiences. To stumble upon a place that is better, not used to be better before it got popular. This bicycle notion, pedalling slow motion, delivered the romance of travel on my Thai and Chinese trip last year. Although the experiences are hard to share around a table in a pub, I'm yet to see anyone 'get it'. It doesn't really matter because I got it and I want some more. That's why I am doing it again. Romance of the road aside, a more pragmatic reason is simply that the season has finished, there is no more work. Sofia is stuck in a contract, so cycling up the west coast of India to drop in on some friends who winter in Goa seems as good a way as any to pass six weeks until she can come and join me. As well as some familiar faces mid-trip, India will also be warm and flat, not like those pesky mountains at the eastern end of the Himalayan range. That's as far as I've thought, and that is the only thought left after the kiss and the uncoupling at passport control.

The duty-free shopping consists of a plug converter and Billy Connolly's biography, but no whiskey, not this time, although somehow I still seem to be the last one to board the plane. MP3, read, movie, steak so tough my plastic fork snaps, damn 9/11, two years on and still denied cutlery that cuts. The red wine flows freely and sleep won't come at all. SriLankan Airlines caters for the insomniac in a way I've never witnessed before. Other than watching my progress across the planet on the screen in front of me, there are also some choice cameras placed around the plane, cockpit view, behind, in front and beneath the belly. As I fly above the planet crushed into economy and thrust into a burning red dawn with red-wine heart burn, I find this screen far more captivating than watching Bush burning fossil fuels in Air Force One to visit Buckingham Palace.

It's not the wrong country, just a long wait

When my body clock says 4 a.m. cabin lighting is intensified to match the squinting sunlight beyond the shutters and breakfast is served. Three hours later we prepare to land; local time is 1 p.m. I watch the belly-cam as we descend, sea, sea, sea, first I pick out fishing boats on the undulating water, then individual waves, and the spray from the breakers, is this going to be a water landing? It's a bit disconcerting. The plane continues to lose altitude, I think I can see the concern on the faces of the fish, my tummy bounces, heart's in my mouth, as wave breaks onto concrete, with a 'bump', we're on the ground, Jesus-fucking-Christ. Some things you're better off not witnessing. That was intense, I may not have slept but right now I've never been more awake.

We are welcomed to Sri Lanka, told the temperature is 29°C and then that the passengers expecting to get the connecting plane to South India are in for a slight change of plan. Turns out there is no connection, they can fly us elsewhere in India, there'll be another flight next week to my chosen destination. After the belly-view landing trauma all I have in me is a calm appreciation for life, it's the easiest decision I've ever made when it comes to location. OK, book me on to next week's flight, I think I'm going to cycle Sri Lanka. I don't make a big deal out of it at all but neither does the airline representative which is almost annoying. Shouldn't she be a bit more apologetic of the circumstances, more appreciative of my leniency? I mean, how many passengers are as flexible as me? Apparently, none. I'm the only one on the plane that's just arrived who expected to connect with one that hasn't. Where's my goodie bag, with socks and toothpaste, where's my inconvenience voucher, my flexible friend-of-the-airline upgrade? My chartered helicopter of compensation taking me to a destination of my choosing? My bike is moving round the baggage carousel so I retrieve it before it disappears to be put on a plane that isn't there.

Right, now the journey has almost definitely started. I change $100 into Sri Lankan rupees and compose myself. I have money, I have time, now let's work on the transport and destination. I start by finding a quiet uninhabited area and unzip my bike bag. This is the point where it stops being useful, but only for a week; I don't want to be thinking about a box, this carrying bag is certainly more convenient than trying to again find some refrigerator packaging. Its reusable and recyclable qualities will soon be utilised. Not sure this one-week layover decision would have been so easy if I didn't have it. The carry bag rolls up to the size of my one-man tent which I don't have this time. Slowly, I assemble the bike, pedals, wheels, adjust the seat, straighten the handlebars and pump the tyres. It feels like meditation, it feels like mental preparation, it feels fabulous. The bike is functional and complete but I have a leak, I'm soaked, dehydrated before I start.

A lady walks over and says I look very organised and she's right, I do, in fact I mostly am, other than I'm in the wrong bloody country – oh, and without warm clothing. However, now I look up, away from the assembling, I see the assembled masses, I've got the attention of distant spectators. Not crowded round like I'd expect in India but just observing as I'm the most interesting thing in the now deserted airport. All other passengers have departed, it feels safe to leave my pile and go buy some water. I've got half the airport staff keeping an eye on my shit for me. OK, where the hell am I going to go now? Conveniently, I spot a big map on the wall. My phone, unlike the latest models for the rich and famous that filled the pages of the in-flight magazine, doesn't take photos and my camera takes film. So I stare at the map and resort to analogue memory storage. Negombo looks close, and on the coast. A security man tells me which way to go and that it's about to rain. I walk out the sweating airport into the humid late afternoon. The pack of taxi drivers are of no threat at all, I give them the metaphorical finger from all those years of being at their mercy. I look at the road beyond the airport, decide that in this country they appear to drive on the left and fix my mirror to the right side of my bar. While I'm doing this it starts to rain, then it absolutely pisses down. However, I'm under the canopy and unperturbed. I put on a thin top and, once again the focus of everyone's attention, I throw my leg over the bike, kick up the stand, push on a pedal and move forward. The journey has undeniably begun. The independence, the liberation, the exhilaration, the delight of being self-propelled, leaving the spectators and looking forward. It feels like I'm walking on water, although cycling on the submerged would be more accurate, the road is awash but I don't care. I am flaunting my freedom like an American at an inauguration as I cycle off into the unknown, or to be more precise the barely known. I came here in '97 with an Australian girl I'd met – we'd made it to the very south of India, so decided to hop over here for a week before heading on up the east side of the subcontinent. Didn't have a guidebook then either. So here I go into the still not known.

Cows are in the road, shit is on the road and everybody says hello – how do they know I speak English? I'm not one to announce my nationality by flying a flag; if you want to know, ask me. I wonder what the last cricket result was. I stop at a roadside shack for more water.

'Where you from, where you go?'

See, if I had a Union Jack sticking out my pannier, I'd have only half as much to talk about.

'England, Negombo,' I say.

They point in the direction I'm going. So far so good then. The driving standard isn't too bad, trucks draw level and youths wave out the passenger windows. An age group that, in England, would either spit or at the very least shout some abuse. 'Oi, ya back wheel's goin' round!' Not here, all I am is welcome. Negombo is, as I was told, in fact very close. I ride right through town. I'm glad I have a mirror, there is plenty coming up from behind, inquisitive and friendly but a threat to my stability – or would be if I was unaware of their approach. I find the beach road. It's not exactly challenging. I'm on an island and I came from the east, keep going west and sure enough there's the Indian Ocean again, but this time not viewed from a camera at the bottom of the plane. I think I saw that wave out at sea, looks familiar. 'Welcome, where you from? All the best.' More waves, more familiarity. I cycle past a lot of hotels and guest houses, I suppose I'd better make a choice, but much like the girls I date, I let one choose me. 'You want room? Come.' He shows me to a windowless room with a private toilet. Although, in fact, everything is private when you don't have windows, but he doesn't use that sales line. He just says 800, I say 500, he says yes, I say yes. That's day one complete. $5.60 spent today from the airport to, and including the cost of, my accommodation. And that right there is why I come away in winter, no need for heating or hot water, I have a cool shower, arrange my panniers and text my parents: *Made it safely … to err, Sri Lanka.*

Now what? Usually, I'm happy to close a door behind me but with only a bare bulb for light I reluctantly hit the streets. It's raining again, I speak to some holidaymakers who saw me cycle in, I walk along the beach, it's a bit early to end my day and I don't know what to do with myself. I go back and read but I can't focus. This is not why I go away, this is agitation, no place to go, no place I want to stay, so I go back out again. I'm yet to find the rhythm of the road, hardly surprising really, I've only been on it for 20 kilometres. I do though find a Tesco, a shack with a store of conveniences, and a crudely painted but very familiar red and blue logo above the door. Painted by some enterprising if not franchising owner, who unsurprisingly won't accept my Clubcard. At a random restaurant I order noodles, and get a pile so big I could hide behind it, it's like the view from my room. I only eat a third and I'm still too full to finish my beer.

I'm in bed for 8.30 p.m. with earplugs but I keep needing a wee, glad I have a private toilet, I wonder what the weather is doing outside. I can't make a decision; shall I leave tomorrow? I need a map. I need sleep first, I've never made a good decision when I'm tired, on an empty tummy, or in a shared bed. Thankfully, I'm full and alone, only one problem left to remedy.

Last time

I'd really not considered the departure decision. However, it makes itself. Someone is inconsiderately banging on my door at the ridiculous hour of … oh, apparently it's 11.30 a.m. They are just making sure another guest hasn't died in their sleep. Another? I do feel lethargic though, the shower fails to vitalise. I don't like this feeling, not lonely, just not very determined. It doesn't feel like I was ever away from Asia, nor from its palm trees, which are for me a symbol of both relaxation and the excitement of the exotic. But they are not doing it for me. Then again, I'm yet to see the sun since I landed, perhaps a window would help. I leave my room and walk to the restaurant and order noodles, I think they are out of a packet. The couple I spoke to yesterday who saw me cycle by say hi but I don't recognise them as she is wearing her hair differently. They probably think I'm rude now, or aloof. There will be no significant distance done today. It's cloudy still so I go to a lounger with my MP3 player and book. I wasn't expecting to feel this way, I wasn't expecting to be in Sri Lanka.

What was I expecting?

A year ago, almost to the day, my delayed flight finally landed in Bangkok. My fellow passengers comprised dykes, monks, paedos, sex tourists and a stag party. Judgemental? You fuckin' bet. A judgement made more credible when police boarded in Doha to remove an obstinate passenger who wouldn't stop smoking. A wig-wearing wanker in an aisle seat tried telling me where the youngest girls could be found. 'I'm here to ride a bicycle, not a schoolgirl'. I got two seats to myself but I didn't have a bicycle, and being a thirty-seven-year-old male travelling alone to Thailand, the other passengers were doubtless equally judgemental of me. A year before I had come here with a girlfriend. 'Why you bring girl to Thailand?' a local had said to me. Coal to Newcastle. This time I was alone and she had a new man and a newborn. Instead, this trip's unnecessary addition was a litre bottle of Bushmills – in a November-dismal duty-free, I felt a duty to exercise my freedom to buy a bottle. Whiskey warms me, blended it may have been but still cheaper than distributing heat to every radiator in a singularly occupied house. I can only be in any one room at one time; however, like a constant volume of music in my ears via a Walkman, with whiskey in my blood I can take the warmth with me as I wander. Thing is, Bangkok being the hottest city in Asia – based on mean temperature, not the beauty of the Thai women – bringing whiskey was as equally imprudent as bringing ya bird.

The Khao San Road had changed a lot since I first saw it in '91. The eleven intervening years had bought 7-Elevens, internet cafés, chain stores, beer boys and the Benidorm crowd. The clientele were now less dope-smoking dippy hippies and more noticeably into harder drugs and heavier drinking, less of the free love and more about paid sex. Don't get me wrong, three of my favourite pastimes, but I prefer my long-time love not to be pimped, my source to be safe and accountable and my drink … *well, actually I'll take a beer.*

The taxi driver from the airport told me, 'King's birthday soon, big celebration', dropped me at my desired guest house and left. It was fully booked, so in desperation my first night's accommodation was better than a dorm but not much more than a hardboard box. No windows for ventilation and the walls ran out before they got to the ceiling. It was nothing more than semi-secure luggage storage and a mattress with a past best not contemplated. The kind of room that makes homelessness appealing. So I took to the street, found a table on the pavement, and sat, watching, acclimatising, recalling. My destination was almost definitely China, perhaps via Laos. However, I always knew I'd start in Bangkok, specifically the Khao San Road, as it is the M25 of Asia – regardless of where you are going or where you are from you pass through here, making flights cheaper and the possibility of buying a bicycle better. My beer glass was less than half-empty even by a pessimist's standards, when among the pedestrian parade walked a fellow pushing a fully kitted-out bicycle with a *For Sale* sign on it. *See*, I said to myself, *that's exactly the kind of thing I'm looking for…* A moment passed. *That's what I'm looking for! Why aren't I running after him?* I ran after him, leaving my seat, and an uncharacteristically unfinished beer. I consider myself to be a good haggler, but panting and approaching from behind was not exactly the indifferent look I was going for. However, the only thing worse than bad negotiating is not getting it at all. How many more opportunities would there be? He said he wanted US$350 for the bike, he was off to meet his girlfriend, couldn't stop now. I pointed back at my table. 'I'll be there,' I said. 'Come find me once you've found her.'

He came back with Ana, whose bike it was, we chatted, we drank, we laughed, we clicked. It had been three years since Stefan had cycled out of Belgium and from Alaska to Argentina – we had covered a lot of the same ground. I realised my research gave me an air of confidence, I knew a little, but he was an authority. He said several people had shown interest in the bike and taken his email address and, to back up his bargaining technique, as we talked more people stopped to look at the ready-to-go bicycle.

'I'm going to fly to Bangkok, buy a bicycle and ride it to China,' I had told my friends before I left. Eighteen years before that, I'd said I was going to America to buy a Harley and bring it back to England … and I did, so there were expectations. This potential purchase was not a matter of checking out the bike, it was discovering the seller, knowing the person more than the product. He was not only genuine but was a wealth of knowledge; the bike would inevitably come with his road-learned wisdom. Impulsively, but with a good gut feeling, I told him he had sold his bike, but I wanted to look at it properly the following day, not viewed under street lights and through weary eyes of misjudgement. Strange how the voices of the obnoxious British beer boys disappeared when I was engaged in enchanting conversations of adventures, listening intently, concentrating, retaining, and about to take the reins.

I woke with the obligatory first-morning hangover, the good gut feeling was gone, the sweat was turning frosty in the cool of the room, not that I was encouraged to break the seal on the Bushmills. I pulled my fleece over me, forgetting I had a sleeping bag in my backpack. Feeling wretched I stood in my hardboard room and stared around vacantly, I could hear the inhabitants I shared a ceiling with. Nothing good happens when you are living in a box. I went to the street and found Stefan's guest house. The bike looked a little worse for wear in the cold, sober light of day, and no doubt I did too. Ana said she hurt from laughing so much the previous night, and that a double room had just become available here, so I booked it. Window, balcony, well-being, I felt better already. We used the bike to carry my backpack from my box to my new bedroom. I was already witnessing the benefit of independent transport. The day passed making notes, listing parts, dozing off jet lag, feeding hunger and feeling exhilarated for all that was to come. Every sensation came with an urgency and was satisfied fully before moving on to the next. The passion I exuded clearly came across in the mass email I composed, judging by the *Jammy git* responses. Planet-aligning luck, nervously excited, turning a long-term plan into productivity and reality; that was how my first twenty-four hours in Bangkok passed.

By comparison, my first twenty-four hours in Sri Lanka have been somewhat less exhilarating and productive. It's already afternoon as I get the bike out of the room and cycle to town. Thinking, *This time last week* … doesn't make me feel lucky, doesn't make the location seem enticing. If the sun would just shine…

I buy a coat for $5, some Pringles because I can't resist them and mozzie coils because the mosquitoes can't resist me. Spice sellers are forceful but pointing out I'm on a bike seems to be an acceptable reason not to buy, if not a logical one. They just don't have a practised retort. '*Big Issue?*' 'No, my lace is undone.'

I leave the bike unlocked when I walk into shops because it feels OK to. I pass homeless beggars, they have nothing, not even hope, looking at them through $300 Oakleys gives the vision some perspective. Supplies are accumulated and I'm becoming acclimated. I cycle back through a fishing village, thatched huts of fishermen and their families' nets hung out and boats hauled up the beach. We would build better for our spades in England, any allotment has sturdier accommodation than their beachfront properties. However, I get a lot more hellos than I would if passing a bunch of bent-over gardeners shovelling shit into their soil for optimum nutritional value in the hope of producing prize-winning vegetables.

In the restaurant with my newly purchased map spread out on the table my route is instantly clear. When I said I'd stay for a week there were only really two choices, down the sweltering coast or up into the centre and cooler Kandy. I've been to both before but the place that eluded me last time was World's End: a location where high plains drop away leaving an infinite view. It was a massive mistake to take a rental Honda XL250 away from the beach, no speedo, no back light and bald tyres, and my two-day foray turned into an extended day and nightmare. Long ride, long story, bad choices, wrong clothing, underprepared, overzealous, low cloud, nothing to see, ride in the dark, flat front tyre, disappointed mostly at my idiocy. I'm going to try again.

The guest house owner tells me what roads to take while insisting I drink Sri Lankan tea. I'm not sure it's an invite or a demand. I suppose asking for Indian chai here is like asking for a Cornish pasty in Devon: close enough to associate; far enough away to offend. Despite his enthusiasm and proud knowledge of the road network, even after borrowing the waiter's glasses he can't focus on the map. That's just fine by me, my whole life I've been misguided by people who don't know my priorities – as a trucker indirect could still be more accessible, as a biker bendier was better, and as a cyclist back roads are healthier. I'm invited to another table and more locals look over my map. I know of nothing more effective at getting company than an atlas opened up on a table, certainly in England I wouldn't be able to pass the peruser by without a comment. I love maps and people love to point at places they know. You will never be alone for long with one unfurled in public. With direction well and truly deliberated over from the coast to the end of the world, I escape to the virtual one, finding an internet café, and send some emails. Sofia said she nearly cried when the forty-two flowers arrived at the hospital and replied with forty-two thank yous.

I fancy a sunset beer and by complete accident find the same bar I was in last night. Same beer still no sunset. With alcohol back in my blood and confidence in my demeanour, I stride off purposefully, seeing a pair of tempting flaming hippy pants, but the price seems high and I don't want to get burned. For the same reason I decline a $7.50 lobster dinner. Something a tenant could easily have paid for, but empty house means empty tummy or at least a calamari compromise. Across the restaurant is a single woman, I consider making contact but she's loud, brash and would be better suited to my local than this locality.

There are flashes in the sky as I hurry home, not speed cameras or the apocalypse, but it makes my humble shelter seem appealing. I make a swift purchase of some less preferred hippy pants on the run to my room to escape the rain. I don't have much to occupy me, I've got no use yet for the private toilet, so I pack everything into my panniers which are now bulging with supplies, suggesting I'm ready to ride. The Pringles are emergency comfort food and I reason the empty tube might be useful, forever the hoarder, it won't be useful, its biggest value will be getting back the space that it is occupying. Phone charging, fan blowing, I lay on the bed, tomorrow the journey will definitely start.

Remember last November

I had more faith in my alarm than the wake-up call I asked for, neither did the job. I can't sleep when I try to and can't wake up when I want to. The only thing my sensory-deprivation room offers is surprise, what will I see when I open the door? My view in the restaurant is a couple of fried eggs in the foreground with a backdrop of crashing waves. The sky looks like brooding winter weather but the air has humidity that would flatten a Pringle. I sit and consider the worst breakfast I've ever had; this isn't it but it's bad enough to trigger that train of thought.

My panniers seem to be bloated. They looked all right last night, but now mounted on the bike they have fat-arse connotations. The guest house owner does his bit to help reduce my load with a sneaky little 10 per cent surcharge. Short-sighted fucker, can't see a map or that I'll be back in a week and won't be staying here as a result.

I wouldn't really describe myself as a beach person, I find mountains more exhilarating as there's far fewer of them on my home-county Essex coastline. However, I do feel a pang of nervousness as I cycle away from somewhere that has become vaguely familiar – and I don't mean the phoney Tesco. The journey hadn't really started when I stopped to take stock but at the same time it was too soon to just ride off. So consequently, like leaving my house, or the kiss outside passport control, there is more longing in the leaving than delight in the departure. The only way I know to cure this is to keep on going. So here I go.

My departure from Bangkok was delayed, not that I had a schedule, and the pre-trip instruction was enjoyable and invaluable. There was no urgency, I had to adjust my tempo to a cyclist's pace. I'd got a puncture before the bike had even been out of my room but maintenance is so easy compared to a motorbike. No bead to break, no axle to relocate, no hydraulically compressed brake pads to part, I can see the appeal. I just turn the bike upside down and remove the wheel – petrol doesn't pour from an inverted tank, no parts burn or break skin, it's so easy. It was a shame I didn't have a puncture repair kit. *I'll put it on the list,* I thought. I had been told of a bike shop and I bought a city map to be shown where it was, thinking rickshaw or taxi. But Stefan put my inner tube in the toilet bowl, found the hole and put one of his patches over my puncture, saying: 'Ride there.'

'Oh, right, yeah, of course.' *I think it's my turn for the toilet now.*

Sharing their guest house gave me companionship without pressure or expectations. I sat at a street-side restaurant, happy in my own thoughts and company as I watched a hundred pretty girls of varying nationalities walk past, feeling an urge I knew could be satisfied with a fistful of dirty baht. However, mostly my thoughts were occupied more with procuring the two-stroke engine than a two-stroke hand job. I settled for a second-hand book, *I'm with the Band: Confessions of a Groupie.* Intellectual stuff. But still I felt I was above the banter of the Brit beer boys and the banana pancake brigade. I was actually quite ashamed at the behaviour of my countrymen, but it was likely more of a shock to me, the steady flow of this type into Thailand had probably prepared the locals and they didn't appear to judge or discriminate, they'll take anyone's money. Not mine, I had a steady flow of whiskey I could drink alone in my room if I chose to but I didn't. I couldn't even consider it. I had a constant glow of humidity on my skin, why would I have wanted to generate more heat within? I could have mixed it with ice but was afraid of impurities in the frozen water. I didn't want to blend my drink with a parasite thawed, reborn and baptised by whiskey with the sole intention of multiplying in my tummy.

What am I doing here? Well, I seem to be averting my eyes from the Sri Lankans I pass, to avoid the inevitable questions. However, the repetitive predictability of the 'Where from, where to?' inquisition would, if I had engaged in this brief exchange, have told me I was going in the wrong bloody direction. I head up to Katana, saving face and finding a pace and place I can reroute. It's a challenging day, the simplest of needs are hard to obtain. Water being the most frustrating. It's not that they don't have it, I just can't seem to convey without confusing. There are plenty of English speakers on hand, almost fighting each other to play their part in my journey. A giant of a man who worked for the English army in Iraq gives me clear directions and still I go the wrong way. Tiny roads make for tranquil riding but disorientation is permanent. Monkeys screech from treetops. Last week I was riding wet Colchester roads under orange street lights, saying goodbye to mates, now I've got primates announcing my approach, I'm not even sure I should be here. If the sun would just shine, I'd have a clue; if I had a compass, I'd have some certainty; if I wasn't killing a week, I'd have some conviction. I come to a main road, read destinations on buses and ask some loitering youths. I need more reassurance than the insecure, more confirmation than a customs officer. I can't find an empty space, nowhere to stop and collect my scattered thoughts, but I'm not hassled. A man with three kids shows me where I am on my map, I'm not really lost as I don't have a destination for today but I'm not really in the right place either. I cross a railway line, if I rode on the rails, I'd be on a path of certainty. I'm not sure which is the right side of the tracks. I pass a temple and gunshots ring out. None of this is exciting me, there is no wow factor, I feel exposed and exhausted. There is no fire of inquisitiveness, no burning ambition, no awe of the unknown, no wonder in my whereabouts. There is a vital ingredient missing – what did I forget, what was it I took with me last time that isn't present on this two-pannier, lighter-load trip?

Last year I'd left nothing behind but an unoccupied house and more of Barry's empty promises. But I was complete, I was whole, I had no reliance on anyone, my loveless life was delivering full liberation and my heart was free to pump as I pushed my load along new roads. This trip my heart is on hold, still fluttering with infatuation, new love and longing. I didn't put the missing into the equation, it's not something I've ever experienced before. Leaving love behind, this is shit, this is what others do. The depressed traveller, the loan diner, doing what their partner can't, not revelling in their solitary status, nor finding comfort or contentment, moving in a manner that makes loss and loneliness their only travel companion. At every available opportunity they voice to newfound strangers how much they are missing. It's boring to hear, heart-aching to write, excruciating to read, entirely the wrong mindset for the road. It's a pointless endeavour to leave the person you most want to share this with, and end up only sharing solitude with every unfortunate who can't escape your monologue of longing. The pain is exemplified with every solo-occupancy room, table for one, sight unshared, every bus and train is a single one-way ticket that takes them deeper into depression. The high point of the trip being the end, and the point being lost before it was ever found. There is no point, the purpose of their existence is to be a couple and now they've split the unbroken, parted from the partner, and what's left is pathetic. Oh shit, that's what I've done, I've left the point behind. I'm loved up and waiting for reunification. I'm killing time, I'm counting days, I'm all alone without my lover and I'm fucked.

After 50 kilometres I'm knackered. Jetlag, sleep deprivation, little more than noodles of questionable nutrition and I'm having the wrong thoughts to drive me forward. The first room I find is 700 rupees so I carry on. At Warakapola I see Western faces at a food stop. The rooms have Western prices too, 3,100 rupees. The next place is full until 3.30 p.m. I say I'll be back. Hot, sweaty and desperate to end the cycling day, I keep going, up a hill and find a place for 500. I'm the only guest.

The shower feels like forgiveness, the dust washes off to reveal burned forearms. That's not fair, the sun wasn't even out, the mirror shows I have a nose to match my arms. It's not even 3 p.m., I'm captive again in a room, I don't want to go out, I don't want to stay in. I'm bored. I lay on the bed with a sarong over me and doze. It rains, I read, I contemplate, look at the map and realise at this rate there is no way I'll complete the intended loop. I see faces at the window, I'm being spied on, dark faces, dark eyes, white teeth, no shame, no guilt. This is true captivity. Fuck this, I go out into a red sky behind a lattice of power lines. In a restaurant I'm gifted some thin flaky pastry, they saw me cycle past, seems everyone has seen me. When, that is, they weren't watching the TV. England, I'm informed, just won the Rugby World Cup, for the first time ever. I don't follow sport, I don't know anything about rugby, but I do know England doesn't win much internationally and I would have watched it for that reason alone. So am I pleased it didn't cause homesickness or annoyed at missing my country win?

I sit in my room, sleep won't come, I think of a prison sentence, thirty-nine more days, this actually makes me feel better. I'm still awake at 1 a.m., bloody jet lag. Last time it passed while I was preparing. Jumping off the plane to do a one-week lap is all wrong. I could have used the week to sit on the beach, my skin would have toned progressively, my body clock would have calibrated steadily, and my stamina could have increased gradually. This is all wrong. And from here to World's End every day will be an uphill struggle.

Push and pull

Rain is coming down so I don't bother getting up, I get a knock at eight. They have a surprise for me, a 22 per cent surcharge, this is bollocks. Next time I'll ask first. It's a shitty end to my residency and a bad omen for the day ahead. However, as soon as I'm on my bike exerting some energy in a positive way I instantly feel better, bloody stinky room, spying boys, sly surcharge. I'm free of it and after a few more curses so are my thoughts, onward into the new day.

Smiley people are waiting for me where I dined last night and usher me in for breakfast, feeding me omelette without asking, and writing down directions without wanting. I leave full of egg, optimism and well-being, not least because the sun has finally decided to shine. This changes everything, that red sky last night was right, I have delight, palms have glory and a blue sky has limitless possibilities. Predictably, the road leads me uphill but I cope, and 12 kilometres of quiet momentum is perfect for peace of mind.

Every independent journey I've ever taken would be done better a second time, but what would be the point in that? The answers are obvious now, I should have got a train to World's End. I could have dozed, and watched, become accustomed to it all as I passed by. Then I could have freewheeled back to the coast. That would have been the way to utilise the week here. Not throwing myself into an instant struggle, it's as clear to me as the day is but I can't see a way to correct this now. I have to carry on up, and with that thought the road descends and I feel the reward. The breeze refreshes as I glide by tiny villages and this morning's moistness dries on my flapping clothes. A good bit at last, instead of missing and counting I'm enjoying, appreciating the value of my choices. Schoolkids laugh and shout, running with me, not after me, and I catch their infectious smiles. There is no problem finding my way today, water is plentiful, I'm feeling strong. Today it's a pleasure to be in my body, it's performing with gratification, both physically and mentally, nothing is holding me back. I have no real appetite but stop at a restaurant shack for a Pepsi to power me onwards. There are five men pushing a truck uphill and they stop to wave, the physics of momentum being of less concern than acknowledging a passing push-biker. I pass an old woman doing her laundry under a waterfall, again no need for the appliance of science, just an endless stream of opportunity. I should have taken a photo, but I seem to have found the right pace to pass through this day, and don't want to lose the rhythm.

In Karawanella I see fat German air-con tourists filling a restaurant. I'd hoped to refuel but it looks expensive and I have the supplies and energy to pass on by and continue on to Kitulgala, where I'd happily call it a day, but there is nothing here to stop me. However, the hill out of town does. It's not an ideal entry into the afternoon: 7 kilometres and nowhere to rest. I hear a truck rumble up behind me, and, just like riding a bike, last trip's technique comes back to me. As he gets level I make eye contact, make the gesture, and get approval. Now I have to push like hell to keep the pace, lungs gasp and only inhale black clouds of burned diesel. I look for a point of purchase behind the back wheels and with my right hand I grab a hold of the truck. In an instant all strain is relieved from my legs and transferred to my arm, I find the tempo, keep the balance, control the breath and, with relief, increase alertness. Check his mirror, no resentment is reflected; check his load, it's secure; check the road, there is still some for me; straighten my back, flex my arm, keep some slack to accommodate misjudgement and feel the power of his engine. The thing is, after all that exertion what I need the most is a drink but it can't be done. I've been towed up many a hill and my usual contemplation was how to reach my water bottle. The right hand is spoken for, letting go is out of the question. The left is what's holding me on to the bike, lift it from the bars and we part company, and it would likely be a painful separation. So now it's the test of tolerances, what will stop me first, losing my grip on the truck or giving in to my demanding thirst? With every uphill revolution of my wheels I'm encouraged to hold on, summoning all my strength because when I let go, I'm on my own, like a discarded rocket booster. I can't even change gear, so when my momentum changes from tenacious hand grip to lurching legs, the gear will be too low to keep up. My lower limbs will spin like a slipping clutch as the truck proceeds beyond the reach of an outstretched hand, said hand now being free to retrieve the water bottle is little consolation.

I manage to hold on for 6 kilometres, not only is it a wrench on my arm but the angles are all wrong. I'm twisted, tense and contorted. I count down the seconds until it's time for the relief of release, then wave my warped thanks and quench my thirst.

Stefan had told me about how to hold on to the back of trucks, I'm not sure I would have had the front before. The golden rule was to be behind the last axle – if you hit a bump and come off you don't want to become a bump as the truck's wheels roll over you. These lumbering vehicles move so slowly that it's easy to grab hold. As the straining engine sound gets closer wave them past, that generally gets a wave of acknowledgement, and return it with a begging gesture to be towed. I've only once been refused. The next bit is a co-ordination of speed as the vehicle crawls past, searching for a suitable point to grab on to. It's a decision that needs conviction. The reaching out is unsettling, regardless of how synchronised your speeds are there is still a wobble with the transfer of force. Once all hazards have been assessed the free ride can be enjoyed. When the strain is greater than arm strength and you part company, as the vehicle pulls out of sight, listen for a difference in engine tone. This denotes a change in gradient, when the revs go up the downhill has begun. Hills have false summits, what looks like the top becomes just another level to look up from. So have an eye for aerials, antennas, transmitters, as they are always at the top, a false peak won't have one, those red and white beacons are at the pinnacle announcing the end of an uphill struggle.

This is why I find it hard to quantify my journey in China. I cheated when it was too hard to continue, I didn't traverse, I was towed, I didn't circumnavigate, I caught buses. It wasn't a quest for charitable donations or to break records, just a bit of a bike ride. In fact I'm unsure I even crossed a provincial line, but I did find my threshold of pain and ascending the mountains I found my level of endurance. I'm proud of my solo, unsupported, independent achievement but to say I cycled across China is a bit of a stretch.

After I've let go of my saviour I hear no change in engine note and see no masts on the vertical horizon. However, plodding on I pass the parked truck, and again wave my appreciation, tortoise and the hare. The name on the cab is *St. Benedict*. I dub it the patron saint of pulling and sure enough on this road we share he gains on me again and for a further 3 kilometres I cultivate a full-blown blister from the swinging chain on the tailgate that heaves me up another hill.

Back to my own power, but it's all gone and won't be coming back today. I try to flag down some buses but they don't want my bicycle on board. I'm spent, all reserves depleted, and then it rains. I push the bike, wet, weary, shattered, the drizzle washes sunblock into my stinging eyes. At 4.30 I have to give myself a firm talking to, I need to be more assertive, the situation is deteriorating; I have to get a lift to the next town. In a desperate plea I flag down a sand truck. My bike is thrown clumsily in the back and I sit on the passenger sack in the cab. I'd prefer to be in the bed. The driver can bridge the distance between here and town effortlessly but the language gap is gaping, awkward and barely traversable. Us truck drivers are not the most highly educated of individuals – thoughtful yes, skilful certainly, but multilingual? No, not really. Also, the sign language is a little one-sided when one side of the conversation has an obligation to keep his hands on the wheel. Still, I enthusiastically persist in the charade, thinking if I can keep it going without a pause there will be no recourse but to bring me along for the ride. We stop at a waterfall so he can fill his radiator. Very useful these cascades, for cleaning clothes and refreshing cooling systems, they have far more function than just stopping the passing photographer. The driver takes me all the way into Hatton. I gush gratitude like a burst hose. He accepts my paper offering which appears to be an appropriate denomination.

The rain comes down again and tea plantations disappear behind clouds. I find a dodgy hotel and shower away today's disasters and misjudgements. My bum is really sore now and I wash my cycling clothes knowing they will not dry tonight in this humid atmosphere.

Feeling refreshed and revitalised I find a restaurant that serves what my appetite desires: meaty chicken legs and loads of vegetables. I've pushed and been pulled to a cooler altitude, calling for combats and long sleeves, with the chill my need to eat has increased and that has to be a good thing. *Bugger, I forgot to ask if the price of the room included a surcharge.* Twice bitten, bitten again. The colder air has not deterred the mozzies and although I have a net over my bed it's ripped and couldn't keep a budgie out. I visualise a Sri Lankan Two Ronnies sketch show, guest complaining to the receptionist the mosquito net is full of holes.

Counting days has not helped my scheduling, tomorrow I'm going to have to catch a train. I find a timetable and make a plan. I feel the need for a friendly face who says more than, 'Where to?' Today had its moments but I only felt fully immersed when it rained. Too cold, too wet and too tired to admire, the feel-good feeling has eluded me, but now I find comfort in the little pleasures of a tummy that doesn't rumble from the inside and is squeaky-clean on the outside. I go to bed at ten but the jet lag arrives at 1 a.m. and stays until 4 a.m. It's infuriating and not helping any aspect of this journey.

Monday 24th November
Hatton – Ohiya
Kilometres cycled: 22

Not the end of the world

I wake again at 6 a.m. If I got up now, I could catch the 7.30 train. I stay in bed with a less than positive train of thought. I get a knock on my door. 'Chai?'

'No, I'm asleep.'

It's a slow start to a new week but days don't mean much anymore, the weekend is just two days beginning with 'S' and today started with too many 'ZZZ's. At 9.30 I have another hot shower and slowly pack my panniers. I can't find my watch. I unpack my panniers, then find it tangled up in the mozzie net. Another hour has passed.

My clothes are still wet but no mozzie bites and I'm not stung with a surcharge today. Funds still need replenishing so I change some money as this is a proper town, big enough to have a bank if not a black market, and so begins the bureaucracy of changing $100 into 9,300 rupees. It's excruciating.

The railway shares my sense of punctual indifference: the train is running ninety minutes late. I check in my bike with the luggage guard and am given a receipt for my 93 rupees, and another receipt for my bike. I'm accumulating a lot of paper this morning, but not the train ticket I want – I can't buy that yet, apparently. So I wander off to find food, some scrambled egg with triangle bread and speak to a man with his three granddaughters. It's easy to find someone who wants to chat, the tricky bit is finding something to talk about. English appears to be quite widely spoken but with limited vocabulary, so conversation travels in circles smaller than my circuit within the country and is often an uphill struggle. The bike is always an ice breaker but the language reaches its limits long before the intrigue is satisfied. Likewise, my food is finished before my hunger is gratified.

72

Back at the station I buy a second-class seat for a third of what I paid to bring a bike on board, because a first-class ticket is five times more. So continues my second-class, second-hand journey through life that affords me so many first-hand experiences. I check my bike is being loaded and get in the carriage with it. I'm expecting to be told to move, but no one is bothered, I'm not even asked for my ticket. I'm little more than luggage now and it's a status I'm comfortable with. I find a bag of rice to sit on and text Tara happy birthday before I lose reception. The station starts to move backwards, from the back of the train the motion is as smooth and quiet as a bicycle, I have a widescreen view out of the open door. I'm not sure I have access to the rest of the train or a toilet but neither are of any concern as we pass plantations on the sides of mountains. See, this is better, I should have done this on my second day, I've got it all arse backwards. It's not just the journey, it's the freedom to be in the luggage carriage, alone and loving it, like a hobo. I try to recall a song, something about 'I've been everywhere' but it's not coming so I put on my Ozzy Osbourne MP3 and find a live version of 'Crazy Train' as I spread my damp clothing around the carriage to dry. Contentment comes as the journey continues, I love a little rebellion, not taking my assigned seat, and not feeling the insecurities of an out-of-sight bike, the serenity of a carriage to myself, this is my kind of first-class, and the sights outside are straight off the cover of a PG Tips box. Best of all, this slowly changing view comes without the sweat of exertion or the pollution of being towed.

At one station about ten backpackers get on. I have mixed feelings, I'm pleased not be part of their practices but also a little disappointed not to be part of their pack. I like that they haven't even spotted me, my stealth increases my feeling of renegade, nomad, wanderer, and actually that little illusion is great company for the rest of the journey. I would imagine we'll all disembark at the same stop anyway. We don't, I'm the only one who gets off, the place is abandoned but for the stationmaster. He thinks I have petrol and oil in my water bottles and I tell him I need it for fuel, for me, and then open the lid and drink it. He's momentarily horrified and then we both laugh. What a strange sound, like screaming or crying, a burst of spontaneous emotion and I realise I've not laughed since … shit, since I got here. That's what's been fucking missing. How awful, I've got to correct that.

The day came when I had to leave the comfort of the Khao San Road and ride, which was basically straight off into the deep end, the toxic streets of Bangkok, wearing a mask with a black circle where my mouth was, not as a locating device but it showed what was filtered before entering my lungs. The bike was so light and fast, whizzing past temples and Buddhas. I was a pin in a blender of bolts and carbon monoxide, weaving and dodging, nimble, swift, slim, and alert. More turns than I could ever retrace. The faster I went, the faster I went, meaning to slow down was to be caught, surfing a wave that would break over me if I reduced my speed. Biking baptism by fire. I could ride a bike, that wasn't the issue, apparently, it's not something easily forgotten, but this, this was like London dispatch riding without the throttle-twisting acceleration to get out of a situation. I had to push with adrenalin-fuelled legs onto metal pedals with calf-lacerating possibilities, and choose a gear that synchronised pressure with performance while always maintaining balance. My translucent white top clung wet with sweat and my full-back tribal tattoo broke through the opaque fabric. I've never seen it without reflection or photo – I've never seen the wind, only what blows past – but the awareness was another notch in my nomadic road warrior illusion. The frictionless rider, gliding, fully focused, primed, thrusting onto pedals, poised over brakes, leaning over and looking out with wild and alert eyes. Level with mopeds, undertaking buses, weaving round pedestrians, finding the rhythm, feeling the flow, anticipating the movement of all that was ahead and forgetting the past like Alzheimer's.

I may have been riding recklessly but not aimlessly, I was actually trying to find an elusive revered bicycle shop. A place of carbon fibre and high-end accessories. A little Western fixed-price affluence in the streets of hard living. It was a place I'd never find again and couldn't really afford in the first place. I walked in like I belonged. My arrival by bike gave me guest list status – well, in my mind, at least.

They had all I needed if only I'd had the money to pay for it, trip gauges and tools, water bottle and mirror, everything I deemed essential before I set off, so I tried not to think of the cost but I did cut a crucial corner by not buying cycling shorts. I can just about handle the Lycra-clad, *Ski Sunday*, downhill-slalom look, but that sanitary-pad-cushioned crotch put me right off. Anyway, I figured my arse had barely been on the seat cycling here. However, the king's birthday was coming, a grand event, and to celebrate, in this shop by the cash register was a lucky dip bowl. I pulled out a coupon that gave me 15 per cent off my total purchase.

My confidence on the bike and having found the shop had me blasting past a bus on the way back. Some Home Counties Hooray Henry with newfound 'left the nest' self-assurance had caught some Bangkok city bus bravado, he leaned out the window, and in his newly acquired Cockney accent asked, 'Are ya fuckin' mad?' I looked up with Oakley reflection and masked anonymity, the ink under my skin the only identification, and with calf-pumped power I declared, 'For the adrenalin.' It was spontaneous, it was pretentious, but in the moment, it had impact, and then I out-accelerated the bus, leaving them with what I like to think was an impressionable moment.

The bike, the company, the accumulating knowledge, the discount and the ability to fly round the streets unharmed, occupied all my thoughts and all my days. I was riding a wave of luck, filled with well-being, faster than a backpacker, and becoming part of an ever-growing crowd. Soon I was joined by a hardcore dreadlocked Czech couple who had hiked across Tibet before cycling here. The girl had a wild beauty and rolled her 'R's with purring sexual enticement, but had very hairy armpits that turned me off like halitosis. She said she juggled with fire – she was either very good or hadn't done it for a while, that sprouting growth had gotta be within singeing range. There was a typically down-to-earth Aussie, he seemed all right on the surface but I got the feeling he had an agenda. He was slightly manipulative and I didn't trust him fully. He was befriended by a young Brit called Pier, a preaching vegetarian who was definitely damaged goods. I had credibility in this crowd from my past travels and motorcycling, and acceptance because of my new plans and bicycle. I listened intently to their tales and couldn't help but learn. Quite literally a world of experience all came with beer, upbeat chatter, support and camaraderie. We talked loads, drank loads, spent loads, laughed loads, and we were all fit, slim and muscular. It was the perfect launch pad, and without trying we couldn't help but become our own entity in a predominantly backpackery environment. I'd found the direction I wanted to continue my travelling in, I was so right for this lifestyle, broadened horizons, part of a new scene. Although, I did have to remind myself, I hadn't actually cycled anywhere yet.

As soon as I leave the railway station the road is narrow and steep, so steep, I can't even keep my front wheel on the ground. It's a ridiculous gradient, I have to push it. A 3-kilometre vertical climb, the hairpins so steep I feel I should crawl or fall backwards. Eventually, the road levels out on to Horton Plains. I can cycle again, glide, ride with the breeze, silently and effortlessly propelling myself forward. So silently that a massive stag crosses my path; absolutely oblivious to me, he stops in the middle of the road. Annoyingly, the Velcro on my bar bag spooks him as I try to get out my camera. That was stupid. I should have just stood silently and watched; it was working for him.

The road is perfect, smooth and unpopulated, the views are uninterrupted by pylons, wires or any human blot on the landscape. I'm so happy I've finally made it here, not quite the kind of endurance I anticipated, not stamina and strength but the dealing with my emotions, jet lag, bad diet, bad rooms, and the transition in general. Still, I've got through it, I've got here. Now I just have to find the guest house on my map. And that's when it all goes to shit. As soon as I allow myself a moment of rejoicing in my achievements I get kicked back down. At the official entrance into the national park I'm told that the two guest houses are no more, and it will cost me $16 to get to World's End – and it's closed, until tomorrow. Well, bollocks. Now I wish I had a tent. Now I wish I hadn't asked. I could easily have avoided the official entrance, innocently trespassing, but now I'm marked, now I'd be breaking and entering. I'm within 4 kilometres of my destination, the same one that was denied me six years ago. What now? Back down the shitty road, just say *fuck it then*, take the train back to town. I feel like going home. What a bloody miserable trip it's been so far.

I put on my new coat and freewheel back down the hill, thinking nothing good at all. Just before I get to the town where the station is, I see a sign for a lodge. There isn't much daylight left but a sign is enough to fire up some optimism, it sends me down a steep, unmade road. Man, I don't want to push the bike back up here, at what point do I turn around? Every corner brings increasing indecision, every decline has to be climbed back up again. How much further am I going to go, when will I give up the idea of finding somewhere to stay? The later it gets the more desperate I become, the more destitute I'll be the further down I go. After 2 kilometres there is a derelict shack. My heart sinks to the level of the altitude I've dropped to get here. But there is someone home, and he speaks English. Are you open? He makes me tea. Do you have a room? I'm the first guest in three weeks. Is that a yes? He seems tired of my questions. We watch the sunset behind mountains that drop down into a Sri Lankan Grand Canyon. Yes, he finally says. There's not much urgency in his manner. He shows me my room and then the guestbook, I'm the first entry this month. But not the first cyclist to come here: the *Method of Transportation* column has its share of proud and bragging 'I cycled' entries. With a guidebook I'd not be here, one little sign, one last hope, my emotions have gone up and down with the hills today. It's been a hard road, draining me of everything, breaking me, taunting and teasing. The bonuses of this week have not been like a fine wine complimenting a good meal, more like an air pocket when you're trapped under ice. It's basically been horrendous with the occasional lifesaver. India will be different. The journey won't be a circuit, I won't have a fixed schedule and there will almost definitely be a shag at the end.

I'm fed a massive curry, it's all good apart from one dish. No guests for three weeks, some things don't keep, not just the secrecy of this place but the food with which he feeds his sporadic visitors. I say good night at eight, have a hot shower and then my bottom explodes, but thankfully once detonated it's disarmed for the rest of the night. Another air pocket under the ice. It's a silent night, no phone signal, no TV, no Westerners, no planes flying over, far from the crowds, far from feeling like I have any more control over this trip than I do over my bowels.

Now where? Now what?

It has been a deadly silent night. If this is World's End it certainly didn't die screaming. I get up at 6 a.m. to watch the sunrise but it makes less effort than I did, so I go back to bed for an hour. Egg on toast, again no menu, and a vague apology from the guest house owner. 'It's OK,' I reassure him, 'I would have ordered this anyway' – *along with bacon, sausage, beans, tomatoes, mushrooms, a fried slice and some HP sauce*, I don't add.

No sneaky surcharge, and I leave him to his tranquillity. I'm on the road for 7.45 – well, path, there is no road. If ultimately I'm still metaphorically trapped under ice then that was definitely a good air pocket. Now where? I know it's 5.1 kilometres to the plains. I push on slowly, the hills don't seem nearly as bad as yesterday, probably because I know where they will end, and I recharged overnight, lost a bit of weight too. See, I said if I did a trip a second time, I'd do it so much better. Research would probably help too, but research led me to believe there were two guest houses on Horton Plains and those expectations had me cycling on thin ice. If I'd not expected that perhaps I would have been more vigilant and found the hidden guest house on the way up. I could torture myself with these possibilities, these *what ifs*. What now? That's all that matters, that's all I can control. I manage to do half a kilometre without stopping, that either indicates the steepness of the incline or the sustainability of stamina, maybe both. I can feel my thoughts are getting stranger, I've been a stranger too long, it's the downside of solo travel, only company can cure this now. As I leave the shade of the climb my phone gets reception and bleeps a reply from Tara as I cycle on to the sunny flat plains. No stag today but my camera's out just in case. Again, presumptions are what come when you're not breaking new ground, the element of surprise is gone – well, I'm not surprised I don't see it. However, right on time the day delivers the much needed and unexpected, in the form of the non-permanent. I meet five English cyclists. Conversation at last, cheery, like-minded, common ground, shared experiences, and on top of all that they are actually well-balanced people.

My bicycle in Bangkok didn't only come with instructions from experienced and congenial company. Stefan and Ana had their fingers on the pulse, their nose to the ground and were aware of who was where when it came to two wheels around Asia. So as my prolonged preparation continued and the in-crowd of long-distance overland cyclists grew, I discovered some fractured minds among those fit bodies. And man, were there some fucked up individuals. Why do people take to the road? There are of course as many motives as there are roads. But some are more common than others. I was escaping – that was a given, on the face of it – an English winter. That escapism is as acceptable as it is doable, perfectly reasonable. But dig a little deeper and the thing I couldn't outrun, not by flying 10,000 kilometres or cycling another 3,000, was the news I'd left England with, that I may or may not have a daughter in Denver. So as well as my four panniers I had this emotional baggage too. However, as a sage once said, we all have baggage, it's how we pack it that determines the ease of our onward journey – and I don't think they meant concealing your whiskey. As my cycling acquaintances became more familiar, the friendships stronger, the conversations more personal, the insights became deeper. Beneath the surface I discovered quite a few of them had grief-stricken, guilt-ridden, self-punishing, over-analysing, deeply depressed, doom-driven demons, baked hard into their heads as they pushed their load around the planet. The solitude was expanding the torment, the hardships were self-harming, the distance was intensifying their torture. The same thoughts revolved inside their heads with every revolution of the pedals, inevitably going over the same ground repetitively compressed the surface, they found their reflections stuck in a rut and then became entrenched in the mindset they'd worn away. And me? Same, same but different, as long as there's someone worse than me I'm managing all right. I remember meeting a French cyclist on a long, lonely road – well, it was long and lonely for him and his red, white and blue flag that was flying in a foreign land without a legion. I had company and an engine, but I always stop to ask a cyclist if they are OK for water – being a two-wheeled brother of the road, I'm not about to discriminate just because they don't have a motor. His nation had just won the World Cup and I congratulated him. OK, I'm no football fanatic but some things like US elections, the Second World War, Darth Vader being Luke Skywalker's dad, you just can't help but have some knowledge of. He, this guy, was as vacant as last night's guest house. His eyes were as empty as the road he was on. I never expect unreserved conviviality from a Frenchman, but this – he was so deep inside his head he wasn't even coming through in waves.

So by comparison these individuals are very well adjusted, although more academic than adventurers, with more intellect than ingenuity and their bikes could use a little maintenance. They have just been unloaded from a minibus – *oh, so you haven't actually cycled here then*, I think, with I'm-better-than-you buoyancy. I don't need to say it, I just need to give myself a little confidence boost, it's been so long since I spoke to native English speakers, and in my defence, nearly twenty-four hours since I last unloaded my bike from some public transport. We chat for an hour, or perhaps I monologue for an hour unloading my loneliness on this captive audience. They say they are going the other way. Ahh yes, that old chestnut. I often go that way myself. However, they do let slip they are going to India. I resist saying 'Me too' to save them squirming, backtracking and mumbling they meant Indonesia. However, they have issues with their bikes: having disc brakes, the levers get pulled in transit when the wheel is removed and that pushes out the pistons of the callipers, closing the gap and making it impossible to get the disc between them upon reassembling. I suggest putting a coin between the brake pads and a rubber band round the lever to keep the pressure on. *Oh, will you look at that, I have value, I've just endeared myself* – well, endear might be a bit strong, but their bicycle clips are bracelets again so body language says prolonged encounter.

They tell me they climbed Adam's Peak, a place of spiritual significance regardless of your beliefs. It could be Adam's (Eve's boyfriend) footprint on top, from when he first set foot on earth … or was that where the Ark came to rest? No, wait, that was Mount Ararat. Or the footprint could be from Lord Shiva or an apostle from India, possibly Buddha, or it could all be bollocks. Whatever, the view is undeniable and the climb sounded daunting until today. They say I could do it easily, but then they didn't just see my half-kilometre cycle between long pushes, or yesterday's train, although going 'the other way' they'll soon see what I've been through. We collectively decide to give World's End a miss; $16 is so disproportionate to all other expenses in this country. Three nights' accommodation, over a whole day's budget, just to walk a 4-kilometre track. We say goodbye and as I cycle off, I think, *No, fuck it, if it were free I'd go, I've come all this way, it's been denied me twice, I can't assume I will ever be back and even if I am it will cost me more than $16 to get here.* So I bite the bullet, pay the fee and walk the track to the end of the world … and it's shite. I do see a lizard though so the trip isn't a total waste. I look at the cloud-obscured view for about five minutes and then walk the 4 kilometres back to my bike.

Now I really am going the other way, I've not been this way before – I'm heading west. The road I want to take doesn't materialise, only a dirt track and that can't be it. I go down a very steep hill, no wonder those cyclists came up in a van. All the way down my back brake squeals for release and the front threatens to dismount me with a head-first stoppie. When it comes to cycling apparel I do now wear the padded shorts but as underwear – I get enough looks without riding along in a Lycra posing pouch – but that's it, I don't go for clinging tops or shoes that clip to pedals and I certainly don't wear a helmet. There are a few reasons for this. Firstly, I'm a child of the '70s and we never had such softy hardware and, secondly, well, I just don't want to look like a twat, and anyway a wide-brimmed hat actually offers more safety here, preventing both sunstroke and sunburn. So looking cooler than a wheelie king, I freewheel into civilisation and find myself in … Pattipola. Bollocks, I don't want to be here.

81

Then I drop my bike. No harm done, but no drop ever goes without some kind of damage. In this case it's pride, perhaps symbolic of my mistake in being here at all, if you care to read that much into it. The town is little more than a train station and, if I choose, it could be the end of my road. In three hours there is a train to the capital Colombo. I consider it briefly, an air pocket or airlifted out of this predicament? I want just one more thing to experience. I take a deep breath and ride on.

Knowing now I won't make it to Adam's Peak, the lows seem more frequent than the highs, the rewards not worth the price paid, the laughter not worth the long silences. It's the 'I will, I won't' ups and downs that are worse than the hills. After this morning's conversation I had my sights set on the summit of the peak and now I'm looking down again. As John Cleese said in *Clockwise*: 'It's not the despair. I can take the despair. It's the hope I can't stand.' But hope won't find me here, I've got to go look for it, so taking my independence once again into my own hands I cycle on, now with the destination of Nuwara Eliya in mind. An old British colonial town, much like the British Empire it's downhill all the way.

I find a room, it's full of flies, I take it anyway, they have hot water and I pay up front so there is no opportunity to add a surcharge. I'm learning slowly. After washing my clothes, body and hair, I walk into town. It's certainly a place of colonial architecture but with corrugated iron roofs. Perhaps the upper classes took their upper covering with them. I find an internet café and lose myself for a while. I don't think Sofia can send me an email that makes me feel better. If I have no message I feel disappointment, if it's a loving one I feel longing, if it's a brief one I feel unimportant, and if it's matter-of-fact one I feel second-rate. I'd be better off looking at my inbox of recipients and subject headings and leaving it there. Opening anything takes me back and I was beginning to make progress.

I return to my guest house, there are lots of Westerners but no one even makes eye contact let alone talks – kill 'em all, I have a massacre of flies in my room, the map has never been so accurate and therefore so useful. With death all around I open it up and confirm that there is absolutely no way I'll make it to Adam's Peak now. Perhaps like World's End it would disappoint, that's the problem with knowing, there are expectations. If the guidebooks enthuse the hordes follow, and take tranquillity, authenticity and affordability away from a place that was once worth the effort. No guidebook predicted a stag in the road or a lizard on a rock and those sightings have been some of the most memorable so far. So fuck the peak and the fabled footprint on top, I certainly won't be adding mine to the well-trodden path. I'll get a train tomorrow, denying myself the reward of the downhill freewheel.

I go out for sunset and take some photos, out of habit more than awe, then eat noodles out of hunger more than desire. I could eat in a posh restaurant with white-gloved waiters but it seems a waste on my own. I don't have the confidence to portray the mystic lone diner. With a cloud over my head even my shade wouldn't be enticing, I'd repel company like Lycra shorts and helmet. I wander the market, the prime commodity seems to be fake Columbia clothing. If I hadn't brought my $5 coat I might be interested but for close to $50 even with a fluffy zip-in liner I think I'm getting fleeced. So I go back to my room and kill more flies. It starts to rain and even a new coat couldn't coax me out. I hope it rains tomorrow too, just to make Adam's Peak a pointless endeavour. If I can't go then I don't want anybody else to either. It's not fear of missing out, it's wanting the weather to intervene and take the point away, just for one day. This week has not worked out at all.

At 9 p.m. they are still banging and building downstairs. If it is not barking dogs, honking traffic or amplified prayers it's fucking banging. I can't help but think working on my Harley in the shed would be more fun than this. I hope India can redeem this trip, there's a lot riding on it but I think it can handle the pressure, though probably not in the way I hope or expect. India doesn't move in a logical or methodical manner, there is mysticism and mayhem beyond Western comprehension, thus creating the magical and memorable experiences. I think the subcontinent is up to the task of redemption. I get a text from Barry, he has a potential tenant – *oh, Barry, pulling me from my dreamy yearnings, you are everything India is not, you have the spirituality and mysticism of an estate agent, the grace of a brick and the wonder of who threw it through the window, the finesse of a cement mixer and the repulsion of a dead rat on the doormat, and to top it off ya too late mate.* I'm tempted to make an appointment just to waste his time like he's wasted mine.

This is my fourth consecutive day without alcohol, which has absolutely nothing to do with my frame of mind.

At 11 p.m. I go downstairs and politely ask the builders to shut up. I think that's what they were waiting for and seem happy to comply, then for the first time this trip I sleep right through the night.

The pull of the train

There appears to be no sign of breakfast, or of anyone at all, that's fine as I'm up ahead of my appetite, away before the surcharge gets out of bed. I'm on the road for 7.40 and I'm going down. Nothing to eat but tea as far as I can see. I try to see the uniqueness of the scene that is spread before me, I've seen it before but will I ever again? For that reason the landscape is worthy of a photograph, taking me past the halfway point of my 35mm reel of Kodak Colour Plus. I can't really capture the sight and I can't grasp the feeling as I'm not feeling it, no one is picking today, and they almost always have a wave for me. I'm aware that I am unaware, wondering where the satisfaction is, and when I'll find it. After seven freewheeling kilometres I'm at the station ninety minutes early. The stationmaster is ecstatically pleased to see me and shows me where I can strip my bike for transit to the coast. Its fee today: three times more than my $1 ticket. Now I'm ready for breakfast, I get a loaf, eight bananas and a glass of warm water, yum. Back at the station I make a marmite sandwich as some schoolkids stare at me. The bravest takes my ear buds to listen. 'Ahh, Michael Jackson,' he proudly announces.

'No, Aerosmith.'

It inspires a poem and I write a bit of verse to Sofia, hoping perhaps that putting my missing down on paper might let me leave my longing on the folded sheet, but I'm so inspired I keep adding to it, the longing and the long poem. The train is dead on time and as I've been absorbed in creation the station has filled with French tourists. I wonder where they came from, France probably. I get a window seat facing the direction of travel and nothing else matters now.

With sounds in my head I watch the winding decline of the road and all the exertion-free miles that would have taken me back to the coast.

What I'm missing brings me down, I did all the hard work and there is no return for my efforts. I really messed this week up; I could blame the map to some degree but the simplest solution escaped me. Train up, freewheel back. I'm annoyed it didn't occur to me. Everything happens for a reason and the reason is: I'm a bloody idiot. I don't feel I've done any part of the journey properly so far. I suffered the increased friction of inclination and failed to enjoy a fraction of what was on offer, out of sync, out of sorts, out on my own, and now out of time, stupid and frustrating.

The train takes a route stopping at Kandy. *Aargh, the agony.* Yes, I've been here before, but it's beautiful, it could have been my first stop if I'd had taken the train from the coast. I was too damn keen to get on the bicycle – understandable after weeks of waiting and preparation. After all the public transport I just wanted to start cycling but if I'd just waited a little longer, given it a little more forethought, I could have got *Jammy git* emails all over again. I've not really been communicating much at all this trip, no one has sympathy for a misery on the road, and it never occurred to me to contact Stefan for advice. He's in a different league, not only as a hardcore cyclist but now back in Chile and working on a family. How very different from my life journey. He clearly has a better map than me.

We crawl into Kandy so slowly I could have hung on behind the train, but now things speed up and we pass through some quite big stations. I recognise some bits I cycled through, even a tree I stopped under for shade and a refill. With this newfound speed, seeming so destination-driven I'm concerned the train won't even stop at my station. I put my head out of the window and see some red lights. The train slows and I pick up my bag which, annoyingly, I placed too close to the parade of feet that trod moist and pungent footprints down the carriage from the piss-soaked floor in the toilet. It's the first rule of Asian train travel: make sure baggage location avoids contamination. But I suppose I got lazy, my last train trip in the luggage car had no such inconveniences. So with the aromatic emblem of travel embedded into my bag I jump from the train, keen to retrieve my bike before it leaves again. I needn't have worried, they have a transfer system more efficient than the toilet sanitation and I see it being unloaded as I approach. My little station of choice is called Veyangoda. I assemble my bike for an audience of one: a staring bloke who gets closer and closer to the main attraction, getting me ready for India. Check directions, get water and fly off in a westerly direction. I want to be off the road before dark, and not fall off it because I can't see the kerb. I'm averaging 26kph, the first time I've achieved double figures this trip, aided by the sea-level air, a week of working out uphill, a flat, smooth road, and the return of confidence and control. I'm sweating hard and I've not got much food inside me but water is flowing freely and that's all I need for now.

In my daze of becoming a cyclist and socialite in Bangkok, I wasn't counting on much, least of all the days, and before I knew it the king's birthday celebrations had begun. The vibe was infectious and gave me yet another reason to stick around – anyway, a little culture away from Khao San couldn't hurt. In the park by the palace, stages had been set up, kids dancing, decorated dignitaries speaking, jugglers thrilling, and always fireworks, even before dark. Thai boxing and rock musicians all with the omnipotent golden Grand Palace as a backdrop. A puppet monarch he may have been, and perhaps those actual proceedings were more powerful than his imperial or political authority. However, the excitement in the air couldn't be denied, it was potent, dispelled cynicism, and it was exhilarating to be a part of this national pride with 50,000 happy Thais.

But the festivities were not without incident. A local lad grabbed Ana's arse and Stefan flew off the handle, creating an ugly scene. Frightening how quickly you are suddenly a guest in someone else's celebrations, my alliance was decided by the colour of my skin and I didn't have the language to calm the escalating commotion. Not something I've ever been party to as a predominantly lone traveller. Thankfully, a higher power intervened: the heavens opened, extinguishing the flare-up and causing a mass exodus.

The next morning, with money and passport draped and dehydrating around my room, there was a knock on the door. My mistrust actually let the dodgy Aussie think I was 'polishing off' rather than let him in to see my wealth hung out to dry. I was leaving the next day and didn't care what he thought, but he had come with a warning and found me at breakfast to tell me Pier, the paranoid, un-joyed Brit, wanted to ride with me.

A week since I had landed and my feet hadn't touched the ground. My bike fully packed was so heavy I couldn't lift it any more than I could a motorcycle. However, when Stefan inspected my packing, distribution and pre-trip preparation, he was genuinely complimentary. Diplomatically, he chose not to cast judgement on the liquid I was carrying that was excessive in both percentage and volume.

There were some sad goodbyes, and solemn promises to visit in Chile. I was given a shark-tooth necklace and then became the centre of ridicule as I didn't have cycling shorts. They said I was going to suffer from the pain – like I was suffering then from being the butt of every joke – and cycling with Pier too was going to be another pain in the arse. I knew he would cling on like a limpet, hanging around me with irritating discomfort like piles. The goodbyes went on until 1.45 a.m.

I'd been advised to catch a train out of the city as there was little to see and no point in wasting a day, or using up a life, trying to exit the sprawling metropolis that is Bangkok. After three hours sleep I left my room before it was light, with a weeks' worth of preparation and advice. The first thing I encountered was some British pissheads still drinking from the night before. They were at the same table I'd sat at and seen Stefan walk past, from which I'd chased after him and changed my future. 'Oi mate, ya back wheel's going round!' And to add to their drunken, cutting-edge commentary and hilarity a dog chased after me. One of the golden tips I had been given was to carry a dog beater. This was preferable to trying to beat a dog, as you might not always be able to instantly summon up the power to outrun a rabid ambush. Having an easily accessible stick, on the other hand, is a failsafe deterrent. I grabbed for my weapon that was to see action before my guest house was even out of sight. I let the larger louts have the last laugh, not that the cunts will recall it. *Now, if Pier fails to recall the meeting time and place*, I thought, *perhaps it will be my time to laugh … or at least rejoice in having escaped the second unwanted contact of the morning.*

A boisterous youth at a bus stop tries to run after me and grab something off my bike, the only negative interaction in the whole of Sri Lanka. His mate pulls him back, showing what a unique incident this is. There's always one and perhaps here there is only one. As he fades out of my mirror's view a rickshaw draws level with me. Three girls in the back giggle and purr over my speed and strength, now if they want to try and grab something …

My map remains inaccurate to the very end but I find the airport and now retrace the road I took a week ago. I'm not exactly sure what my frame of mind was then, but my body has certainly improved. I speed past traffic with assertion and high stamina, I feel light-headed, close to perhaps what a runner might call 'hitting the wall'. Back in Negombo, I ride straight to a beach guest house but it's out of my price range. However, I'm directed to another, newly built and German-owned. It's wunderbar, clean, convivial, inviting and enticing me to go over-budget. I think I deserve it.

I shower and then sit in the sterile, airy room and contemplate what I've done and what's to come. The people I'm going to visit in Goa I've known less than a year. I met them on my Chinese trip, an educated and well-spoken Kiwi, at least by nationality, although truly international and unidentifiable by accent which has an uncanny similarity to that of C-3PO. His friend had characteristics which confirmed his country of origin: aloof at first, on a guest house deck suntrap with nowhere to sit, he'd occupied two chairs, one for his German arse and the other for his feet. The Kiwi was a habitual traveller, a few bases but no home; the German had taken early retirement and wintered in Asia. We've been in touch over the last year and it occurs to me the reason the Kiwi doesn't get burned out being permanently on the road is he tends to stay put for two weeks at a time. I can see how that strategy conflicts with my afternoon arrival and dawn departure. I'll slow the pace when I get to India, take a lesson from his well-practised habits.

I go out for a sunset beer, send my poem to Sofia and end up in a lonely pizza parlour where single people sit at separate tables. I have a second and third beer. I manage to miss my guest house on the walk back, proving I can get lost even without my map. I've gone a long way before I'm convinced I've passed it. See, that wouldn't happen if I was to stay put for a while. Maybe I'm drunk, I can't seem to get the mozzie net to cover the bed and the opportunist bloodthirsty bastards feast on my mistake all night long.

Thursday 27th November
Negombo
Kilometres cycled: 13

For a few rupees more

Now the reality of the ride is over I can dream, and did I have a good one – hanging out with a rock-god legend, one of my favourite recurring ones. Last night I was even singing songs with him. Clearly a dream as I can't even sing 'Happy Birthday' in tune. I get up for a wee and go back to the dream but I have to get rid of him, he's stressing me out. I can't host someone used to life's luxuries; I find his desires exceed the limits of even my dreams. So even in sleep, it appears that I still can't escape my frugal budget.

Still, this is a very sumptuous room, with a Western as opposed to squat toilet. Regardless of technique, hovering or seated it's the first time I've faced the door in sixty hours. One tends to keep track of such things, and stats like these will be the envy of many when I get to India. I do laundry in preparation for my change of country, and have the best meal of the journey so far. Mango and unknown tropical fruits, yoghurt and honey, eggs and fresh bread. Perhaps it's because I've paid more than usual or it's got the Germanic influence but the meal, room and general surroundings come with a bonus of serenity. Possibly this is the reward of the return. Sometimes the hardships become commonplace, a gradual decline into a menial daily grind. No one willingly walks into an unpleasant situation; the transition is a subtle one. During the last seven days I've systematically taken pleasure out of my perceptions. Especially when I think of my prolonged leaving party, I was thrown into the lonely world without a *Lonely Planet* and the sentence was solitary liberation. I closed up to keep myself complete, I may have held on to some kind of comfort but the clenched fist of possession repels invites and opportunities. Now I feel I'm opening up, my whole body is unfurling in warmth and light, voluntarily vulnerable, happily approachable. I'm

91

not going to catch anything nasty on white-tile floors, and this ambience of net curtains bellowing in a sea breeze, fragrant, fresh healthy food, hygiene and high standards all add to my blossoming.

Pier, my partner to be, was not at the prearranged meeting place and there was nothing else on my mind but to leave the dirty city behind. I waited for him just long enough to justify my commitment to our being a couple then gladly left without him. I was nervous. It was the first ride with my ridiculously heavy load, it was dark, I was unsure of direction and had a deadline. Half a kilometre from my destination I asked a tuk-tuk driver for confirmation and confidently cycled the last leg into the central station. I found the platform my train was leaving from, took off the panniers, checked in the bike and, just as I was feeling fully in control, annoyingly, Pier came and found me.

The journey was seven hours long and over the course of it I heard everything – albeit in a tone so low I had to strain to hear even though I didn't want to. He was another anguished victim plagued by his past. I think perhaps his antimalarials were not helping his mindset, I've never seen such paranoia. He was convinced that every discarded and unravelled roadside cassette tape contained code to be passed around the underworld.

'Yeah, and every bottle has a message in it,' I retorted flippantly.

I didn't get a laugh, I got a look.

'Only taking the piss,' I continued, 'and that's what you'll get if you're on the verge of checking every bottle for answers.'

He actually thought the other passengers were making subtle signs. Communicating by rubbing noses, and scratching ears, they were all seated strategically to spy on him. *Ya not that fuckin' special mate*, I thought to myself, *or maybe you are.* He had been inspired to travel, he said, by watching Mr. Benn as a kid.

'Did you see that one where he put on a rubber suit and gag? Mr. Benn-over.'

He hadn't, he didn't have an ounce of humour in him, just a monotone monologue.

As paddy fields passed by, we got on OK, he had more cycling experience than me, so I mused I may as well let him tag along. I had no real plan anyway.

We disembarked early afternoon onto the quietest road I'd seen since I arrived, with squashed snakes and flattened frogs, so there was clearly some traffic. Stopping for coke, I was invited into a car by some Thai lads playing 'YMCA', all insisting I sing with them. It was not quite a dream come true and I would really rather have stood, as my arse was aching already. I decided to leave my bike with Pier so they could take me to find a guest house. It was so easy, but when I picked up my bike and told him to follow, he decided to stay elsewhere. This night's accommodation had its own restaurant, and food was included in the price, assuring all guests ate there. This was the reason I found myself in the company of two Polish girls. I suppose, I thought to myself, that travelling with Pier during the day might work as long as we split every night, but then he appeared, hovering over us, and his drone soberly ruined the vibe. He had to go. Actually, I had to go – something had disagreed with my insides and urgently wanted to exit.

But the next morning he came up trumps, redeemed himself, found a bike shop that stocked cycling shorts. It was not so easy to dump him anymore. We cycled off alongside canals and found a Wat without tourists, without restraints, without anything, you could have lived in it, no one would know. Then more 13th-century architecture, and a Buddha by a moat, all uninhabited, peaceful, and I was overwhelmed by the benefit of having a bicycle. Through a gap in a stone wall I saw an absolute giant of a Buddha on the other side, making me gasp, 'Jesus Christ,' before realising the inappropriate faux pas. It was really quite intimidating. I touched its painted nails, looked up at its humbling eyes. The place was like Angkor Wat without the hype or any inhabitants, and I wandered around temples, carvings, sculptures, moats, palms, cut grass and ruins. Then we cycled off to find shelter from the rain, to talk and take in what we had seen in utter awe. But Pier wouldn't laugh, couldn't find happiness in his tormented soul. When the sun shone again, where I saw a rainbow, he saw a downturned sad face.

I had tortured guts, progressively getting worse every day, hampering my actions, what to eat, where to stop. Bangkok belly, but I'd brought it with me along with the whiskey. Both were unwanted. I've got a story of debilitating diarrhoea for every stamp in my passport. I have the head for wanderlust but a stomach more suited for the life of a hermit with an en suite. Stop and fast is the best fix I've found, staying put for two days and nil by mouth, but sweet black tea always rids me of the runs.

I stuck with Pier and rode on for a few more days but opted in the evenings to get my own room where I could spend some time by myself. Although, during one night of heavy rain, I dreamed so deeply my demons came to life. Their suppression rarely caused depression. Does extreme physical exercise require an exorcism, had they escaped from the darkest recesses of my psyche or the bottle I wouldn't abandon? I woke up very confused, was his delirium contagious? When I ventured out of my room the humble Thai owner confided in me with distress: 'Sir, your friend was playing too roughly with my child.'

I was not entirely surprised to hear this. I knew he was damaged but I didn't think he was malicious, not a danger to anyone but himself. Perhaps I was being naïve, I'd given him the benefit of the doubt, assumed he was just not used to, or comfortable in, the company of children and didn't know the appropriate way to be with them. Perhaps, I thought, he'd do better to avoid kids and I should work on trying to accept that I have one. Anyway, like the Bangkok arse-grabbing accusations I felt guilty by association and could only respond with, 'I'm sorry, I'm leaving him tomorrow.'

Volatile and unhinged, among his other inappropriate behaviours was – as a sanctimonious vegetarian who hadn't bothered to learn enough language to convey his finicky diet – the fact that he would righteously throw the meat that inevitably arrived with his meal onto the floor.

He borrowed my speakers – yes, as well as a litre bottle of Bushmills, a pair of high-top trainers and a library of information and documents I needed for China, I was carrying some stereo speakers – which were powered by heavy batteries. I could hear his music through the wall, using my non-renewable power. His lack of consideration increased daily. He was habitually dependent to the point where pretty much every sentence out of his mouth began, 'Have you got …? Can't I borrow …? Could I use …?'

It climaxed one morning when, as I waited, all packed up, he approached with his toothbrush in hand and said: 'I've packed my toothpaste. Can I use some of yours?'

You really are a bottomless pit of need, aren't you? Mine's packed too and I'm waiting for you, I thought. However, I recalled a phrase I had once heard, although it was perhaps meant for a different circumstance: Just Say No.

On the way to Tak he waited for me when I had to squat at the side of the road as another explosive expulsion occurred. It splashed my shorts and hand. Little more in life will make you feel as wretched as getting covered in shit – but at least it was mine. I was getting weaker and weaker, my tolerance for his behaviour lessening daily. His delirium was debilitating and he wasn't helping himself at all. He was on a road to oblivion; it was hard to have sympathy for someone so resistant to helping himself and taking so little responsibility. I don't mind helping out, but I couldn't have begun to fix this, he was fucked up beyond belief, a total liability. Eventually, I shut myself in a cell with a toilet which was promoted as a room in a guest house, and let him and his polluted blood go on ahead, so that I could cure myself of the crippling stomach bug.

'Look I'm going to have to stop here,' I said. 'I can't continue this way.' It clearly wasn't a half-arsed excuse, I was wholly suffering from a bum that was running out of control.

'I can wait,' he said. It was not an offer of support, more the case that he continued to need mine.

'No,' I said with all the assertion I could muster, which was limited as the majority of my resilience was being summoned to clench cheeks. 'I don't know how long I'll be, you carry on, perhaps I'll catch you up.' Even he must have been able to sense the lack of sincerity in that afterthought.

'OK, I'll email you when I get to the next town,' he said.

Damn that internet connection, I thought. It never used to be that way. The parting of ways had been final, other than a message on a guest house noticeboard or a poste restante box, you were free of the obligation of reuniting.

I did free myself of some things though and left that horrid concrete place of rehabilitation having ridded myself of two parasites and rode on with liberty – well, until I came to a hill and had to hold on. The journey went on increasing in intensity expediently.

The few extra rupees I threw at this place have paid me back already. I sit and read but even here the flies have me waving my hand repeatedly like I'm riding through a plantation of tea pickers again. I get on the bike and fly north in search of an idyllic beach without pests on the wing. I don't find one but I settle for an air-conditioned supermarket and get some Sellotape to stick my diary pages together. It rains and I run to an internet café but still don't feel like composing a mass mail. I don't want to lie and I don't want to moan so, basically, I don't want to make contact at all. I think it's time for the emergency comfort Pringles. I've carried them there and back on my inner-circuit tour and not even popped the top. Now I just want to see them gone.

Sitting with the German guest house owners, I feel they are as fresh as the accommodation: unscathed, enthusiastic, hospitable, every conversation is a new one. I cynically think that with dipping mattresses, damp patches and cracked tiles the rotation of repetitiveness may lose it appeal. For now, we are all unique and interested. They persuade me that cycling to the airport tomorrow is by far the best option. We talk about missing people and how we handle it – well, how they do, I'm not bloody handling it at all. I tell them how I spent a year learning Chinese before my cycle trip last year, but when asked which dialect I can't even remember if it was Cantonese or Mandarin, which isn't good for my credibility. 'OK, I'll say some phrases I remember and you tell me what language it is.'

I take myself out for dinner and am waved enthusiastically into a restaurant. I get the feeling the waiter knows me, have I been here before or is that his tactic? He's certainly friendly and I get spicy prawns and rice. He has a voice like an approaching train. He creeps up from behind and with increasing audibility he says: 'Would you like some desert?'

He shakes my hand vigorously when I go to leave, like an old friend, maybe we are, or perhaps he thinks I'm someone else, which actually I am.

A gin and tonic nightcap with my German hosts and then I pack all I can because this *wunderbar* idea of taking myself to the airport means I'll have to get up at 5 a.m. This day of staying put has been most agreeable, which doesn't bode well for the continuing wandering that is to come. Well, I'm sure I must have learned something from this short circuit. Now, if I can just remember what it is …

The sweet taste of budget dining

I sleep about as well before a flight as I do on one, so at 4 a.m. I stop trying and start my day. The guest house owner is up, or still up, and offers me tea but I can't put anything inside me this early. Predictably, it's still dark when I get out on the road. This doesn't deter me. There isn't much else about and I speed the 13 kilometres to the airport, slowing only for the armed guards on the entry road. 9/11 was only two years ago – well, there's one every year, be it the 11th of September or 9th of November, like 24/7, those two numbers have one implied association. Consequently, security is still twitchy and I don't want to irritate a trigger finger. My backwards trip of cycle uphill, train downhill concludes as I dismantle my bike where I assembled it last week. Only now with even more precision, dexterity and efficiency. I've got butterflies again, and a little foreboding too. It's illogical, like homesickness, just a feeling that will disappear with some good company and conversation, two comforts that rarely come on cue. However, I've found that with a bicycle on past trips they do arrive faster than without one.

Repackaged, I check in my 29 kilograms and wander off with my carry-on. No departure tax, no window seat, no breakfast, so I've still got $50 worth of rupees that I gamble with, assuming I can change them at a better rate in India.

This week, as promised, there is a plane, and my recompense for being the flexible, reschedulable passenger is a broken seat. I point it out, sensing an upgrade or at least a window seat but am shown to a vacant aisle seat next to a Finnish couple. Now seated further to the front my inedible food is served sooner, warmer and taken away quicker as the descent starts. So it's with a very limited view that my re-entry into India begins. I left here five years ago having travelled solo for six months, although you are never really alone in this country whether on the backpacking trail or the road less travelled. I came back to the UK sun-bleached and forever altered. I enthused at every opportunity, as someone does who has made a life-changing discovery – be it finding Jesus, the path to enlightenment or a new band. I declared that a visit to India should be on the national curriculum, it opens minds, changes views, and if nothing else gives you appreciation of your lot in life. I swore I would never complain about my first-world problems again, but of course I did and still swear constantly. But much like a junky or a gay person can spot a kindred spirit so there is an unseen and unspoken alliance among Westerners who have had that, some might say, spiritual Indian experience. Not a package holiday to Goa, that doesn't count, Goa is India-lite and on an all-inclusive deal is exactly how I got there the first time.

My first two weeks had all the culture of a Club 18-30 holiday, but it was an ideal place to acclimatise before I left my package entitlement, choosing not to embark on the return flight and instead enter the real deal. I returned to the UK in late spring to find Blair and his Labour government were now in control, a kind of coalition with girl power, namely the Spice Girls, who were omnipresent from crisp packets to fruit machines. It appeared that mobile phones were really becoming quite popular too. I was a wide-eyed Westerner back home and nothing would ever be quite the same again.

Neither would be returning to India it appears, for once again coming back comes with preconceptions and anticipations. My beginner's mind now has experience and expectations and as we touch down into the dusty, parched plains of the airport, I see the faces against perimeter fences and tarpaulin-covered poverty next to skid marks and landing lights. 'Well, it's a little noisy, leaks in the rain, there are rats, no sewer or running water, but it's very handy for the airport, no parking problems at all,' says the slum realtor. So the questioning begins, the unfathomable gulf in wealth, living an outstretched-hand-to-mouth existence underneath an opulent flight path. I put on my blinkers and focus on my immediate needs.

I ask the Finnish couple where they are heading, hoping to hear Varkala, but they say Kovalam. A taxi to Varkala is $20 so, forever flexible, I share with them for $2. They seem a bit put out by the size of my luggage, even more so when theirs fails to materialise at all. Saying *Don't worry, it will probably arrive on next week's flight, I did* is not going to cheer them up. It's an awkward drive, but distractions are everywhere and I watch our route avidly. I'll be riding back this way in day or two. Not unlike Goa, this beach locality has tourism attraction at the cost of authenticity, so it's a gentle step – well, for me perhaps, as Sri Lanka has also prepared me. I think perhaps my fare-sharing friends have just been thrown into the deep end and they don't even have a change of clothes. I'll leave them to find their feet.

We are besieged by a tout attack when we arrive at the coast which is ideal actually as I let myself get swept away to a big room which I negotiate at $23 for three nights. I only wanted to stay for two but I'm told Sunday is not an auspicious day to start a journey … *I bet you say that to all the cyclists.*

How does it feel to be back? Well, I'm not sure I want to let India into my day yet, I need a menial task, a familiar focus, I need to feel my liberation is not an illusion in this fully catered-for haven of holidaymakers. I'm different, I'm special, I'm a cyclist, I want to fly my flag of independence and uniqueness – well, if not fly it, at least unfurl it and connect it to the flagpole. I assemble my bike again. It had a rough trip but seems intact. At least it arrived. The Finnish couple have got off to a bad start by beating their bags. I play an MP3 as I rebuild the bike – Aerosmith's 'Taste of India' – and ceremoniously remove my watch. I won't be needing that for a while. In a month I meet Sofia and that's my only obligation. She had said to me, 'If you're not at Delhi airport to meet me consider yourself dumped.' To which I had replied, 'If I'm not at the airport to meet you, consider *yourself* dumped.' The jest failed to impress or entertain.

My food poisoning in Thailand was crippling for a few days. The room I had to endure was a concrete cell. It was horrendous. Small windows at the top of the walls let in little light and allowed no sights to be seen. I was inside a poured-concrete block, with peeling paint and leaking pipework. A squat-hole toilet in the corner and a metal bed frame with a slice of stale mattress on top. I shat, I sweated, I stank and drank water. After two days I was empty, drained, wrung out, emaciated, weak, white and wretched. When the poison had passed I walked outside to find sustenance. I found a stall selling bread and took a tiny bite, chewing slowly and swallowing carefully. The pellet of wet dough fell like a golf ball into a goldfish bowl. But it didn't bounce back up and it didn't fall through a fracture either, I was on the road to recovery. The next day I walked a little further and found a white marble hotel with guards outside, palms and plant pots, manicured lawns and a glide-in entrance. *What a wonderful place to be ill*, I thought. Clean sheets, cool breeze, a TV to distract and a fan to keep the frosty sweat away. It was sometime later, having been pulled up some hills to a populated place, that I learned the posh hotel had easily been within my budget. I had just assumed that, like cosmetically enhanced cars and fast, sleek women, it was out of my league.

As soon as I head out, I get a nod from a proverbial long-term Western loafer, his dreads swaying with an upbeat bounce in his stone-head steps – it's just a nod, not even a welcome, but its acknowledgement feels like acceptance. *Ahh India, there is no judgement, just us.* I go to the beach for breakfast and, at last, a proper Indian chai. The butterflies have flown away and from a landing balcony I look over a banana-curved bay with a dominant lighthouse at the southern protrusion. I watch the fishermen land this morning's catch. It's a frantic ritual, with possibly hired hands, waste deep in the surf, chanting and splashing as both ends of the semicircular net are hauled towards the beach. Doubtlessly, some Hindu god is summoned to fill the heavy net with enough to feed every hungry mouth and fill their empty pockets. There is an utter frenzy as the net reaches the shore and I expect to see a mass of flipping fish, perhaps the rent-a-prayer ritualists do too, but it's a disappointing haul. Well, plenty more gods in the sea, sky, cosmos and within, cast thy net again and pick another spirited deity.

My pockets, too, fail to be lined with rental income and now that I know the exchange rate I sit in a hammock chair and work out my daily budget. It's as disappointing as this morning's catch. I'm going to have to reel in my spending, opt for lassi and chai over beer and spirits. Last time I was here I regularly made my own sandwiches; in this touristy mecca I may have to resort to that again. In the intervening five years since I was last here the world has seen some significant changes: 9/11 gave paranoid authorities the right to take away liberty, but that was substituted with mobile phones and the fact the internet has become commonplace. There were no internet cafés in India five years ago – well, not that I was looking, I didn't need one, I didn't even have an email address, it was inconceivable, the thought of a personal electronic letter box you could access from anywhere in the world. I wrote to friends on paper, and then tried to find a post office. The letter told where I expected to be in six weeks so the recipient could mail their reply to a poste restante. That kind of communication had a romantic inconvenience, my route was dictated and often uncompromised by my wanting to receive replies. It didn't always work and I hope to retrieve some of my seven-year-old mail this trip, hence the want to go to Varkala.

It's definitely more expensive here than in Sri Lanka. I see a used *Lonely Planet* and get the price down to 350 rupees but it's still too much. So is a fish dinner; I settle for fish-flavoured curry. It's one of those places that screens Western movies from loud TVs and my eye keeps getting caught by *Pirates of the Caribbean* being watched by tables of couples who have nothing to say to each other. I'm looking forward to hitting the road, getting on budget, eating locally, leaving the alcohol for a while and focusing on feeling fit, running efficiently and finding the thrill of what I'm about to embark on: cycling in India.

Can't afford friendship

Twelve hours' sleep, what a great way to spend the weekend. Now if I can just get through the next twelve with the same expenses I'll be adjusting to my Indian budget. Money is on my sleepy mind, I need to change that, so I take to the dusty paths that connect traders of tourist requirements and find a black-market money changer. With two $100 bills I'm able to haggle the rate up to 45.3 rupees to the dollar, but he doesn't want my Sri Lankan rupees, no way, not for any price, couldn't give them away. What am I going to do with them now? Sometimes you just want fixed-price ease, but there are always better deals to be had than the advertised amount and after all that sleep I'm refreshed and ready. I know the best tactic when haggling is a smile, and it helps to have patience too, even better is not even being arsed whether you make a purchase or not, there's nothing like indifference to secure a good deal. They are shrewd businessmen, the Indians, especially when you are purchasing with white riches – well, white in places, tanned in others, burned in the rest. That's the look of the cyclist: lattice tan through Teva sandals, an even spread on calves and lower legs, positively growing forearms and a radiant nose, and the rest is ashen. I have the appearance of a zombie who leaned against an electrified fence. I hope to even out my tan as well as my expenditure over the next few days. The shade a November Essex boy has toned to determines his length of stay and therefore how green he is, and the starting price of a product reflects this. The pasty Fins will have a high price to pay; mine depends on what flesh I choose to flash. The other single biggest way to secure the best deal is to play to their Achilles heel, the first-sale-of-the-day superstition. Today the *Lonely Planet* guide starts at 550 but I secure it for 300, because if I walk out that shop without a purchase, the belief is, so will every other non-customer today. I buy banana and bread and come back home to make breakfast on my balcony. I've still got enough left over for tomorrow, so I've eaten for 33 cents. This is better. I walk to the beach; the money changer spots me and says, 'No friends?'

'No, just money,' I say. 'I'll buy some friends.' But I don't. I walk the bay alone and can't spot anyone I trust enough to leave my bag with while I have a swim. Anyway, it's cloudy and I'm not that keen to go in. I find internet instead: an email from Goa, my friends who winter there are eagerly awaiting my arrival, which feels good, and I check out a cycling site. Some dude, I have no idea of his nationality but he goes by the name of Mr. Pumpy, has pretty much covered the planet by bicycle and documented it well. I see what awaits me on my route north, nothing too untoward. Bring it on – when, that is, the planets permit it.

Eager to leave my cell, I got back on my bike prematurely, cured but still weak because nothing of nutritional value had stayed in my system since Bangkok. It all passed through, the good and the bad, and I was truly depleted. But just to be back on the road was revitalising. The warmth of the morning sun, my driving light, the tunnel was behind me. Unfortunately, the hills were ahead and beyond them my ridiculously optimistic destination. It was 87 kilometres to a fabled pizza restaurant I'd been hearing so much about. The hype was almost deemed to disappoint but it was driving me on, my Italian target.

The day had started with a Thai man on a moped riding level with me and telling me that his mum lived in the UK. Then I went the wrong way, but everyone smiled and waved, and like a marathon runner at the end of his energy it spurred me on. As I left the town of pedestrian pleasantries the baton was picked up by police, truckers and road workers, with thumbs-up encouragement and occasional comments. The waves moved to farmhands, and fruit pickers all had words of reassurance. Then came the incline, the boost was behind me and the hills were beyond me, in such gruelling situations the mind tends to count. Lowest gear, my legs did nine revolutions and I covered 10 metres, having to stop every 150 metres. My speed was 5 kph, the least I could do without losing my balance. It was a pathetic pace, and it got me nowhere fast. The aluminium handlebar stem creaked like it was cracking with the strain I put on it. The noise quickly became irritating and alerted me to my ill-placed exertion. Sweating wet, sucking down water and slumping over my bars. Not the energy to dismount, another corner, another climb, balance barely kept, calves cramping, perhaps I should have stayed another day. Ironically, my tummy felt better than any other part of my body. I'd been plagued by its decline for over a week. It occurred to me that it wasn't the last two days that had weakened me, I'd been liquidating anything I ate almost immediately for some time and now I was literally running on empty.

And that's when the truck grabbing began. Towed at 7kph, it was a slow way to be saved, a brief downhill, before I let go and left my lifeline behind. But with the next hill the trucker passed before I could grab back on. My arms were no stronger than my legs and soon I'd be back to my 150-metres-and-rest. Droplets of sweat exploded off my face with every violent exhalation. Water, crackers, peanuts, try again. Another truck, another hill, another tow, this time to the summit. The driver waved enthusiastically, almost seeming honoured to support me. Then down, 62kph, my fastest so far. I overtook trucks, sped through police checks, broke speed limits, determined to milk every last moment of the momentum. When the freewheeling free progress faded due to flat roads and friction, I found a bus shelter, pulled my airline pillow from my pannier, lay down and dozed.

After more bananas, more fuel, I set off again, but the recharge was inadequate and it took me an hour to do the next 10 kilometres, averaging only 8.4kph. Short downs, long ups, making it to my chosen town was looking doubtful. But then a pickup came from behind. I gestured vigorously that I needed a tow and he complied. I held on until the plains came into view, whooped and let go. Flying the last 10 flat kilometres, I glided into town. That was exertion, that was achievement, that was bloody stupid. I treated myself to an air-conditioned room with a hot shower and collapsed on the bed. It had been my hardest day of physical endurance since … since I had hiked Torres del Paine in Chile nearly two years earlier, also underprepared with inadequate equipment. That was where, coincidentally, the idea to do this stupid bloody self-punishing escapade had been planted.

The end of this excruciating day – that demanded more than I had to give – also represented the end of my Marmite diet. I got my first hot food in forty-eight hours, my tummy gladly accepted it and I felt elated. I took my jubilation to an internet café. Waiting for a computer to become free, I noticed one screen was not displaying the customary blue of a Hotmail account. The open page was about coping with loss and I realised with horror the back of the head in front of the monitor belonged to Pier. Having unintentionally honoured my empty promise of reuniting I was inevitably updated but thankfully not involved in his latest predicament. While I'd been recovering he had progressed to this place a few days before, got shit-faced drunk and had his bicycle, photos, documents and money stolen. It was sad news but not surprising. Getting the embassy to send him home was his best hope.

I spend the rest of the day sighing a lot, looking at my guidebook, looking out to sea, the situation is not helped when I speak with Sofia. The phone call doesn't go well and I'm all the worse for it. We are in very different places and I don't just mean India and Surrey. She is of course preoccupied with work and surrounded by room-mates, and I'm feeling very alone and not even cycling, due to some bloody auspicious prevention. My ceaseless enthusiasm for this country was infectious and having successfully travelled in Australia and New Zealand she was ready to up her game and add India to her spice of life. I don't want to be the tour guide, we'll cover new ground together but, regardless, I'll get to see afresh through her eyes and everything will have an incomparable newness. I'll share my experience if she'll share her awe. The common place will become wondrous again, complacency replaced with curiosity, she will give a new lease of life to my journey through life. Unfortunately, I can't wait, don't want to wait, am not enjoying the waiting, want to fill this gap between here and New Year,

Kerala and Delhi, cycling and seeing her. Her waiting is full of obligations and preparation, mine just feels a bit empty somehow.

I fill myself up with fish and rice and walk the whole length of the beach looking at happy groups and feeling very lonely. Another American movie blares out of the restaurant so I wander back to my peaceful balcony as a bunch of rowdy Brits turn up. I get bitten, and go inside. Earplugs and back to bed, unconsciously killing time until the planets align and I'm allowed to leave.

Net and gross

Another ten hours sleep. I'm not sure if I need it. Are my reserves replenished, fully stocked to embark on the journey, or am I most at ease when unconscious, eyes fixed on the future and not wanting the awareness of waiting for it? I watch again the morning fishing ritual. It doesn't feel inspiring or uplifting, the chanters seem apathetic, going through the motions. Perhaps I'm reflecting my own mood on to this scene, and with the power of my pessimism the net is pulled out of the water empty. I suppose the more fish caught the more inclined you are to chant harder: no fish, no fervour, it's catch-22. I can empathise with the effort exerted not being worth the reward received. An argument ensues, the angry boat owners with empty nets chastise the chanters. 'You didn't worship hard enough – replenish the depleted fish stocks or our tourist income is over.' I've got to get out of this mindset. How am I going to leave it behind?

Having got rid of Pier it was almost a worry-free stopover, but my Thai visa was expiring with attention-seeking ticking, not dissimilar to a woman's biological clock. I seemed to have reached a point in life where, as a solo passenger on a plane to Thailand, I was assumed to be a sex tourist. Yet should I have actually wanted to date, available girls my age were either single mothers or desperate to cohabit and conceive. Their luxury of having time to wait for Mr. Right was running out. There were of course options in both scenarios: I could have skipped across the bridge to Myanmar for an afternoon and my visa would have been renewed on my return. And the childless and yearning girl approaching forty had the 'adopt a Chinese baby' option – in fact, a large percentage of the pupils in my Mandarin class were doing just that, not crossing rivers to renew visas, but learning Chinese before they flew over to pick up a baby. Strange really, as I would have thought you could teach a newborn any language you like. I was wary though, not of being adopted by a Myanmar family, but packing all I had and crossing a border on my bicycle could involve lengthy customs searches. Likewise, if I walked alone and couldn't get back, I wouldn't be much better off than the situation Pier had found himself in.

The hills had not only whipped out my energy, they had me seriously questioning my next move. Was China going to be beyond my capabilities? Laos, it seemed, was now a compulsory destination; everyone was heading there, which sounded awful. I'd visited a few years ago and caught it just before the onslaught. It was ready and waiting and I felt I had seen the place at its best and didn't want those memories tainted. I hired a bicycle and cycled to the Chinese border. It had mystique, a forbidden fascination, or maybe that was the opium, this time I could cross to the other side. Maybe Kathmandu would be a good place to fly to, most directions from there were downhill and there were rumours of roamers and cyclists who had got across to Tibet. OK, Everest may have been in the way but, beyond that, when I heard *Tibet* I thought *plateau* and that meant flat. And I really wanted some level-ground cycling, although perhaps 15,000 feet above sea level it would have taken my breath away.

This was not really a place for research and worldly first-hand advice from travellers passing through. There was a high density of American aid workers, who somehow brought a military-base atmosphere to the place. They were not travellers by any stretch, and they had taken the exotic out of the location and replaced it with a kind of righteous objective with religious overtones. On the plus side, this wealthy Western influence had benefits: the enterprising Thais inevitably catered to their needs and I was able to find a shop that had a good selection of Christmas cards. As I recuperated, I wrote twenty cards. My list was much shorter this year, and not to save weight but perhaps face. I'd disowned my American life, which had been my second home, a place I'd been escaping to for nearly two decades. I was still unable to accept the implications of having a newborn daughter there and disillusioned when many of my American friends I thought I could lean on actually offered as little support as an overseas call centre. With zip codes crossed off my Christmas card list, I had headed to Asia hoping to seek solace in my newfound liberation and selective solitude.

There was also a selective choice at the book exchange, where I traded in *I'm with the Band*. The confessions of the groupie had been disappointedly tame: the author seemed to enjoy name-dropping more than dropping to her knees. I exchanged it for *Far from the Madding Crowd*, same, same but different, that harlot with her inheritance jumping from solider to farmer to bailiff. The evenings were cooler here and every day when the sun went down I sipped a little more of my whiskey away.

Late one morning, having locked myself out of my room without knowing it – and maybe with embarrassment – I spontaneously decided to restart my riding, hoping I'd found the balance between rested and regressed. The temperature was certainly more tolerable and at one point I realised with relish that I'd daydreamed up a hill, a welcome distraction from my previous all-consuming awareness of overexertion with every push of the pedals. I selected gears subconsciously and kept momentum effortlessly. I was rewarded with views of rocky cliffs soaring out over clear rivers where I soaked my hat and hair for air-conditioning as opposed to hair conditioner. I was now in deepest Thailand, albeit on the Myanmar border – well, perhaps not deepest, but certainly the most authentic. I'd ridden back in time to tiny villages without modernisation. No electric cables were strung across the skyline, no motors broke the sound of chirping crickets or squawking from the canopy of shade. There was a delicate aroma of burning wood in the air, far more preferable to the potent pollution of exhaust fumes. However quaint, picturesque and untouched it may have been, it was still a scene I had to enter as supplies needed replenishing. It seemed intrusive to cycle down a private access path, and safe to leave my bike on the road. So it was with all senses on full alert that I crossed the undefined threshold into a tiny community, indicating I would like water in a plastic bottle and any food it may have been possible to purchase. It's not that they were uninviting, just a little intimidating and I couldn't help but feel I was trespassing. They were as welcoming as they were intrigued. The problem with places that hadn't changed in generations was they rarely had change. I either had to purchase more than I could comfortably carry or pay more than they asked for. It was around this time that peanuts started to become a big part of my life. I'd been told they were the ideal fuel for the cyclist, high in protein, readily available and instantly edible, no preparation needed, keep them in you bar bag, grab a handful and fill your face. An addiction was about to begin.

There seemed to be more transport with four legs on the road than four wheels, but what few cars there were seemed driven by English-speaking businessmen. They were invariably in the teak trade and always wanted to chat. On one occasion I was shown to a beautiful bamboo bungalow, and left with *rice and vegetables* written in Thai – ข้าวและผัก – for future orders. The guest house was in a jungle setting, clearly built for more affluent travellers but, taking what they could get, they allowed me to stay for my usual fee and even offered ice for my whiskey. I was increasingly feeling that my bicycle gave me access, a rite of passage, it put me in a different category. I always felt welcome. A lot of this was thanks to the Thai persona, but something told me it was also to do with my choice of how to travel.

The only challenge I seem to be facing this trip – having reduced my load to two panniers, my road to sea level and my budget to suffice – is how to deal with this pathetic longing and loneliness. Banana and marmite breakfast again, so some things are the same. I finish my Billy Connolly book and trade it in. The bookshop man says this is a very expensive place to be which gives me hope that once I'm out on the road my budget will afford me the food I really want. Knowing from the contents of the net this morning that there is nothing in the sea, I bravely go for a swim and thankfully spot the 20-rupee note as it flows out of my pocket. I don't have money to drown so we both dry on some rocks. I soon remember, due to the stench, that anywhere out of sight in India has a primary function of being a place to shit and stink not sit and think. This is not a sanctuary for the antisocial.

In my Sri Lankan rooms I killed flies with my misleading map; in this one I kill time with a book I can't get into. When the sun is low enough I justify going for dinner. Somehow, the manager manages to sell me fish, god knows where he got it from, or Shiva knows, or Brahma, Buddha, Vishnu or Ganesh, who knows? Being one of the earliest diners I'm given the remote for the TV, so I can play god with the channel changing. I hate this pressure, it's like being DJ and no one's dancing. Another American movie plays, some Stephen King shite, and I'm tempted to just turn it off and say, 'Anyone fancy a chat?' But actually I don't. I leave the remote and the restaurant and any chance of a conversation becomes more remote. Back in my room I pack my panniers as best I can. I can't even compose a text message in my head let alone a mass email. My thoughts are negative and introspective, why am I back here?

The thing about the Indian experience is that, much like recounting any story, what you witness is personal. I see it like attending the Glastonbury festival. Goa would be the backstage area. There is clean, solid accommodation, catering, all needs are met, but you really are quite isolated from the festival goers without whom, let's face it, there would be no festival. There are the organisers and instigators, like in any community, who are inaccessible to the majority of us, the politicians and mafia types, who therefore lack a true insight into our side of life. But how you choose to see India depends on how you choose to read your programme, or guidebook. You can keep to the popular places, the Taj Mahal stage, see the big names, or venture to the other stage, the slightly alternative but still well known: Dharamsala, Darjeeling, Rishikesh. You could retreat to the green fields of ashrams and communes. Or be a volunteer cleaner and do your bit to maintain functionality like one of the many NGO's witnessing what most fail to find. You could choose to never leave the campground, surround yourself with people in the same situation, just managing to survive outdoors although out of their element, much like sticking together in a gap-year crowd, coping and not feeling too out of place. The darker side might be to roam the cities by night, eye-opening extras, people sleeping on streets, curled up in the rickshaw-backseat bedrooms that transform to transport and earn an inadequate living in by day. This unequal economy, the night-and-day difference, could perhaps be likened

112

to the utter hedonism of ultimate debauchery, the Hunter S Thompson, and Pete Doherty blown of mind, working creatives in a waking dream of questionable reality. You could integrate with the service workers, the man who pumps out the Portaloos, the lower castes who are equally human but less desirable and approachable. Regardless, you will have your own micro-impression based on the magic of India, the mini moments only witnessed when you walk alone. The girl with angel wings breastfeeding her baby, the man with a bowler hat and umbrella rolling a joint, the white galleon held above the heads of strolling visionaries, the stilted jester leaning on a tree. Getting a connection at the STD phone booth as a marching band of three trumpets and bass drum parade past. The beggar on the station gifted an ice cream and that unique look of surprise, confusion and delight mixed with distrust, hunger and need. The young woman in a sari with a baby tied to her, brushing away the endless dust of the day in a futile attempt to keep the country clean and earn enough from hand to mouth. An ashen-faced sadhu contorted cross-legged and somehow hovering a little higher than the ground he's not sitting on.

India, like a festival, is nothing but an endless stream of images, many beyond comprehension, sometimes misinterpreted, fleeting glimpses in a concentration of passing life. An overwhelming stimulation and occasional uncomfortable interaction, glimpses that instantly embed into permanent memory, visions of previously unknown lifestyles that are as intriguing as they are frightening, leaving you teetering on the edge of your comfort zone. India will push you to the limits – of your tolerance, of your observations, and later your recall. It will deliver more than you ordered, not what you ordered, it can't be returned and inevitably there will come a point when you've had enough. You will see many who have had too much, the trick is having the wisdom to know your soul is full and take it away to a place of tranquillity for processing.

And what quite often happens is that data is discarded, deleted, forgotten and on occasion reformatted and retold to sceptical natives of Western countries, often leaving only the storyteller with an overwhelming urge to return and do it all again. The site may be the same but the programme will be forever altering. Voyeur, participant, artist, volunteer, India is a living being and therefore every breath is different, evolving, revolving, and under no obligation to comply with your plans, it's not going to sit still waiting for you to revisit the best of what you saw last time. It's not a Las Vegas residency, it's a wave of change, a live flow of unpredictability, a rush of humanity. That's what makes it so addictive to those whose wild blood has stagnated in their sterile Western environment and so repulsive to the comfort seekers out of their depth of soft furnishings and basic certainties.

Tomorrow again I hit the road but for the first time this trip it's from a place I planned to be, heading directly to where I want to be. It has to be a turning point.

The point of return

I reluctantly get up at 8 a.m. and willingly shower away my greasy sleep. New week, new month, new country to cycle in, same budget, same breakfast. Saturday's supplies are eked out, so that's 9 rupees a day, less than $0.20, this will get me back on track financially if not keep me on it physically. However, a hard and hearty dump is a great omen for the start of my journey, long may it continue. What little pleasure can be gained by solidity of excrement is taken away when I torture my weak will by entering the internet café to check for an email from Sofia. There isn't one and that really is shit.

So I pack up, the planets are apparently appropriately aligned now and I'm more than ready to push off onto the dust track that depicts the beginning of my journey, or at least another beginning. I'm instantly stopped by a Western girl who wants to talk about me and my bike, bloody typical. I've been in some kind of self-imposed ostracised solitude since I got here, conversing only with waiters, traders, money changers and an astrologist innkeeper who couldn't possibly know that it was a year ago today in Bangkok that I bought the bike. Now I'm ready to leave I have a reason to be delayed, but perhaps that is the auspicious in action, it's all above and beyond me. The road ahead is steep but I have the strength to get above and beyond it. I recognise the way from Friday – well, the road if not the incline.

A couple of well-dressed Indians in a car pull level with me. 'Where you go?'

'Goa.'

'Aah,' they respond, having had their question answered, then the comprehension of my comeback kicks in. '*Goa?*'

Ha, yeah, I'm a hardcore motherfucker, motherfuckers, I think to myself, and find the main road to Thiruvananthapuram quicker than I can say it. Their reaction, their look was not one of respect or dismay, but more *Why? Why, wealthy Westerner, are you cycling when you can easily afford a train, bus or plane?*

This is why.

The traffic isn't too bad – I mean, in levels of death-destined drivers the intensity is dense but that's India, I never expected anything else. I doubt any Indian folk songs sing of lonely roads. Lonely anything, over a billion of them, a sixth of the planet's population and they all want to know 'Where you go?', 'Where from?' and the more eloquent 'What is your good name, sir?'

Now I feel it, now I remember – like an overloaded truck of grain with nothing but a blessing for brakes it's just hit me why I'm doing this. I am instantly immersed; every sense is besieged. I'm sweating from the heat, stifled from the smells, diesel fumes, sweets, sewage, perfumed flowers, smoke from wood for cooking, plastic from waste disposal, and also from poor judgement, overworked brakes, electrical short circuits, discarded cigarettes on the verge and tired valves and piston rings. My nose would be feeling singled out and abused but my ears too have audible overload: the constant horns, the two-stroke rickshaws, the cowbells and blown exhausts, and that's just the traffic, there are temples screeching a prayer, hawkers attracting attention, music clashing from every direction, shouts, whistles, high-decibel chatter, and if that all disappeared, I'd hear a plane land, a dog bark, a baby cry, a bird sing, a breeze in the palms or a coconut fall to the ground, and always the omnipresent hammering. I feel the grit on my face stick to a film of smog coating my skin, the warmth of the air and exertion on my legs, I feel the pressure as I push forward through it all and into more, and that's when the eyes get their reward, which makes me whole. This is an instant, momentary insight into lives, I pass life, engaged, inescapable, contributing to, coexisting with, I have become part of the bedlam, part of the day, as unexplained and intriguing as the man with half his face bandaged, a woman carrying metal signposts, squatters, passengers, people pausing to stare at me. Me? How did you even spot me in this high-speed parade of every possible life form all making more noise than my silent passage through this pandemonium?

You may see this from a bus or a train but I'm not seeing it, I'm feeling it, I am it, and it's un-fucking-believable. Street lives, the street is alive and I'm living on it. I'm riding it, again the surfer analogy comes to mind, like in Bangkok, I'm riding a wave of a cityscape and I dare not stop as it will crash over me. When I take a wrong turn people clap their hands for my attention. How do they know where I should be going? Who goes this way? Why can't I?

I pass the airport, not a single part of me wants to catch a flight now, eleven days since I left the UK, nearly two weeks of dragging my sorrowful load up, down, round and going nowhere, getting nothing out of it and now I've found what I went away for. To feel alive, to dodge the constant obstacles in my path, to have a new challenge every moment, a new experience, new sight, new questions, new purpose.

As I leave the city behind, I catch my breath, the air is cleaner, the pace slower, the scenery quieter. It's not serenity by any stretch but the blender I'm in has been turned down from whisk and whipped to mix and merge. The road signs confirm I'm on Highway 66. Kicks? You could say that. Directional markers are adequate, the buses are utter bastards, overtake and brake, cut me up and stop, pass again and not a hint of consideration or apology for invading my personal space and confiscating safety. I just give way to them, I really can't argue with a bus and come out on top. Lots of 'hello's, lots of water stops. Hooting traffic is bearable, the pollution breathable, uncertainty palpable, the progress sustainable, it's all better than I thought, way better. I'm soon over halfway, assuming I stop after the same distance again.

I turn off for Varkala, there is familiarity, it's been nearly seven years. I stop on top of a cliff and take a photo then head back to what I recall was a kind of hippy community. The price of a room certainly suggests they cater for the deadbeats. One hundred rupees, or just over $2. I was paying $8 at the last place, maybe the bookseller was right. Kovalam is an attraction for people who are dropped out of the sky, with no comparison or transition, for a two-week package. Of course the traders will adjust their prices accordingly, and perhaps their standards too. Varkala has maybe never seen a better day nor a higher standard of clientele. The evidence being that among my fellow travellers I meet a dreadlocked

English single mother living on a UK welfare cheque, and Israelis just out of the military. From Patagonia to Dharamsala, Israeli occupation generally signifies you've found the cheapest place available. I was on an equally low budget last time I was here, as were my travel companions, and I seem to recall the place had a similar vibe then too. However, having only been in India for less than two months, at that stage I was less judgemental. Naïve, wider of eye, taking in everything, talking to everyone, processing, deciding, and concluding, hence my now more opinionated views. I'm happy to be older and more first-hand-informed from my travels, worldly wiser, but what I miss most about those innocent days of wandering the planet is the accepting awe of all I saw. More and more often with age, I find my immediate reaction to many scenarios is cynicism. It seems to have become a defence mechanism, it's as if now I'm tired of considering and accepting, it takes more to impress me and make me question my direction. So much I see now is summed up with a 'been there, done that' condescending scorn. It's not all-consuming, a sticker-festooned pannier will have me humbly kowtowing with reverence, but I see little achievement in the ability to be able to score your drugs abroad and bumble about in a bubble of bewilderment.

It's only for one night. The delicious shower is followed by tasteless noodles. I recognise some faces from Kovalam as I walk around. I remember the Hanuman Swami Temple, and 'The Tank': a place for washing, bathing and swimming. The green water in a concrete pool had more concentrated contamination than all I rode through to get here. And there is the post office of disappointment, which after four weeks of anticipation in the beginning of '97 failed to have a single letter for me. Some things don't change. Either the mail never came or they recklessly threw it out and it's not even been seven years yet. Now, during this visit, my expectations that they'd have something for me were low but I had to check. Wouldn't it have been cool? Like finding a cobbler's receipt in your returned effects at the end of a long sentence, and picking up your resoled brogues from the son of the shoemaker with an expression like you'd just dropped them off the week before.

I try to doze in the room but I'm bitten by ants and other things. The price I paid came with satisfaction to find I'm back on budget. The power goes off at dusk – power cuts, I recall, are as frequent as sunsets, not enough current to go round the subcontinent, so the darkness is shared around the country. After our allotted loss of electricity I get to my room just as the lights go back on and see fleas jumping on my bed. However, being back on the bike I'm only ever anywhere for one night, I can handle this effortlessly. Although I still think I may try and go a bit more upmarket with my accommodation tomorrow. I lie on my sarong, and put my shirt over the pillow, sleep tight, hoping what lies beneath doesn't bite.

Invites and offers

I lie waiting for the alarm. I've not even taken off my panniers, the less at home I make myself the easier it is to accept this shithole I'm sleeping in is a one-night mistake. I'm ready to go at 7 a.m. but the guest house owner insists I drink his 'special' coffee. I expect enema but get energy.

I got my bites, my itches and scratches and don't need any more kicks, so avoid Route 66 and find a pleasant back road on a spit of land, sea on one side and the backwaters on the other. Kollam isn't like the map at all. *Lonely Planet* maps are habitually inaccurate but it's impossible to relate to any road or landmark, turns out I'm not in Kollam, I've got another 5 kilometres to go. I find a post office but they don't sell envelopes, I find an envelope shop but they don't have airmail. It's a long procedure but eventually I send Sofia my Sri Lankan rupees, to take a little stress out of her long Sri Lankan layover before she gets her Delhi connection.

When I was here seven years ago a trip to the post office was all I would schedule for a day. It was a prolonged procedure, the posting of a letter or postcards internationally, the various counters and queueing involved. Making sure you saw your stamps getting stamped, so they weren't peeled off when your back was turned and the correspondence thrown in the bin. It wasn't uncommon for the operation to overflow into the following day, of those six months of travelling a lot of it was spent in queues.

I can't find anywhere to eat but a backwater boat leaves in ten minutes. I don't want to travel that way though; I've done it before, this time I'm going to cycle. I settle for veg curry and soda for less than 50 cents and cycle onward. Today feels lazier, less intense. Kerala is renowned for being a laid-back state; the men wear dhotis, a kind of sarong that is doubled over and hangs above the knee. They seem to need constant adjustment and fiddling with, but there's lots of time and little else to do. I get lots of hellos, lots of water, Coke and Sprite breaks. I'd intended to stop at Kayamkulam but it looks like a dump so I keep going and manage to miss the temple, its only redeeming feature. At one water stop a man offers me a lift in his van, he has sweeties and everything but the road is flat and I really don't need his assistance. Another man on a moped pulls level with me and invites me to stay at his home. Is it my blond ponytail, are they friendly or confused? Home stays with utter strangers come at a high cost, generally squirming embarrassment and best behaviour to the point of impeccable posture. It can be bloody exhausting.

I took up an invite in Thailand because I was bloody exhausted.

The route alongside the Moei River was where I learned some important lessons. Not wanting to face another tribal village with my requests, it was possibly Pier's constant neediness that had me acting the opposite and thinking I had more independence than I did. My ข้าวและ ผัก piece of paper was working wonders and feeding me well, I was feeling strong and let a tiny village down a steep decline pass by without making contact. Soon after I was faced with some challenging hills and had to double back, to stock up on water. Wasted effort and time, no need to write this down in any language, note to self: *Don't pass up opportunities.* But there was another lesson to be learned that day.

The road got harder, there were no opportunities left, not for water, food, or a place to stay. Supplies became depleted, traffic was scarce and my attempts to flag down a car only resulted in returned waves. My emergency water was all used up, as I'd once heard that when a dead and dehydrated body is found in the Australian outback, they invariably have water still on them. An engine rumbled slowly behind me, a bus, an air pocket, a lifeline, and for some inexplicable reason I let it pass. Now I wasn't even thinking straight. The road was dirt and it was tough to get traction. I threw my bike down, the gradient too steep to use the side stand, and I sat and sulked. When I realised that wasn't working, I got up off the dusty track and found

I'd sat on the only bit of tar for miles around and now I had that black sticky mess stuck to my shorts. Pushing the bike seemed the most efficient expenditure of energy but the situation was beginning to get serious – *should have* was not helping my circumstance. I was out of oomph and out of water, no more momentum at all and nothing but jungle around me. I didn't have the supplies to stay or the reserves to leave. My shorts had stuck to my skin and a Sting song was stuck in my head – 'There's a little black spot on my bum today …'

Ahead, the density disappeared slightly. A tiny verge of grass. I could pitch a tent there but that wouldn't cure my water problem. As I approached, the trees thinned and there down in a valley, I saw a misty settlement of smoke and palm-thatched huts. An air pocket in the form of another settlement, a scene this time I was desperate to be a part of. Some children saw me and came running up to greet me. I showed my empty water bottle, they took me to an irrigation hose. 'Yeah, great, but my tender Western tummy requires it be boiled before I can drink it,' I said, and they seemed to understand. I was taken to a hut on stilts where a village elder lived, he invited me in where a fire blazed in the corner and water boiled above. Indebted for receiving the fuel I needed to continue, I poured some into my bottle and went to leave, overflowing with gratitude. It occurred to me I wouldn't be seeing hot water again for a while and poured a bag of instant noodles into the bottle for nourishment, ignoring my inner urge to escape this increasingly uncomfortable situation immediately. There was no threat at all, just the inability to communicate, which can take embarrassment to the level of excruciating as the miming continues.

The delay bought about a scenario that was to etch itself permanently into my memory. Back by the attractive grass verge where I'd left my bike was a parked car. The obligatory English-speaking teak dealer had stopped with his wife, I'm not sure why. I asked how far the next town was, the answer was too far and it was pointed out that it was getting late. The driver spoke to the village kids, an elder was summoned, I was told I could and should stay with them tonight. This air pocket that was bequeathed I'd rather not breathe. But suffocation and suffering were imminent. I was ushered back to the elder's homestead to sit on the floor where, between the cracks in the wood, pigs and chickens could be seen running round beneath me. The children sat in a semicircle behind me and watched as plate after plate of cooked and unknown substances were bought for me and the elder to eat. It was as awkward as fuck, no language, no clue, no real want to be there, captive in his hospitality but protected to some degree. The only alternative was to cycle into a dusk jungle just to escape my social discomfort. As night fell more adults joined us and I was shown in what area of the communal hut I would be sleeping. It was however one invitation too many; I insisted on erecting my one-man tent for a little privacy and a break from being the spectacle of the community.

Everyone watched as I set it up and got inside, saying good night. I lay on top of my sleeping bag, sweating in the airless, synthetic accommodation thinking to myself, *there'll be no sleep in here tonight*. I needed a piss. I waited as long as I could and then quietly unzipped the tent. There were the spectators, they hadn't moved since I'd got in. Sitting and standing, watching on in bemusement like I'd stepped into the Tardis – unfortunately, upon stepping out, like them I was in the same place. It was agonising, one of those well-I-dreamed-so-I-must-have-slept nights. Damp, clammy, sticky, smelly and that bloody tar had got everywhere: sleeping bag, clothing, flesh. There were sounds of droplets falling onto my tent all night, either moisture dripping off the heavy, hanging tree or perhaps an exorcism was being performed outside. *The power of Christ compels you!*

Despite those tormented memories, what I recall with the most uplifting feeling was at dawn, as I rolled up my dew-soaked tent and tar-covered sleeping bag, I was given an instant coffee. A man grabbed my arm and took me round to the other side of the hut – *to show me where to shit?* No, there was a view down the valley, and a stunning red dawn. I felt he had understood something about me, knew what my soul needed. I love sunrises and perhaps he was proud of his, maybe embarrassed last night at his meagre life, he could now show off his greatest asset. 'Welcome to my jungle, we've got sun and rays.' A stunning back garden by any standard, his wild, untouched and infinite surroundings, his life-learned survival, his harmony with nature and his respect and appreciation for it. Standing with him watching those colours as the sky lightened, I felt something, a gap bridged, I felt a connection, it was an honour – albeit an awkward one – to be invited into their community. However, the cherry on top was sharing the moment when a crimson sun rose out of the mist. There was absolutely nothing more important either of us could have been doing with our day, we both watched in reverence and silence. The memory still makes me shiver.

I tried to give the villagers something for their hospitality. They wouldn't accept a thing. Again they filled my water bottle and eleven hours after I'd pulled up outside I was waved off. I didn't know if the community even had a name for their collection of huts. No roads, no cars, no electricity, it existed in a different dimension and I was an independent traveller passing through. I wouldn't have wanted to do that every night, it was a hard hospitality to accept, but it remains a moment I've never forgotten and no guidebook will ever ruin that place.

So no, Mr. Moped Rider, I won't stay in your home tonight, but thanks for adding to today's feel-good factor. I hope my refusal didn't take yours away. However, I should start thinking about stopping. I glance at hotels en route but they are noisy and appear rough. It's looking like it's going to be a long ride today. Another stop and four Indian lads look over my bike touching everything, I feel like I'm playing the shell game trying to focus on the cup that has the coin under it, as tricksters' hands shuffle faster than the eye can follow. It's not exactly relaxing; I'm highly suspicious of their hands-on appreciation. The experience is the first indication that I'm approaching a place of tourism, the mentality has changed and I feel like prey, the calm transition has turned to a toll of transit. I'm not getting looks, I'm getting stared at, particularly as I pass a petrol station. *What? Obviously, I'm not going to stop.* When I go in a shop for water, I'm offered a seat but I feel suspicion, I want to see my bike, and anyway the last thing I want when I leave the saddle is to perch my arse on something else.

I find a frontage road expecting a reprieve from the masses but the onslaught changes to trucks and the black smoke in their wake leaves a taste I can't swallow or spit. I find bananas and chocolate tend to cleanse the palate. The great thing about cycling is you can eat as much as you like as often as you can afford, it's all burned off before bedtime, and today it's not enough. The last 10 kilometres are really tough, my back aches and no posture eases the discomfort. As I pull into Alleppey I remember it a little bit, probably because, like my friend in Goa tends to do, last time I passed through at a pace even slower than cycling, spending days not hours at any given stop, planting memories which now bear the fruit of recognition. I remember also my promise to set my standards higher and book a room on the third floor of a hotel. I put my bike in the lift and cycle along the corridor because I can. A hot, cleansing shower, then I lie on white starched sheets. The top of a palm sways outside my window and then the mosque shrieks into life through tinny speakers. I don't mind the mantras from this soft mattress but the faith seems to have no regard for quality of sound, opting for boy-racer amplification over enthusiast purity. Obediently, I leave my room but not to pray, it's time to replace my mosquito net. Over the years it's protected me better than birth control but it's hard to stretch over a double and I fear the holes are now holding little back. For less than $3 I buy one that meets my criteria if not my colour choice but at night the putrid pink will be more subdued than the call to prayer, which I'll hear even better now I can keep the window open and not get bitten. The first 60 kilometres today were fun, going on was wrong but I didn't want to stop so early in the day. I don't recall this conundrum from the last trip. I've got to find a way to pace myself through the day.

Moving forward, flashing back

My body clock is adjusting to dawn departures, but curry for breakfast is still a bit difficult to stomach. I've packed more compactly today and given away to a beggar my Sri Lankan-purchased coat and old mozzie net. Not that he has a ceiling to hang it from. I seem to feel more gratitude in the giving than the recipient does in the receiving. I assume this must either be due to the liberation of the now superfluous or my self-declared charitable offering. This lack of acknowledgement would have me wishing I'd gifted these items to someone else if this act of generosity was not actually for my own good. If only he knew what the mozzie net had been through, and how little had been through it.

I head north-ish, but not enough, come to a beach and have to turn around. There are no claps of attention, no redirections; my onlookers' assumptions have been presumptuous. I double back a bit and reluctantly resort to the main highway. The morning is still fresh and so am I, it's my favourite part of the day, food is being prepared, shutters are lifted, stalls stocked, and I'm open to everything. With heat the thrill is burned away, with tiredness intolerance becomes more prevalent, making every movement a chore. This cool air by comparison puts vigour into my body and actions. India is a place of instant karma and you regularly receive what you reflect, I just can't keep it up after noon and above 30°C.

With my refreshed alertness I notice the different reactions I get from groups I pass. Whispers under veils and nudges through saris, outright yells from blue-jeaned youths with bumfluff moustaches, energy-conserving nods from grey hair in the shade, blatant in-my-face laughter from bratty, privileged and uniformed schoolkids, bashful giggles from children in rags. And everybody else? Well, they all say 'hello'.

'Good morning, India, how are you on this glorious day? What a wonderful mood I'm in at the moment, it's my pleasure to share it with you, but can't stop now, toodle pip, must be oorf.'

My predicted 56 kilometres are announced on the first yellow and white painted concrete roadside stump distance marker as actually being 65 kilometres. The mood goes down a notch. I stop for a mango juice, I'm seated directly under a ceiling fan, it's such a perfect location I order another. Again it's little things like this you don't have the free will to do when discharged from a tourist bus for a comfort stop. Which is why I feel all the more appreciation for them. The mood goes up a notch. Sitting on this wooden stall with a condensation-covered glass of undiluted goodness, I can concentrate on what matters and get the best from it. It's not a bio break, it's a well-being top-up.

Back on the two-lane carriageway I play cat and mouse with a bus. It's really quite infuriating, he passes me, obviously, then stops for a waving passenger, of course, I pass him, he comes up from behind again and passes, this repeats like one line from an irritating song stuck in my head. There is no escape, no variation, no way to avoid it. I pass him, he overtakes me, if I stop, I get an instant audience, and when I move on it will be same shit different bus, if I speed up … I'm not going to bloody speed up. I really want to check my map, see if I can find an alternative route. By accident, I realise if I squat in the shade of my bike, it's assumed I'm having a dump and I'm left alone. A handy trick. I find what I'm looking for, a quieter road, and ride across a bridge seeing naval ships and shiny hotels. I stop to take it all in, you can't do that on a bus. Then I watch as a man lowers a kind of Chinese fishing net with umbrella mechanism into the water while I have a chocolate break, all with the satisfaction of knowing I'm travelling to my own, possibly auspicious, schedule. A youth high-fives me as I leave the populace and join a more reflective road.

I'm never far from the backwaters that are one of Kerala's attractions; I see a brick factory and have a flashback.

It's another example of first-time wonderment, travelling before judgement had set in. I'd caught a bus to this area with a Brummie girl, she bumped into a Kiwi bloke she knew, he was infatuated with an Aussie Sheila. I wouldn't say the couple from down under were inseparable as later Sheila came with me to Sri Lanka. However, the four of us travelled harmoniously, with matching budgets, compatible pace and mutual interests, namely being in the bubble of bewilderment. One morning the girls were apprehended by some sailors of sorts, who were leaving on their wicker-covered boat to pick up a fare downriver. Wanting a paying cargo, a killer deal was negotiated to take the four of us on their luxury floating accommodation on a tranquil tour of the backwaters with food included. It was one of those 'I must take this opportunity even though it's above my budget' moments. The company, the circumstance, the occasion, the accommodation were all idyllic. We had two punters, a cook and a guide. So basically a staff member for each of us. When the two-storey, crowded backpacker boats would shatter the silence speeding past with their big outboards and too many on board, we'd recline on creature comforts reaching for another fresh fruit picked from the last riverside community where we'd quietly harboured. When the cook wasn't cooking he'd pick a palm leaf and creatively craft a chillum out of it, a cone-shaped pipe popular in these parts. Upon passing round his handiwork for all to admire he'd promptly fill it with hash and hand it round again. As the unfeasible orange sun silhouetted palms, we would anchor midriver for dinner and marvel at the tranquillity as our pace slowed to punt and current. It was undeniably a serene trip and one evening there seemed absolutely no reason at all not to take some LSD. While the staff slept, the Kiwi and I decided to take a swim. It wasn't a boat designed for easy disembarkation, especially if trying to be quiet, so diving or jumping was out of the question – with single-minded determination however, we found a way to lower ourselves into the water, hoping that reversing the procedure would allow us to reboard. Predictably, with heightened senses, slowly immersing my body into the still water produced a multitude of sensations, not least liberation from the boat. I trod water and took in the surreal situation. The current kept me alert and consciousness came in waves. I found myself in an undeniable warm pocket in the water, I voiced this observation to the Kiwi who, through power of suggestion or shared experience, concurred. It felt wrong, sinister, slightly scary, and we climbed back to the safety of our woven craft. We became aware of an industrial noise coming from the shore. Although some distance away, we had tuned into the obnoxious night-time production from a brick factory and, like snoring to the light sleeper, it couldn't be ignored. Something had to be done, so with the girls' help we quietly weighed anchor, took the bamboo punts and, without splashing, pushed our vessel out of earshot from the nocturnal manufacturer. It was exhilarating, made all the more intense trying to stifle giggles as we made our silent passage. The physical exertion of the punting had the acid pumping. I stared with wild eyes into a black night that sunk into the inky, sparkling water with a haze of purple and I knew without a shadow of a doubt that I was 'the nomadic midnight river warrior on the edge of time'. It was an image that stuck, a prophecy in fact, a direction, a way to live the rest of my life, a saucer-pupiled vision, a realisation. The only eyes that were wider were the crews', when they woke to find we weren't where we had been when they went to sleep.

And there it is, that offensive brick factory, possibly pumping its pollution into the river and warming the water that freaked out a couple of unsuspecting and not quite innocent hedonists … yep, been there, done that.

I head towards the city of Ernakulam, and the craziness increases, impatience becomes part of every vehicle's disposition. After my tranquil ride and mind's recollections, my reactions have subdued. I spot an old man riding a sit-up-and-beg Henderson bicycle sedately along the street. Seemingly in synchronisation with the other traffic, not swerving or braking, not cursing or sweating, but on a steady trajectory, unperturbed by all that is going on around. I don't think this is his first day here on a bike, he seems to have found a way to outlive the odds. So I follow his lead, copy his technique and adopt his style, all the way to an affordable-looking hotel. So affordable, in fact, that there are fifteen youths crammed into the one room. I say I'll be back, hoping for better and for an extra 33 cents I find it, and I've got a balcony. Which is where my freshly laundered cycling shorts are soon drying.

Finally, I feel like I've got something to say and head to the internet café. I've got excitement to relay and respond to Sofia's email with gushing enthusiasm for all that has happened over the last few days. As I type feverously it occurs to me that I could reduce the online fee, and with just a little alteration. What I actually have here is a mass mail, I'm finally ready to communicate with everyone. I bcc my group in, and even remember to add Erica, before sending the mail to many, keeping my online time short and cheap. *Excellent, job done ...* and it's then, with a shudder, I realise I've just sent everyone Sofia's love letter. If they chose to scroll down, they will see her intimate words to me. *OH, FUCK!* That's the problem with instant communication, it can't be retrieved, no putting my hand inside the letter box, or waiting for the postman to collect. It's sent, it's delivered, and sending another email chasing after it saying *please don't scroll down* will be futile. I shiver. Oh god, I realise actually it was a stream of correspondence, *Re: Re: Re:*. It's killing me as I recall the words.

I go for dinner on the rooftop of an eight-storey building, taking my anxiety with me but unable to throw it off. I am literally kicking myself, squirming, I don't recall ever wanting to travel back in time so desperately. I once said, watching *Blind Date*, 'Is it possible to die from cringing?' I survived that agonising viewing and this is worse, so much worse. Over fifty people across the planet whom I've shared various parts of my life with have just received the most intimate of intimacies. This is my equivalent of the leaked celebrity sex video, but without bragging rights, no macho performance, no legendary libido. In fact, I've been a bit pathetic up until recently, hence having little to say to anyone other than my absent lover, seeking comfort from her words of affection and consolation. Oh shit, her address was in that email, for me to send the rupees. It's getting worse.

My faux pas follows me, inescapable, excruciating company. My instinct tells me to run and hide, but I am already alone on the outskirts of some foreign town, how much further can I go? My isolation from anyone I know is not helping at all. My uncensored, typo-infested love life is knocking on everyone's inbox. See, this didn't happen last time I was in India, there was no internet. Nothing I can think of releases me from this agonising torment, nothing can change this situation, who can I talk to? 'You'll never guess what I've gone and done?'

'Oh I know, we all know.'

I lie on the bed, defeated under my new putrid pink mozzie net which glows bright from crimson-cringing embarrassment. No biting pest will penetrate this net and get to me, any more than I can infiltrate the internet and stop what's gone to everyone.

A journey defined by the stops

Now knowing well the benefits of the early start and enjoying the beginning of the day most, I have decided I want more beginning, so my alarm wakes me at 6.30. I think with every day I'm getting more and more into road mode. I should never have expected it to be an instant transition but those first few weeks were really unexpectedly agonising, mostly awful in fact. Especially looking back now from this position of waking earlier each day in anticipation of the excitement to come. All that's left now is the agony of accidentally telling everyone, although despite still being curled up with cringing like an embarrassed hedgehog who accidentally mounted a broom in front of his mates, I do feel more liberated from my longing. Perhaps like finding the right mindset for the road, it's also taken time to get used to my own company again, and inadvertently sharing my missing has reduced it to much more tolerable levels. Then again, it could just be that the journey's newfound thrill and fascination has fed my forlorn soul and there is no room left for yearning.

My balcony is perfectly positioned to watch the sun come up out of the dusty haze of the eastern side of the city. I watch it rise, put on clean, dry cycling shorts and am on the road for 7 a.m. The streets are cool and relatively empty, like an illicit lover I've left town before it's woken. I find myself on a much narrower road than usual which means more tree shade, a little unexpected bonus. I know I'm running parallel with the beach but I never see it.

I have a little epiphany: it occurs to me if you eliminate the hills, you lose the scenery. I never factored that into the route. All I wanted was easy, flat and warm, not hard, hilly and icy. I consider previous cycling and hiking challenges, they were excruciating at times and it wasn't always physical. The Thai jungle village home stay, for example, and also my ill-prepared hike in Patagonia, but those hardships I put myself through came with overwhelming rewards, the ecstasy of achievement. I'm not challenging myself at all this trip, not physically anyway. I came away wanting and expecting easy and I've got it, along with its limp handshake of acceptance.

This situation has strong similarities to my truck-driving career. Before I was even old enough to hold an HGV licence I'd drive a little van round London having multiple deliveries and only a black and white A-Z to navigate by. That progressed to European long-haul loneliness, not least because us truckers are not known for our multilingual capabilities. Dealing with unionised dock workers, antisocial-hours, night runs, unscrupulous transport managers, lazy forklift drivers, and unhonoured booking-in times by the very corporations that demanded them. Delivering every commodity from tractor cabs to molasses, food to prolong the imprisoned life of scientific-experiment animals, roofing joists taller than telegraph wires, mini skips and fish from boat to Billingsgate. From dustbin trucks to paper for passports and over-size Portakabins requiring police escorts, I've taken nearly everything everywhere at every time of day and in every type of truck. Which got me to the point of luxurious lettuce logistics. Turn up at dinner time to a loaded trailer, take it to the same place every night, tip, reload with empty crates, back the way I came and leave the truck on the loading bay in the early hours for the day shift to deal with. No loads to secure, no new roads to navigate, no badly addressed delivery notes, no hidden businesses to find, no borders to negotiate, no traffic jams holding me up. No more working for shitty family-run transport companies with no regard for drivers, orders from ignorant authority in privileged positions, not earned but handed to inept sons born into haulage who had never been behind the wheel. Like every hill I'd ridden in the Himalayas I rose above it all, and then there was nothing, nothing new, ever, every night was the same, the easiest job ever and subsequently the most boring. No challenge, no recompense, like trying to write a book telling only one story, and now I'm on the straight and narrow, the flat and featureless, the dull and banal, the seaside insipid. It's not actually that bad, India thankfully delivers mystique wherever you may roam. Although on this route palms will never be replaced by pines, the sea breeze will not drop to wind chill with altitude, coast won't change to cliffs, and fishing villages won't be elevated to mountain settlements.

There may be no mountains, no prayer flags flapping from frozen peaks but, as I've discovered, it's important to appreciate the little things. Like the fact I've travelled 27 kilometres this morning before I stop for a cup of chai which, like yesterday's mango juice, soon turns to a second. And also riding with less intensity I can consider other things and I'm beginning to understand the language of the road. The behaviour of the drivers is not as random as I first thought. A little flap of the hand out of a rolled-down window appears to say *I know I'm cutting you up, go this way, I can see it's OK.* There is some courtesy in the confusion, it's classic Indian culture, unfathomable to Western logic, they are not bloody-minded just bloody hard to understand. That hand indication may be tantamount to saying: I may be about to throw you overboard but I'm at least pointing the way to shore. But it's still an acknowledgement, a fair warning, and that somehow takes some of the severity out of the seemingly selfish manoeuvre. Their turn signals too are a flash of confusion. They drive on the left – well, more accurately, the steering wheel is on the right, and they drive all over the bloody place. However, a right flashing indicator doesn't necessarily mean a right turn; it can mean 'pass me'. We sometimes flash the left one in the UK to indicate the same invitation; even if the indication is misconstrued nothing too awful can happen passing the right side of a left-turning vehicle. However, having your line of trajectory cut off by the truck you're halfway past turning right, means hard braking or terminal breakage. Thankfully, I'm travelling at a pace that observes this action rather than being an impatient participant in this passing practice.

37 kilometres before breakfast, which today is chicken curry and chapatti – easier to swallow after this distance, it's not really a dish associated with breakfast in bed. The day is defined by the stops I make, in fact any journey is. When I have a soda an older gentleman takes great pleasure in telling me his life story. He's heading to an elephant festival that's north of here, to me that says noise all night and no rooms. I half want to see it but that half doesn't control the pedals and direction and I miss the entire town. My next stop is at a Muslim-owned shop and the wizened shopkeeper performs exaggerated mannerisms with mute hilarity

and a smile that turns to deadpan if he gets a reaction. He's messing with me, making me laugh and then pretending to be offended that my reaction is inappropriate. When I recoil, he goes off again in animated gestures and a sly grin. Is he like this every day to everyone? Another of India's infinite mysteries. I buy pop, bananas and chocolate from him and leave with little confidence in my deduction of the interaction but with a confused smile that stays with me longer than the chocolate does.

I'd had to do miming of my own fashion in Thailand after getting that tar all over me, my shorts and sleeping bag. But before the miming could begin, I had to find the appropriate audience, someone, anyone, so my request would not fall on deaf ears. I left that hillside settlement with renewed energy but it wasn't enough, within 10 kilometres my legs were as tired as they had been the night before. Again I resorted to pushing the bike up hills, stopping for a Marmite sandwich and depleting the last of my supplies. I missed a truck I could have held on to, but then the road turned to ruts and potholes so nothing was lost at all in the end. It was unrideable. I couldn't even push the bike, my feet just slipped on the dusty track. Again I sat and sulked, now coating my tar-covered shorts with a layer of dirt. A small tribe of ... well, tribesman, walked past, authentic dress and traditional style – at least to my eyes, what did I know? Maybe they thought I was straight out of the Tour de France. Anyway, feeling exhausted, deflated and having had no interaction with anyone but Thais for several days I just looked up at them, smiled and said, 'All right, boys?' I got a convivial response.

When the third vehicle in two hours passed, I flagged it down. They happily let me and my bike sit in the bed of the pickup. Up and down, on and on, impossible roads for a bicycle but some great views of cloud-filled valleys, I never would have been able to ride this. I'm taken all the way into the next town, then asked if I'd rather be dropped at the one after. 'Yeah, OK,' I replied. I could easily have done that last flat, smooth 25 kilometres, which, in the case of today's effort, would actually be the first 25 kilometres of my cycling day. I was in civilisation by 10.30 a.m. and, like last night's hosts, the driver wouldn't accept any money. So I got a room, shower, ate and was then ready to face the day's next challenge. I found a pharmacy and approached the man behind the counter. I calmly mimed the painting of my nails and then, without urgency or losing his attention, I proceeded to remove the varnish. He totally got it and, from under the counter, produced a bottle of nail varnish remover, which soon became tar remover. After that I took the rest of the day off. Reading my guidebook and discovering there was a ferry along the Mekong River from Thailand to China, my plans changed again – considering a slow boat to China.

I'm far more independent this trip and have done over 100 kilometres today, and it hasn't been that hard. The worst thing has been the kids on bicycles trying to overtake me but, like hysterical teenage girls running after an overhyped heart-throb, they aren't quite sure what to do once they have caught up. I think it would be inappropriate to use my dog-beating stick but the thought does cross my mind. I'm hoping for a beach hotel but I don't hope hard enough, or try hard enough. As I ride into a town of unknown size and ready to end my cycling day, I get the first place I see. It's a cesspit, the worst so far, rooms with no doors, walls with no colour, corridors with no light, floors with no covering but scurrying cockroaches, and furniture with broken legs. I have no glass in my windows that look out over the main road to a noisy, polluted, dusty bus station. I might as well be at the elephant festival. I go for a shower but there is no shower, only foot disease lurking in a damp, dark concrete cubicle with a dripping tap. I pour buckets of water over my head, then lay on the lumps and tufts that by their position on a metal frame must be deemed a mattress. It's only 4 p.m. This is undoubtedly my least favourite part of the day. Too early to eat, much too early to sleep and too tired to do much else. I go and find an internet café. I've kept my cringing at bay for most of the day, there has been enough stimulation and distraction to keep my confused thoughts focused. I open my email and just see the heading *Oops* as the power goes off. The embarrassment comes back with a vengeance, and it's killing me all over again. I don't know what's best, not being able to read the responses or knowing now with absolute certainty, despite my desperate wishes, that the email was indeed sent to everyone.

Left with little else to do I watch life go by from out of my broken window. It's full on, the street's procession of traffic, throngs of bus station passengers swelling and dispersing with arrivals and departures. The advancing tide of traders, hawkers, beggars and taxi drivers who gravitate round the new arrivals. I don't trust this room, especially now it's getting dark and still no lights. I lock my bike and take my valuables to find a place for dinner. I order a vegetarian meal, as the cooking is questionable with no power, and a raw carrot will do me far less harm than undercooked meat. I work out that now with a daily average of over 100 kilometres I can be in Goa by next Friday. I'm not sure how I feel about that, it's as if the journey has only just started and now an end is in sight.

I lie on my bed, the noise from the street more amplified from two storeys of elevation. I've really got to raise my standards, this place is appalling. Through restless sleep I become aware of the fan whirling and the bare light bulb glowing. The power is back, I don't know what time it is but I get out from under my mozzie net and kill the light. There is banging at my door, *oh, what now?* It's three lads from the internet café. 'Come back,' they say, 'the computers work again.'

I've got to smile. Three, *three*, of you have all decided to come and find me to give me this news. I suppose I'm grateful but the next time I leave this room it will be forever. *Goodnight, India, please try and keep the noise down, I've not got glass in me windows, ya know.*

Friday 5th December
Ponnani – Calicut
Kilometres cycled: 97

Followers before me

Early nights make for early mornings; shite rooms make for swift exits. At 6 a.m. it's barely light but I now know the sun, like me sleeping on a revolting mattress in a nasty room, is keen to be out. Sure enough at 6.30 as my tyres make contact with the street and I'm springing fresh into the world, morning is breaking. A Muslim man on a bicycle pulls out from his house onto the road as I pass. He invites me back to his for chai. I, like him, have only just got going; unlike him, I feel the need to keep my momentum, and so decline. He is really disappointed, there is no agenda to this decision other than my want to ride in this, my favourite part of the day. But it's already ruined as I regret my reaction. That was an opportunity and I wasn't ready for one so soon. In much the same way as I remind myself to be aware and take pleasure in the little things, so do I also get remorseful at the silly and seemingly insignificant, but it was a wrong decision. It was just chai, but the infinite possibilities that interaction may have had I will never know, and I recall the refusal with more clarity than a hundred chai's I've drunk alone.

The road turns a corner. This is where the hotels and guest houses are. Damn it, I really did stay in the arse end of town. There is choice and temptations; the only temptation in my chosen accommodation was to leave. I stop for a chai, hoping the dejected Muslim gentleman doesn't ride past and see me. I get into an intense discussion about whether this is the right road or not. It's funny as it doesn't even matter to me that much but my indifference causes even more distress as my map is scrutinised in excruciating detail. Today the delays seem to be the journey, I should have started the stopping earlier.

I manage to miss the coastal back road and find myself on the highway for nearly three hours. A road full of fast traffic, when I wanted tranquil, the sweat is pouring off me and I wanted sea breeze to cool me, as opposed to being buffeted by truck turbulence. The road undulates with overexerting inclines and not enough descent to recover; I'm inland and I wanted to witness crashing waves not close misses. I've really screwed this morning up. I should have paid more attention to direction at the chai stop, I am no longer indifferent. It's busy and noisy and there is nothing available that resembles breakfast. After 36 kilometres I stop to buy bread and make a Marmite sandwich in a quiet corner of an abandoned building. I should know better, there is life everywhere in India and the wall I've leaned against has an army of ants heading up to the roof, and I'm bitten through my sweat-wet shirt. Every inch of this country is occupied. I convince myself my map is wrong because there seems to be no turn-off to the beach road. I decide to ask and instantly get a crowd of thirty people around me. Catching sight of hands trying to steal my bag off the rear rack I accelerate away with previously untapped energy. I leave the smooth but undulating highway for a bumpy and undulating back road. There's less traffic but more people and none of them seem to have anything to do at all. I'm the most interesting thing to pass by in anyone's living memory. This must be how Lady Godiva felt, all eyes are on me, I can't even find a place to take a piss. I stop for a soda and again get surrounded, stared at, not talked to; *come on, you've seen someone drink from a bottle with a straw before, surely*. I'm so perturbed I leave forgetting to pay. Still, no one said anything.

I take a wrong turn and a moped gets level with me. Both rider and passenger just stare, no comments, no facial expression that I can read, just a blatant gawping escort, with two-stroke irritation in both noise and fumes. *Oh, for fuck's sake*. I see a path to the beach and just stop, pushing my bike to the sand, still populated but not permanently, this is a place of squatting, all taking a shit and watching me, it almost makes the room I left this morning seem appealing. Back to the road, it comes to a river and ends; no bridge, that's it. I've got no option but to turn back, no wonder they all looked at me, this road goes nowhere, I can't imagine many people come this way and now I've got to bloody go back. Obviously, they knew this and now everyone has come out to gawk as I double back through my discomfort. I'm followed on foot and bicycle, it's not threatening, not in the slightest, just really bloody annoying. *Fuck off*, I'm panting under my breath. Much like a hunted and distressed fox will eventually make a mistake, I take another wrong turn on to a road that crosses a railway track. The barrier is down and no one is held up, hand-operated by a man with a handle, on a pulley he mercifully lifts the gate for me to ride under. A moment's respite from my followers. It's around this time the line 'There's always someone looking at you' from a song by The Boomtown Rats comes into my head and keeps me company for the rest of my ride.

A lone man with a wooden barrow is selling veg. I buy two misshapen and not quite ripe tomatoes. He weighs them on his balance scales, wraps them in newspaper and ties them with string. *Come on*, I'm thinking, *they are going to catch me up*. I put them in my bar bag and hurry on past a bend in the road. Feeling I've outrun the throng, I sit down and make a sandwich; they remain the tastiest tomatoes I've ever eaten. Not aesthetically pleasing but full of flavour, every tomato since has always seemed a little tasteless by comparison. But there is little time to savour and no option to return for more, my audience has caught me up. With Benny Hill characteristics, I ride off, the crowd chasing at a pace that I can easily outrun … usually. But my tyre is flat and a pack of schoolkids are coming from the other direction. This is bad, this could incite a riot. Mending the puncture is out of the question, I get out my pump and frantically try to inflate the tyre, I have about twenty people in close proximity and many more loitering further back. The tyre inflates away from the rim, that's enough, that will do, I swing my leg over the bike and just ride. So distraught, I'm not even sure of my direction, then the fucking road ends again. Another river, maybe the same river, I've not had a moment to consider, but there is a jetty, I cycle onto it and the crowd follows behind. The tyre is flat again, at least here I only have an audience behind me. I take off a pannier and the wheel as a tiny rowing boat pulls up, more spectators? But no, they offer to take me across the river. 'Yes,' I say, not even asking the price, passing them pannier, wheel, bag and my bike. They fend off the rabid kids with a plastic bottle. I laugh out loud with both relief and the absurdity of the situation, then they cast away and we are free of the onslaught.

That was intense. I use the crossing to replace the tube, never once looking up and taking in the scene we are sailing across. Saved for 10 cents and with the help of a plastic bottle. The bike is assembled, upright and ready to ride again. I pay the ferry man on the other side, just about finding some humour in the situation as this really is the only way to survive.

My Thai jungle back-road tracking was coming to an end. The Mekong River beckoned. But before I could leave, I was told with expert assurance there were three hills between me and the river at Chiang Mai … and they were all up!

'Really? All up?'

Clean and refuelled, all tar removed, I found asphalt where it was most appreciated, a newly surfaced road. The going was still hard, I'd not seemed to have built any stamina or strength, and it had been a week since I'd got over my food poisoning. I set myself a 10-kilometre distance before I would allow myself a break, and as the marker approached so did a truck from behind and I reprioritised, postponing the rest, grabbing a rope dangling off the back and getting some easy momentum. Even when the road started to flatten out, I wouldn't let go, my hyperventilation inhaling the black smog. The road became blocked with resurfacing equipment and the driver had to stop. It was only a 3-kilometre tow but those kilometres were crucial steep ones. As the road continued up, unsure if it was the same hill or the second, I found that with the correct selection of gears, I could manage to keep a pace, develop a rhythm, albeit a slow and repetitive one. But it was steady progress and sure enough I reached the summit and freewheeled until I saw a shelter to take a rest. My left knee joint was hurting so I put more strain on my right knee, applying uneven pressure on the pedals. Now there was traffic again, petrol stations were becoming more frequent. Filling up on Coke and crisps was about to become common practice as those commodities had begun to become such easy prey.

Unfortunately, it appeared that I'd become prey too. As I ate and relaxed in a bus shelter, I encountered the only negative Thai of the trip, who disturbed my rest, wanting money or food, or just to fuck with me.

He failed with the first two and I freewheeled away, finding the second hill and a pine tree research station. They were just closing up for the night so I offered to keep an eye on the trees while they were gone and camped for free, alone, safely locked inside the gates of the institution. It was a sound sleep, with a night-time of unknown noises from the canopy of trees.

I'm pining for some privacy and sanctuary today. Only 10 kilometres to town it's still tough, it's been tough all day. Ahead of me is a very wide load held off the road by four legs, it must be an elephant. Hessian sacks are roped onto its back and a kids' tricycle is tied above its tail. Using one of my precious 35mm exposures, I wastefully take a photo of its behind as I approach, keeping my camera out to capture the trunk as I pass. I feel a bit of an arse when I realise it's only an ass, it seems as disappointed as I am that I don't want a photo of its face. Sometimes as a truck driver, away for long periods with only my own company, I would feel a heightened sense of perception, often seeing what I had only recently contemplated, like a word I was singing simultaneously appearing, printed on a passing van. It was a thin line between insight and insanity and would never, could never, happen if I had a passenger. Perhaps the laden donkey was a precursor or an outrider because not long after my misidentification comes an unmistakable manifestation. Three men in dhotis walk in reverence behind a big elephant's behind. The animal carries only a man on his back wearing a burgundy tunic and half a palm tree in its mouth. I have a photo of both rear and head. I've just ridden past a working elephant, *I'VE JUST OVERTAKEN AN ELEPHANT*, that's cooler than collecting seven-year-old mail. I wonder if the rider is the new owner, bought it from yesterday's festival and treated it to a coconut tree to keep it going. Regardless of the reason, it's a spectacular sight.

I continue on the trunk road into Calicut and find a hotel, it's more than I want to pay but I just want a door I can close behind me. Annoyingly, that door is on the third floor and it's an unnecessary strain to take my bike up, but equally unnecessary stress to leave it out of sight. I have a long shower with cold water but it's not cold enough, then collapse onto the bed. Bloody hell, what a day, fucked it up from the first interaction and it got worse from there, saved by the last overtake of the day. I doze a little but have an underlying knowledge that I have to face my inbox, so I go to find an internet café. Yes, everyone got my and Sofia's email. Some people include an account of their year in the Christmas cards they send, not me, I send a mass mail of my love life. The main response is just taking the piss, which is actually fine. I only ever considered the faux pas, never the reaction, and actually I didn't hurt anyone, it wasn't malicious, only my and Sofia's intimacies were betrayed. I think the recipients feel my embarrassment, and only laugh at my idiocy. It's OK, I can deal with this. Erica didn't reply, ever, I have to assume I copied her email address wrong. The only slightly sinister response is from someone who said: *I didn't scroll down.* There would be no need to say that if he hadn't. I suppose if he needs to satisfy his fetishes vicariously through me then I'm happy to oblige. Hope he learned something, should he ever find himself in a similar situation – that being: far from home, missing a lover who misses you equally and looking forward to reuniting after your independent foreign travel challenge. But I don't think he'll ever be able to relate to a single day in my recent life, and certainly not be able to live it, he'd never handle the pace, how many faces have I seen today, how many have seen me? So I exposed myself, I feel all right about it now. It's just another day on the road, like no day I've ever had before. I limboed under a level crossing, hailed a boat to escape my frenzied entourage, and passed an elephant. Scroll and snoop all you like, keep up with my life if you can, no one else today has managed to.

Saturday 6th December
Calicut – Kannur
Kilometres cycled: 99

Counting threads not kilometres

Who needs an alarm when you've got Islam? The chanting cuts through the night, the window, my mozzie net and into my sleep at 5.15 a.m. I have no issues with any faith – anyone's actions at all, in fact – as long as their activities don't interfere with my life. This amplified prayer is unignorable, shattering the night, because it is night, it won't be light for a while yet. Still, when in Rome … or Mecca. I've inevitably established a routine, I don't roll out my prayer mat, face east and get on my knees, but I do roll up my mozzie net, wash my face and pack with ease. I have to wait for the receptionist to give me my deposit back but he forgets to charge me tax so I win.

Out onto the hazy streets, ready to accept any invite that comes my way but, today, typically none do. So I invite myself, when, after 10 kilometres, I see a sign for a beach resort and take the track, the opportunity, and advantage of my freedom to choose, to see what's down there. It's well posh, $35 a night to my usual $2, bungalows right on the beach. I immediately decide a breakfast treat in this refinery is the order of the morning.

A tablecloth cleaner than any bedding I've seen this week. Evenly tanned toast, butter that's yet to liquify, and jam without ants. Chai poured from a bottomless teapot and a copy of the *Hindu Times* to read; it is a truly decadent start to the day. What I'm missing in cool dawn riding I'm making up for with these sumptuous surroundings, served by smartly dressed, attentive yet reserved waiters. It's slightly disconcerting to know that my skin colour alone is my rite of passage into such premises. I look like what I am: I've been living out of panniers, sunburned and windswept, road-worn, and perhaps slightly worldly. But I am Western and that alone makes me worthy of admittance. *Now hurry along, my man, and fetch me a serviette to wipe away the dirt that has already accumulated in my laughter*

143

lines this morning. I spend an hour feeling genuinely relaxed and fully catered for. I could spend longer but every night here would take a week off of my trip. It was just a little taste of how things could be, a flavour I savour so infrequently that it's all the more appreciated, be it the thread count of the linen on the table for breakfast or on the bed for the night. This cycling thing is not a self-inflicted endurance test, allowing a little luxury into my life is essential and I deserve these treats.

Twelve hours passed in the pine tree sanctuary and research station, the sounds of the unknown and nocturnal were an exotic lullaby. No threat, just a constant background noise, like snoring but without the want to suffocate the perpetrator with a pillow. The moon was brighter than my headlight, but I chose to load up and leave with the transition of dawn illumination, pausing mid-task for a Marmite breakfast sandwich. The security of the sanctuary, the satisfaction of self-sufficiency in provisions, the reassurance of being independent in transport, and the well-being of waking from a free night was a cause for a modest celebration. I like to acknowledge a wild camp or cost-free accommodation with a treat, and to cater for my desire, as soon as I left the park there were food stalls waiting to supply me with tea and noodle soup.

Best of all, after my second breakfast the road was downhill all the way … well, to the bottom at least. Down and down, freewheeling to the point that wind chill became an issue, but it was a small complaint in the great scheme of things. Into a valley of captive cloud the moisture accumulating on and then soaking into my clothing, a novelty for dampness to come from the outside in. I found myself actually hoping for an uphill climb just to warm up a bit, aware that such a wish was tempting fate. But the freewheeling continued into the outskirts of urban where a bridge crossed a fast-flowing river with sandy banks which the sun shone on. Seemed like a perfect place to stop and warm before my nipples snapped off.

The river widened and slowed and the road followed its descent all the way into the district of 'Hot'. This easy morning had given my left knee a much-needed break. The discomfort in the joint was seeking more of my attention and therefore concern. My 50 kilometres were already complete and it was only 10.30. I cycled round looking for accommodation, even asking at the post office and police station – apparently, there was only one, a hotel, and I couldn't find it. It was not the ideal decision but, lacking options, I continued north, now convinced I'd left the mountains behind, although I never did determine what hills were up and how many I ascended.

The following 30 kilometres were some of the flattest since I had left the capital. Unlike Bangkok they didn't seem to accommodate travellers in these parts: no hotel, no guest house, no pub, no restaurant. I headed towards the park and found a 'porn hotel'. Pretty Thai girls sat on the steps, but somehow, they looked cheap, not in an affordable way, just a bit sleazy, layered with tainted love, not radiant. They had a beauty but it was brutal. They had company too: young Thai military types, gobby, full of bravado and cum. There was not a single part of me that was attracted to any aspect of that scene, strangely not even the sex. Something was occurring, something I'd never experienced before in my life since puberty. I didn't seem to be thinking about sex all the time, none of the time, my libido had never been so low. I was a little concerned. It was new to me, I could go off on a long train of thought as I cycled and never once got sidetracked by sexual desires, derailed by yearnings from the nether regions or fantasies coming to the front of my mind. I could think straight, unperturbed, undistracted. *Is this what a eunuch feels like?*

Anyway, the porn hotel had no attraction. So on I went for another 7 kilometres to a sort of holiday camp, where, for my usual nightly budget, I got a two-bedroomed apartment with a kitchen and a large lounge, including a table to socialise round. Which was about as useful as a porn hotel when you'd lost your mojo somewhere on the road and were travelling solo. In the grounds was a pool of sorts, a three-metre circle cut into the ground and walled with rubble and pebbles, resembling a well and fed by a natural spring. So I got a beer and sat in it, and was soon joined by two Aussie men in their mid-fifties. They were most definitely the camp

145

in this holiday resort, queens of comedy, upbeat and bitchy, a double act of pert-lipped put-downs. I realised I was now, having left Bangkok two weeks before, a cyclist; I only had cycling stories to tell, I couldn't seem to come up with anything else to talk about, but they humoured my tales, appearing bicycle-interested.

In the evening I cycled behind their moped following them to a restaurant, keeping up easily without my panniers. I led the way back chasing my shadow in front of their headlight. Then I invited them for a Bushmills around my socialising table, which I never for a moment thought would see guests so soon after my arrival. They ripped the piss out of me for all the stuff I carried, having set the table with whiskey, stereo speakers and relaxed into my evening attire, spreading my luxuries around my posh and palatial apartment. Such extravagances occurred once in a blue moon and that night was my full moon party, although not exactly Ko Pha Ngan. Three rooms but no mushrooms, stereo but no techno, although, like the Flintstones, we had a gay old time.

I know my place and it's somewhere between bedrock and high end. It's certainly not this beach resort so I get back on the saddle and back on the middle path. The sun has gone up in elevation and taken the temperature with it, my favourite part of the day may already be burned out. Then I see a motorcycle accident, nothing too serious, smashed indicator and a damaged flip-flop, bad for the injured party but good for some perspective. We are none of us immortal, spend it now, make sure the last cheque bounces. After yesterday's manic puncture solution, I'm riding without a repaired replacement tube and no glue either. However, punctures are a regular occurrence, and bicycles, like rats, are commonplace and often nearer than you think, so it's easy to find someone who sells the supplies I require. I buy a big tube of puncture repair glue for 15 cents and have a Pepsi too. As I stand taking in the little parade of shops I'm parked in front of, I see a place that sells fridges. It's called Sell Fridges. Brilliant.

The day is flying by, or at least I'm flying through it, 70 kilometres by lunchtime, but I can't see anywhere that encourages me to stop and I think I've got another 20 kilometres in me. The road keeps crossing railway lines, or perhaps it's the other way round … depends on whether you're on a train or not I suppose … *uh-oh, there it is again*. I need some Western company, my thoughts are getting weird. I'm hot too, very hot, that could have something to do with it. Delirium may be germinating in my head.

I see a sign for *drive in beach* and head down to see what it's all about. It's just hard sand, be easy to ride on, shall I? Yeah, why not? Best decision of the day, totally peaceful, only the sound of the waves, smooth and flat with land-speed-record aspirations, no friction holding me back. I take my camera in my hand, holding it at arm's length and, as I ride with the lens pointing towards me, I press the shutter button taking a photo of myself. I wish someone would come up with a term for this act that is shorter than the thirty-two words to describe the action of taking a photo of one's self, it would save a lot of room in my diary. I'm able to look into the lens as I ride as there are no obstacles to watch out for the first time since … well, ever, I suppose. I could ride with my eyes shut – *shit, why did I think that?* I ride with my eyes shut, it's as exhilarating as it is stupid. With normal vision resumed I see an attractive hotel up ahead, but it's full of noisy Indians. If I have to endure noisy, I might as well act like a bird and go cheap, so I make like a tree and leave. Somebody help me, I need company.

Back to the main road and into town with a huge choice of accommodation. First one is full, the second has no door, the next only has a room on the third floor and only stairs and I'm not dragging my bike up three flights again. Then I find an idyllic little room: the window overlooks a garden, birds tweet – well, they always do, but I can actually hear them over the horns of the traffic. The sun shines through pleasing leaves in a cool breeze, palms and plants flicker shadows across my bed, crickets sing. I hang my sarong in the window and just lie, listening to this refreshing new song. No traffic at all, its absence so noticeable now, it simply never stops, there is no getting away from it, obvious really when you choose to live your life on the road.

I eat dinner at a turfed rooftop restaurant: a very natural floor covering, although perhaps not what a structural engineer and damp proofer would

147

consider a natural choice. When I pay the bill, the waiter points the way to Mangalore through the latticework of streets below before shutting me in a lift and pressing the button for the ground floor. Seemingly certain I'll find my way to a major city alone, but not to street level without his help. I get a text from Mum, she and Dad are decorating the tree. No pangs, nothing at all, I don't miss Sofia any more either. I have arrived, I am now a nomadic road warrior on the edge of time, no more air pockets, I've broken the ice.

Burning calories and a burning desire

The mosque calls, Fajr, dawn prayer, but my atheism doesn't get me up out of bed or down on my knees for Allah. Then there's the sound of a siren, if it's fire I can jump out of the window. I continue to not believe that there is a saviour above or the threat of an inferno below. In fact, as I lay in denial of everything, I believe I will take the day off, and with that fact I compose a mass email in my head, in my bed. It's just such an agreeable little room, I feel relaxed and simply want to stick around a while. I put on some music just as a generator, as opposed to a creator, fires up below my window and I smell emissions from an exhaust pipe that does as little to dampen the noise as it does to filter the fumes. It's just like being back on the road. I find a bloated mozzie inside my net, too fat to hide, too slow to escape, and now I have my blood on my hands.

Deciding to have breakfast in bed, I reach for my bread to find the ants found it in the night. The bread in India is often sweet and sugary. I used to ask when I purchased: 'Is there sugar in this bread?'

'Oh yes, sir,' the seller would say, 'very good bread, how many you like?'

'No, I want bread without sugar.'

'Oh no, sir, no sugar in this bread, very good bread, how many you want?'

Ants know the difference and these sugary slices are not an ideal canvas to paint the savoury taste of Marmite on. Evicting the invaders is as futile as picking out the sugar and now I have no foundation for my sandwich any more than I do for my faithlessness. So the idea of breakfast in my room goes out of the window, literally, and I hit the streets for bread, chai, bananas, nuts and jam.

Travelling by bicycle may not require petrol but I burned a lot of calories and used a lot of fuel in the form of food. Hauling speakers, whiskey, warm clothes and high-top trainers, my appetite grew as my bodyweight decreased. Even though I'd reached the fabled flatlands of northern Thailand, stocks needed replenishing, and so began a day of gluttony. I highlighted my food intake in my diary entry. Breakfast was delivered to my apartment at 8 a.m.: *two fried eggs, sausage, chicken, toast and two bananas*. The Aussies came by with a list of recommended guest houses for my onward journey. After 2 not exactly arduous kilometres I saw my first 7-Eleven since Bangkok and stocked up: *Toblerone, Nestle Crunch and Oreos*. Just in case I got famished before lunch. They were giving away stamp-sized sticky holograms in celebration of 2003 which was only eleven days away, and the stickers sparkled on my handlebars as I cycled in the sun. I like shiny things and wondered how many more I could collect before I left Thailand.

The road to Chiang Mai was flat, easy, dual carriageway. There was a lot more traffic and no one was interested in me anymore, no hoots, no waves, as invisible as a motorcyclist in a supermarket car park. I'd left my elite status in the sparsely inhabited hills, feeling a drop in my significance I opted for some comfort food: *crisps and Pepsi*. It was clearly high-octane fuel as I was steaming along averaging 16kph and that included my three snack stops. Food and distance were not the only things on my mind, there was a decision looming, bigger than the hills behind me – *what will be next?* A choice I was both apprehensive and excited about. Chiang Mai was where I'd make the onward plan. Where to and how to get there. There was no time to procrastinate; my visa was running out. It was a big and popular tourist town, where I expected to find information and means. What happened there would determine how I spent the next nine-week truck-driving sabbatical from my lettuce-logistic-free life.

When I'd first come here back in '91 this had predominately been a place that had launched the jungle track into the Golden Triangle: an area where the undefined borders of Laos, Thailand and Myanmar meet, and an ideal environment for growing opium poppies. It had been heavily populated with backpackers even then. A well-trodden route that had ended every night in a jungle village where a black-toothed and bent-double tribeswoman, dubbed the Opium Queen, had shared her wares in what had seemed at the time to be a near-spiritual ritual. However, I was in my mid-twenties then, and was much easier to impress, having had far fewer dealings to compare to this nightly procession of pushers. It was a wonderfully blissful state of ignorance to be in, and the opium high had only accentuated that pleasurable condition.

It seemed, entering this town after my twelve years absence, the jungle and Golden Triangle was no longer the biggest attraction. It had been replaced by a different jungle, the Pubic Triangle. The sex trade seemed prevalent, and it was easy to guess the clientele it catered to, judging by the Tescos and other English firms and franchises. I'd ridden into a place of white Western faces and big, fat bellies. I couldn't help but cast my judgement with my unwelcome newly lowered libido. Even more so when I was eating more than Pac-Man, yet was slimmer than Sonic – without the need for speed.

I found a place that could be my last stop in the country. Keen as mustard, I hit the streets and found a travel agent where I was informed there was no slow boat to China, no fast one either, no boat at all, but I could fly to the city of Kunming for $100 including a visa. I needed to digest this information and got a *club sandwich and crisps*. The pavement cafés were full of fat, old foreign fuckers. That's exactly what they were: beer belly, belligerent and here to shag pretty young Thai girls. I walked the streets doing my research, not anthropological, although I couldn't help but make a few presumptions. More demanding than demeaning thoughts was the need for a decision, where, how and when. I was adamant, there was no way I was staying here for a moment longer than I had to. However, there was much to consider, definitely a deliberation that needed lubrication.

Back on my balcony with a *Chang* beer, I looked at all my acquired information and made a plan. I was aware that this was a significant moment in my journey – my journey through life in fact. I'd been studying Mandarin Chinese for nearly two years in preparation of what I was about to embark on. I had said I was going to Bangkok-☑, to buy a bicycle-☑ and then cycle to China-☑ … well, *ish*. I *was* going to China. It looked like I was going to have to fly, but at least it would get me there, and soon. I hated the place I was in, but I loved this plan. With map, guidebooks and notes spread all over the floor, bike leaning against the wall of my room, I felt the euphoria of a dream that I was now as close to achieving as the charmless obese in this town were to getting laid. I decided I would do a circuit in China, back through Laos and then down to a Thai island for a full moon party in two moons' time. That would be my grand finale before going home. It felt great to have a plan, and equally good to eat an *Oreo* and then wash it down with a few *Bushmills* because I had to get to the end of the damn bottle.

I watched the sky change as dusk occurred over the rooftops. It was like a Thai *Coronation Street*. And then I went to the Rovers Return – well, an Irish pub actually, for *Singha beer, steak pie, mash, gravy and a loaf of bread* for later. At least, the intention was to eat it later, but I ate most of it on the way home. I saw the night market that I recalled from the previous millennium, resisted the banana pancake, and went home to put *Marmite on the rest of my loaf* and have *a Nestle Crunch* for dessert.

God, I never used to eat this much as a stoner. I hadn't even got the munchies, I just couldn't stop eating. The energy I was using didn't justify the calories I was consuming, and my sex drive had disappeared completely. I wondered, *am I going through changes, is this the menopause cycle?*

In the Indian internet café, I'm tempted to look at trains to Goa. I feel a big decision looming but I've got an upbeat mass mail in my head and I'm determined not to be rushed. Equally, I don't want to lose all I compose, it's happened before by power cut or some blip in the matrix, although most frequently it's due to user error. Whoever is on my mind as I write tends to sway the direction and content of the mail. Unfortunately, thoughts lead to my creative writing course and that takes the confidence out of what

I'm compiling. I also feel the need to apologise for the last mail, at least acknowledge my faux pas without inciting those who missed it to go back and check.

I go to the train station just to see what the seat situation is. I've not got a plan but just want to explore some options. There are no seats, so that's that option eliminated. I realise as I walk the streets that this town is real India, the contact I have, the commodities on sale, they don't cater for tourists here, I'm not unique but I'm not conned either, there only seems to be one price, Indian price, and I'm happy to pay it. So much so I get a Christmas card with a pop-up Taj Mahal inside, it's so tacky it's beyond nauseating. With the Christmas shopping done, I take a ride down to the beach, which, like my card, is equally tacky to the point of repelling. I stay for a Pepsi and head back home.

I'm getting a bit bored now, lie on the bed and wonder why banana tree leaves are so big, read, doze, shower, and with little to occupy my mind, annoyingly, my thoughts turn to Sofia and I decide to book a hotel in Delhi for her New Year's Eve arrival. The booking agent, like the train station, says, 'No.'

'What, no hotels, not a single room available in the whole of the capital with its twenty million population?' *So there is no way to get there and nowhere to stay if I do.* It's lucky for me I'm not a believer.

Same rooftop for dinner, fewer staff, less friendly, and they won't let me order Rogan Josh. 'No, sir, I think it is too hot for you.' *Well, what will you let me eat then*, I feel like saying. This day off has got me sighing again. When the going gets good, it seems I should keep on going, because today has been a bit rubbish really.

Decisions have been made

Imagine if the mosque slowly escalated the intensity of the incantation as the dawn slowly illuminated. Imagine if they complimented each other: a gentle, inspiring, uplifting, chanting prayer, acknowledging, announcing, and introducing the new day. Inviting the faithful, anyone, in fact, to come join the celebration of daylight into their life, feeling the joy of living, having thanks to give, help to offer, warmth to radiate and gratitude in mood. That would be the theme of my presentation if Islam were recruiting freelancers to promote their faith. Because to my ears what they've got wrong is this hysterical screeching-tyre-road-accident alarm, with no warning, over-amplified with atrocious sound reproduction. Imagine a 'Wish You Were Here' intro, a 'The Battle of Evermore' tempo, imagine a sound all around that vibrated the goodness to life, pulsing well-being to the surface, love to spare, love to share. How did you sleep, tell me your dreams, let my intonations kiss your ears. Come into this dawn and all will be well in this world, while we keep our calling simple and step with awareness from bed to bathroom, from dark to light, from dreams to reality. The mosque has the power to construct a welcome that attracts good and defeats desires at the expense of others. Imagine if that was the awakening, the world would live as one. But no, you screech this fucking high-pitched prayer into the air, with all the subtlety of a plane flying into a skyscraper and it's really not doing you any favours at all, mate. I refuse to have my opinion swayed by agenda-driven Western warmongers and one-sided media, but come on, if you want the West on your side give a little thought to your actions, or more specifically your sounds.

The wake-up call fades away but sleep will not return, I'm left with an agonising battle in my head. My momentum since I started cycling in India has me outrunning the despondency I'd experienced as I pushed on through much of Sri Lanka. The journey started in a downpour but even when the road was dry there was still reflection. However, I persevered and cycled forward into contentment, now off the road, deliberation has come back to meet me, caught me up, and it's not something I want to ride with. Stopping only for a day has lessened the stimulation of distractions and my thoughts have returned to their default doldrums. Since I've been in India my dawn direction was always clear, the sun shone on my right side every daybreak as I cycled north. It had been such a good week on the bike and just one day off has changed the mindset. Not helped by a chill in the morning air. This is not why I'm here.

I'm out of my room at 6.30 a.m. and can't seem to find the coastal road. Again I'm on the national highway, traffic and horns are even more intrusive after our brief separation. My bike is making a clicking that is felt rather than heard. It's more annoying than worrying, the anticipation of irritation with the revolution of the pedals. At a chai stop I oil the moving parts. I do love the morning chai, more and more, in fact, the best part of any journey, not just by bicycle.

My first ever Indian chai is not indelibly ingrained in my brain but, like having a favourite cassette, that became the backing track to my initial visit to India, the taste of that beverage accompanied just about every experience.

My first encounter with 'the real' India didn't occur until I had left sanitised Goa. I'd already witnessed the unrestricted wanderings of the holy cows but now other national beliefs and customs became apparent. The country ran on chai and the vehicles, it seemed, ran on faith. Blessings were bestowed upon commercial vehicles prior to crossing a mountain pass, but brakes blatantly ignored, the endless wonderments of India were just beginning. Everything after the coast was beyond me, the incomprehension of ancient ability in the form of architecture. Temples and intricate remnants, remains of past civilisations, the untold history, captivating creativity, structures that were unguarded and inviting the paradox of an overcrowded country with deserted ruins. I was entranced, and that was just my first day away from the beach. I continued my immersion for a further six months, and was to be forever affected. I met wanderers who had gone so far there was no hope of return, I kept a tenuous grip, and now I'm back, to see it from a different perspective, from the saddle.

It's got appeal, this bicycle, but going to the train station yesterday has stirred a dormant memory. I recall my first second-class sleeper. Bombarded with all India had to offer, both inside the carriage and beyond the window. The parade of peddlers chanting their wares with a repetitive and distinguishable tone that announced their approach in a pitch that cut through the commotion: 'Chai, chai, chai, chai, coffee, chai.' The awareness of their presence roused me from my sleep, I would purchase a cup, roll a cigarette and wander to the open door. Watch a sunrise over paddy fields, parched hills or attractive arable land. Between the stench of the toilet, the taste of the air outside, the warmth of the chai in my hand and the first inhalation of some Dutch tobacco, I don't believe there is a better way to enter a day. India instantly stimulates all senses, not always in a good way but frequently a memorable one. The second-class sleeper never stopped: food, fruit, padlocks to secure your luggage, toys to entertain, shoe shiners in your face, beggars at your feet, amputees dragging their torn bodies playing on heartstrings, vagabond kids pulling at your sleeves, a bejewelled and bereft widow mother enclosing a baby like a joey in her sari with an outstretched arm and pleading palm. Everyone had something to sell and if they didn't, they just asked for money, urchins and fake sadhus, they all passed down the carriage, the parade punctuated with the call of samosa, pakora, veg, non-veg, another chai, another fag, resisting the urge to over-eat or drink so as to limit the trips to the contamination of the toilet that rocked while you squatted, and soiled a steadying hand if you chose to stand.

The appeal and temptation of the train is back at the forefront of my thoughts – thankfully though, smoking is no longer a habit that controls me. It's been so long, in fact, that be it alcohol buzz, the last fork of food, or captive in traffic, the habitual reach for relief is gone. There are no associations with tobacco, after seven years the addiction had been beaten into submission, although it seems not totally conquered. The consideration of train travel and the memories it evokes have stirred a dormant addiction, to construct a cigarette from raw materials, and fire it up with the morning's first sip of chai. The two just complement each other, and addiction can justify anything. Do I want to catch a train to lessen the strain or due to a weakness I apparently can't quite refrain from?

So this morning's chai stop is just that, no fag, it's a drag, a real drag, and the other big struggle is the biggest of all cyclists' dilemmas: the hills ahead. Do I want the slog of dragging my arse uphill in exchange for the reward of variety in scenery or to continue the coastal sameness which to be honest is getting a bit dull now? I catch my mind not counting but wishing away the kilometres rather than being in awe of the surroundings. And much like a chai evokes smouldering memories of smoking, a ritual best performed on a train, again my thoughts turn to terminating the cycling at Mangalore because a second-class sleeper is something this trip has been deprived of. But I don't want to give up. If I'm even considering it, then I have to acknowledge there is reason for dissatisfaction in my current predicament. I should never have stopped; it was all going fine until I took a day off.

The road takes me over a vast river. To the east another bridge runs parallel, I see no traffic on it, which points to track lines, and again the train taunts, teases and beckons. The kilometres though are going by fast this morning, there are some benefits to taking a rest day, I've covered 74 kilometres in four and a half hours. I take a banana and Marmite sandwich break after a level crossing. The fort in the next town is signposted. So is Bombay: 1,200 kilometres away, *arrgh, two weeks of this?* Following the coast to get to the biggest city in the subcontinent. Yuk. This is the decision-making in progress, this is justification germinating, the excuses accumulating, the reasoning resonating, the explanations escalating, and they all seem a little one-sided. I feel an aborted mission is not far ahead. And this is possibly another downside of solo travel, with a partner I'd have someone to bounce the idea off, different objectives, opinions; or perhaps, like two recovering addicts, we would talk our way to the mainline and head for a station.

I find a room, and do my end-of-cycling-day ritual: laundry, shower, doze, eat, doze again and then force myself to go out and look at this fuckin' fort. It's a 5-kilometre ride back the way I came. The entry fee is 5 rupees for Indians, the price of a chai, and 100 for foreigners, the same as I just paid for a night's accommodation. Imagine paying £35 to enter a London museum? You don't have to, they are free, all of them, regardless where you are from. I look past the ticket booth, into the fort, it's just a wall, well, four, but when you've seen one … I decide to give it a miss.

In the internet café I look again at the website of Mr. Pumpy, the cyclist who has been everywhere, to see what he has to say about the road ahead. Mr. Pumpy says it's bumpy, hilly and busy, that's it, mind made up, although to be honest I think perhaps it already was.

Flying to China was an easy decision and I had four things to do before I could get out of Chiang Mai and Thailand: change money so I could book a flight, which meant applying for my Chinese visa, and for that I needed a passport photo. So actually five things, as first I had to make myself photogenic. Shave and hair wash. Beef noodle soup breakfast, far yummier than it sounds. A dish I had been tempted to try on the streets of Hanoi a few years before, the noodles instantly becoming my South-east Asian staple.

There was another typical Southeast Asian surprise in store for me, although it really shouldn't have been. Yesterday's price had gone up 20 per cent, you bastards. I went next door, which was cheaper, and let them apply for my visa as well, finding I actually had an old passport photo in my folder of all things important. And I could pay with plastic too. Within ten minutes I was holding a ticket to China in my hand. The flight left in a week, the day my Thai visa expired. There was nothing more to do that day.

As I walked back to my room there were the grey-haired Brits drinking beer in a pavement café at 9 a.m. It clearly took some dedication to grow those potbellies. *Wonder if they had to set an alarm, or perhaps when their hired lover's meter ran out, they ran out after her and stopped at the bar for a breather.* I loved being this disapproving, I mean I really got an evil, sanctimonious, pleasure from it. However, behind my sneering was a searing denial, I was yet to believe and could hardly conceive that I had a daughter. The bicycling by-product of suppressed mojo was only one factor of my celibacy, perhaps I just didn't want to get into any more trouble, and that willy of mine had made some atrocious decisions over the years. It may have controlled my head but it had never gained access to my wallet – well, not directly, money is used for romancing not hiring.

I walked on with an air of achievement in a plan put into action and the self-righteous willpower that had got me to this point. And while I was at it, I weighed myself: 152.2 lbs. My smugness increased as my weight was the lowest since I had started keeping track. The tracking had begun with a gym membership when I lived in the US. I'd do physical construction work all day, Mandarin classes in the evening, and in between working under the table and exercising my brain I'd be working out. All that exertion was not solely to improve fitness in preparation for the cycling, it was more to unleash my anguish. Hitting the gym had seemed like the healthiest way to deal with pent-up anger which formed like ice with the steady crush of my spirit and the erosion of my confidence from the mental manipulation that was the product of a fucked-up relationship. I knew I was living on thin ice with my illegal cash lifestyle, that's why I invested in getting my back tattooed. When the threat of deportation loomed, the ink under my skin was the only thing that couldn't be confiscated. Consequently, it was all I took with me when I ran for the airport. There was no time for duty free before that flight, it was just my duty to maintain my freedom. I cleared security, threw my phone in a bin and with stealth and purpose headed straight for the departure gate, a narrow escape and a dramatic death to my American dream.

But I was now over that, I'd moved on – albeit slowly. I had a bicycle and a purpose now, and I thought to myself, *I think I'll have a beer.* 'Oooh, very early,' said the guest house owner. *Listen, mate, I don't need to be reprimanded by you and what's more 'early' is subjective, I wonder what your basis of comparison is. Clearly not the beer-for-breakfast sex tourists, this action is absolutely justified by me due to this morning's level of achievement. I now consider that I've just completed eighteen months of planning, and a celebration of recognition of this is the order of the morning.* At 10 a.m. I was on my balcony with beer in hand and the sun shining on my legs. I read my book, looked at my map and worked out a northern Thailand eight-day circuit. From my vantage point I could see a fridge being delivered and so

I wandered down and asked if I could have the box to make a flight case for my bike. My landlord was ecstatic, his face had lit up when he looked inside his new fridge, and he told me they had to keep the packaging for seven days in case they had to claim on the guarantee but then I could have it. Perfect, absolutely perfect. I rebooked my room for the next week as collateral on the coveted box.

Another beer, a little doze, and I headed to a cycle shop I'd spotted. It was like a local liaison point for the foreigner in Chiang Mai who engaged in less popular yet more wholesome physical pursuits. I'd met other Western cyclists and was fed with information I hadn't known I'd needed. Everyone was heading to Laos and every time I heard that, I was less inclined to join the throngs. It just sounded ruined now. I was told my chain was knackered and I needed to replace the rear sprocket too. It wasn't the news I wanted to hear. I said I would do my circuit and assess the situation upon my return. Back at my guest house, I did my daily duty and tried to get to the bottom of the bloody whiskey bottle – like China, it was getting closer but I still wasn't there.

Christmas music drifted out of the streetside restaurants. I tried to find the night bazaar. It took a while and was the usual stuff. 'Hello, sir, you buy? Special price for you.' The place was vast, I couldn't find my way out, and when I did, I was at the arse end: big hotels for big Americans, KFC, Burger King, McDonald's, Pizza Hut, *got to have ya good ol' American food, keep ya appearance up*. It was fucking awful, I was walking quicker and quicker, *gotta get out of here*, I lost my bearings, found the moat that I'd ridden around that afternoon and still went the wrong way. I hadn't travelled with such purpose the whole trip, I just had to get away from this hideousness. I didn't want to talk to anyone about anything – horrendous, absolutely horrendous place it'd become. No amount of opium and ignorance could have taken the cynicism out of my assessment. I supposed that you had to be in populated places to begin and end a journey, from Bangkok to Chiang Mai, and soon on to a tiny Chinese town of just 6 million people.

After my internet research – or was it my confirmation? – I check my email. The lettuce people have a letter for me, a speeding ticket has arrived at their office. Those bloody roadworks on the A12, no fucker to be seen at 2 a.m., no traffic, no workers, but still low speed limits apply and the cameras flash and collect revenue to pay for the reconstruction, and I've been relieved of two weeks' travel budget.

My ground floor room has a porch that faces the eastern plains and I watch a full moon rise with some Europeans. They go for dinner seemingly without wanting my company, so I eat alone and am stared at with every bite I take. I'm glad to be back on my porch, briefly. An Italian girl passes, I feel she is missing some vital social civilities and within two minutes of conversation asks to borrow my bike. No bloody way. She has no collateral to offer, other than the guilt I'm left with by my refusal, guilt I doubt she'd suffer from should she bring the bike back damaged.

Tuesday 9th December
Bekal – Mangalore
Kilometres cycled: 66

Accepting I went the wrong way

I don't need an alarm any more. The body clock has adjusted. The body, however, has a problem.

I'm on the road for first light but can't get past the pain threshold. I'm always a little stiff in the morning – *ahem* – but it usually eases as I warm up with the day. Not this morning though, my legs ache and I've got a sore throat and runny nose. Perhaps just reinforcing my train decision. I manage to strain for 22 kilometres before a chai stop. I have some fruit, bread and butter biscuits too, oil the chain, have a wee and carry on, munching the biscuits addictively, but I can't get in the flow this morning. My bum hurts on the saddle and my legs won't stop complaining. Today is all main road so no risk of wrong turns, lots of river crossings but a bridge over every one of them, not like before, I'm still on Route 66 but no longer getting kicks out of it. One of the rivers is a boundary and I cross it into the state of Karnataka.

But the sights remain the same, I'm not seeing any more, no more awe, not privileged to be a part of it, it's become part and parcel, no fun in the fundamental, now it's just a commute.

Into Mangalore looking for a recommended hotel, I just can't find it, I stop and ask, go round in circles, find other landmarks but not what I'm looking for. When it does appear, I know I've been past it already, in fact I stopped opposite. However, the place is worth the effort and I put my bike in the lift and bundle into my room. Have a shower and devour the rest of the fruit bread. Can't stop eating – well, I can if I start drinking and have a juice on the street en route to the train station, which I can't locate either. Now on foot the endurance continues and it's still not easy movement. I even stop for monkey nuts to munch on as I continue on my quest.

There is a lot of queueing in the ticket-buying process, some things haven't changed at all. They only have seats left in the air-con carriage, which is not nearly as exciting, because it's more exclusive, only the ticketed are allowed in. It's a lot more expensive too, $24. *Ouch!* But my mind is made up and I'm prepared to pay the price which actually turns out to be $4. *Brilliant!* But I'm on the waiting list. *Bollocks!* Kerala, despite its network of backwaters, is actually a dry state, if you find beer at a restaurant it's often served in a teapot, undercover and out of sight. Everyone knows it goes on but they pay their bribe, and make token gestures to disguise the illicit sales. Here, beer is in your face, very noticeable after such abstinence, so it would seem rude to ignore it. I buy a cold one and take it to my room, and then go out and buy another and some crisps and nuts too.

Inevitably, I doze off and totally lose two hours. It's dark and I'm disorientated, like I was drugged, that's beer for you, lost my tolerance, lost track.

I couldn't wait to leave Chiang Mai, or at least I thought I couldn't, but I kept prolonging the gratification, noodle soup, 7-Eleven for more supplies and a French stick to eat en route. I tried to find a pharmacy too, I wanted something for my knee, I didn't know what, a replacement maybe. It was funny how when my bike was fully loaded everyone wanted to talk, it had intrigue and credibility again now it was loaded, which meant I did too. It seemed everyone who had cycled anywhere felt the need to tell me. I needed to remember this, so as not to burden the next cyclist I saw with my mundane monologue, especially if that cyclist was clearly keen to get away before the heat of the day.

I'd been wondering what the weight of my bike was, even more so when it was booked on a flight. An Aussie guy assisted me on some street scales. Balancing next to the bike on the pressure pad platform, the gross weight was 120 kilograms. So the same as most of the Brits here. However, this self-righteous Brit weighed 69 kilograms, so my bike was 51 kilograms including two litres of water and a nearly empty glass bottle of Bushmills. More stats to list in the diary along with distance and speed. I headed north, redistributing the weight by putting biscuits and chocolate from bar bag to tummy. I just couldn't stop eating. It was obsessive, compulsive. I supposed I must have needed it; I assumed the fat Brits probably said the same with a beer at 9 a.m. It's a thin line and wide waistline between need and want. Yesterday I wanted a beer as a kind of rebellion celebration, a sort of 'I can drink this early too but it's a choice', and to prove it, what I want more this morning is to be leaving and food is the fuel my body demands today to drive me forward. It was a busy road but the traffic was considerate and passed me with room to spare. I glided into an immaculate western-styled, modern Shell petrol station with a polished forecourt, smooth and clean, digital pumps, uniformed attendants, and then into the shop where chickens wandered around the tubes of Pringles and crates of Pepsi. There must be some kind of regulations if you want the franchise of a fuel station but it appears inspection doesn't go beyond the forecourt. Perhaps in the cashier station they were accepting applicants for a further franchise, possibly KFC.

I sat on the grass eating crisps and drinking pop. It was the proverbial lovely day, but then every day was. However, with my onward route confirmed, my head was clearer and my outlook brighter, which made the sky bluer, the grass greener, and the temperature perfect for sitting in the sun. As I continued north the traffic subsided and palms and banana trees became more frequent. Still touristy, this was where the jungle trackers, bungee jumpers, elephant riders and white-water rafters went. Some may call them adrenalin junkies, but they hadn't cycled round Bangkok.

As the route narrowed and traffic lessened, up ahead was a snake in the road – not a chicane, but a real snake. I was not sure if it was dead or just feeling the warmth of the tarmac. Would it strike, could it lurch for me? I tried to find something to throw at it, and as I reached into the verge a lizard scuttled off. *Shit, that made me jump.* I could throw a party like a rock star, but seemingly I could throw a rock with the accuracy of an imbecile. It was pathetic; a shit shot that perturbed no one but me. I looked at myself like I'd left my body – there I was on the road, afraid to pass a snake that might not even have been alive. I decided just to go for it, fast and noisy, but would that make it jump, would it retreat or retaliate? However, slow and quiet might seem like a threat, creeping up for the kill?

Shit, what to do? Sing a song, announce my arrival? *I'm clumsily coming your way, toot toot, stand back, please.* Perhaps a decoy, scrape the road with my dog beater outstretched, *bite that, bitch.* Spray some deodorant onto the sole of my sandal, underarm underfoot confusion? All these tactics were based on the assumption that it bit, but what if it was a constrictor? I had my Swiss army knife poised with its decompressor component ready to loosen its death grip. I'd pour the last of my whiskey into its slanty eyes, then torch it with a lighter. I had an armour of defensive tactics and no conviction in any of them. I couldn't camp there, waiting for it to move on. *Fuck it, just face it.* I rode past; it was dead.

My knee had been clicking and grinding for a few days, and suddenly there were shooting pains up my leg. *Ouch*, I stopped and put on what was left of my embrocation and some Tubigrip while being hassled by a tribal woman, begging, selling, I didn't know. 'There's nothing left for you.' Thankfully, the road declined into a valley. I just wanted to stop, and tried several attractive-looking guest houses but no one seemed to be home. It was most strange, I couldn't find a soul. I took a side street and saw some appealing properties set back off the road, with well-kept gardens and inviting driveways. One place had a sign for accommodation but a freshly killed dog lay on the road outside, blood flowing from the gash of impact, which I assumed was from contact with a car. Unlike the snake, my dilemma was not how to pass but to turn around. This animal was not one of the numerous strays but a healthy-looking, loved pet – well, healthy until about ten minutes earlier, and it was right outside the guest house entrance. I didn't want to stay in a place of grief and mourning and certainly didn't want to be implicated in the death or even be the one to point it out. Too awkward, bad vibe, a place of no people and a dead dog, had there been an invasion?

I turned around back to the main road feeling doubtful, until I saw signs for a much-hyped cave – where there is hype there is accommodation. With my extended journey, I had dropped my criteria from 'Can I see the room?' to 'Have you got a room?'. By this point it didn't matter as long as it had a bed. Perhaps something was lost in translation as a long bed is what I got, it went on and on. In a corridor of a room twenty feet in length was a wall-to-wall bed, clearly designed with an orgy in mind. There was a TV and every wall was windowless, this was a very private bedroom.

My leg was feeling weak, and the need for company was getting stronger, increasing in intensity. I formulated a plan. I had now dragged that bloody whiskey bottle within reach of the Chinese border. I took it from the pannier certain I would not be taking it any further. I figured with a little swig I'd have some toxic-breath confidence to go off to the cave area, find a restaurant and socialise a little. I took a little swig and decided it would be best to wait until later, arriving at the prime dining time. I put on the TV and lay alone, spread out like a starfish with a bottle by my side, a remote in my hand and a throbbing in my leg. I almost finished the bottle, I almost numbed the pain, I almost went out …

I woke next morning and saw the bottle by my side. I took the final swig, and rode away wondering where the hell I'd been all night.

In preparation for my train journey to Goa I find myself in an air-con restaurant, full of attentive waiters. I can't even pour the water into my glass, it's taken from me and they top it up. Their attentiveness clearly doesn't stretch to perceptiveness, they have not considered I'm a tiny tipper. It occurs to me I've eaten every meal this trip alone, or at least not with company at my table. Sometimes that's just fine, but then this evening, when the realisation hits me, I know that some changes have to be made. I don't mind leaving the *Lonely Planet* bible fraternity behind but I've been confined to solitary dining for too long. I'm glad I'm going to Goa, seeing some familiar faces and finding some purpose in the escapism. I had it for a while, purpose, I don't need company, but something has been repeatedly lacking this trip. My light load, my easy route, my destination-driven desires, the underlying admission that I'm killing time, the inevitable comparisons of returning to a country I have only good memories of.

In '96 I arrived alone and left by myself the next year, but in between I was never left alone, company was an unavoidable part of a national pack of wanderers, multiple travel companions as diverse as the country.

You can only travel solo for so long in India, but you can cycle significantly longer with very little contact. I have found the interactions are the journey, be it native or newcomer, and I've alienated myself, elevated my status from backpacker, and in these rarefied heights contact has been a rarity. I've got something wrong, the exclusive reclusive, the A-list celebrity alone in his mansion, the castaway, cast out, ostracised, rejected, took the road less travelled and left belonging behind. Give me a mountain range to myself and I'm content, the bigger the vista the less inclined I am to share it, it is all consuming, all fulfilling, I'm happy to consider the vastness, the greatness, the majesty. Experience the solitude, feel my insignificance, be it gazing at the Taj Mahal or at the edge of the Himalayas. Those places had romance of their own, it was an honour to be part of, I felt a belonging, a presence, a sensuality. And it's recalling that which leads me to believe that this choice of coastal route isn't the right choice, it's not providing enough variety in my days, stimulation in my soul, distraction in my thoughts.

My feet hurt from all the walking, everything just seems worn out today and filling my body with food hasn't helped much either. Well, I've broken the 1,000-kilometre threshold since I left the UK. In some aspects that's an achievement worthy of some standing; in others, it's nothing and I'm stuck on the negative side.

I'm not sure I'll do a long cycle trip again and I'm not sure where I'll go next – Bolivia, Peru, Colombia? And I'm having a crisis about work too: I do not want to get back behind the wheel of a truck, I think I've just had enough of the road in whatever form it takes. In fact, I don't want to live in Colchester any more. Dissatisfaction seems to be the default feeling in every thought I have. I need company.

I'd be mad to go on

A newspaper has been pushed under my door, its intrusion has the intrigue of a tip-off. Is there something contained within the pages, a coded message, an invite, a warning? Maybe, if I were taking antimalarials. Turns out it's just a newspaper, still a new experience nonetheless.

Today will be a waiting day as I'm on the waiting list. I decide to be my own waiter and hit the streets in search of food, it's not a difficult quest and soon I'm back in my room making and eating copious amounts of Marmite sandwiches, followed by bananas. Then I taste-test a pack of biscuits and accidentally eat them all, they were meant to be for the train ride. I read the paper. Things are happening,

The US dollar continues to decline in value, which is annoying as the majority of my travel money is in that currency.

The parliament of New Zealand votes to ban smoking in all offices, clubs, pubs, restaurants, airports and schools. That will never happen here – anyway, I'm pretty sure there was a smoking ban in my school and that never stopped us.

Australia has hit 20 million, I assume that's population not runs in cricket, still a fraction of India's population and possibly its cricket score too.

And President Putin's party has won the Russian election. He seems quite responsible, better than that alcoholic Yeltsin, how can you possibly make good decisions when you're a drunk?

Anyway, I don't need this awareness, I've got this far without it and likewise I'm sure the planet will continue unhampered on its line of trajectory with or without my knowledge of what's occurring. I head out again and find the post office … effortlessly. There is no queue – typical, when I have time to kill. Back in the room I have little else to do but leave and attempt a photo of me and the bike in the lift with the help of the mirror on the back wall.

The train station, it turns out, is less than one kilometre away when you know the way and, again, I'm saving time I would rather be spending. It's three and a half hours before the train arrives and I don't even know if there is room on it for me. I queue and find I'm still on the waiting list. So I stand against a wall for an hour with shades on and earbuds in listening to Iron Maiden, looking like a late-thirties dirtbag, baby, and singing the lyrics to myself I've been mishearing and misquoting for nearly twenty years, *Lost Somewhere in Time,* which actually makes my version of the song an ideal anthem for this trip. I pretend to be invisible and it works really well. So much so I invite myself into the vast waiting room which is filled with railway employees. There is an award ceremony for station cleanliness being staged. My concealment allows me access, the unseen voyeur has absolutely nothing else to do. I wonder if the winner feels any sense of achievement and honour as he walks to the makeshift podium to receive his award, it all feels a bit superficial. Will today's events be squeezed into tomorrow's newspaper to be pushed under the same door into someone else's awareness? Well, I saw it live, and when it was over and the winners, losers and officialdom leave, the only evidence it ever happened is a carpet of paper cups left on the ground.

At 12.30 I queue again and I'm told I'm on the train. I go get a pineapple juice to celebrate, I'm actually whistling I'm so happy. I voluntarily show the squeezers around my bike, gears, trip computer, etc. They top up my juice for free and say I'm welcome anytime, and from that point on time flies. Putting my empty cup in the bin I half expected to be approached and offered an award for my contribution to the cleanliness. But I'm too busy to accept, and book my bike onto the luggage car, grab a thali and the train rolls in right on time.

A/C isolates like wealth, there is no parade in this carriage, a little more luxurious perhaps but the price I paid comes with seclusion. I'd gladly downgrade to second-class sleeper if only they had room for me, not to save money but to gain humanity. However, I get some new experiences with my heightened status. My seat is by a big Indian family who besiege me, I want to look out of the window, listen to some Van Morrison but the glass is tinted and anyway they are having none of it. They feed me sweets and cakes, engage me in everything they can think of, conversation, a card game, fashion consultation from a magazine. I'm introduced to every branch of their family tree and I'm shown how every limb is connected. It's done with pride, it's done with inclusion, it's done unquestioningly, it's done with duty and it's done naturally. I came to a conclusion when I was here last that, for Indians, especially a family, a train journey is significant. Booked months in advance, they are almost always on their way to an event, a celebration, and, strangely, rarely ever returning from one.

The man of the family has a bottom lip that hangs down like he's been disappointed and downtrodden his whole life, as if everybody gets at him. But that's just his look, he can't help that and absolutely nothing gets to him. He's as upbeat as techno and as buoyant as Beyoncé, his positivity would turn a glint into a diamond and he makes me smile. Until, that is, an arrogant woman comes along, giving me some lip of her own and claiming my seat. *Whatever, bet you won't become an honorary branch of their family tree.* She'd look lovely in something long and flowing, like the Ganges. I go stand by the door, taking the good vibes I've been gifted with. I look out over hills, I'm so damn glad I'm not cycling them. Now I play Van, look at palms as they lose their colour but gain appeal, showing their silhouette seduction, through low light not tinted windows, and I love what I'm seeing. The warm wind blows my hair, the sun sets into a clear western sky as the train passes a giant statue of Shiva. Not destructive like the woman who took my seat but recreated like this view I have now, then a near full moon rises. I feel fabulous, I think my change from bicycle to belonging has already begun.

That whiskey-swigging morning could have been seen as my rock bottom, but it was far more positive, like casting off ballast. I could have painted a picture of hopelessness but it was more about weightlessness. I could have just left the unemptied bottle but finishing it that morning was a statement,

I wasn't exactly sure what it was saying, but that unnecessary weight that had held me back was now behind me. Although, actually, with haircare products relocated to the cardboard tube I really didn't feel any difference at all. The whiskey and therefore the weight had slowly been decreasing and all that'd been discarded was an empty bottle. The increased space was barely noticeable, but then again my judgement may have been impaired this morning.

Cocks crowed and there was no sunrise to be seen through the mist, which called for combats and a fleece. Heat and humidity, like the Bushmills, were now part of my past. My left knee was bandaged and my right was doing most of the work. It wasn't a problem – in fact, I was impressed at the strength I had built up. It was an uphill day and not causing me much difficulty. I recalled childhood days when the bicycle had been my only means of transport. I never arrived tired, never felt the strain of self-propelled transport, never sweated, and was never late, it was the only pace I knew. Even in my teens, at 4 a.m. I would wake and ride three miles to begin my weekend milk round, listening to the second half of the *Friday Rock Show* on cassette (I would listen to the first half and then press record at 11.15 p.m. to get less than five hours sleep). I'd hump milk crates and run up 200 driveways for the next six hours, then cycle home with energy to spare and the £2 I'd just earned. I bloody loved it. I even used to cycle the 11 miles to school sometimes, just for the fun of it. I never arrived uncomfortable, tired or ravenous. In Thailand, I couldn't say that I had reached that level of youthful stamina yet, but I did find I was daydreaming for longer, not fully focused on the effort required to move me forward, even when it was uphill.

I stopped after 40 kilometres, despite the lack of view. It turned out I was at the summit. So I rolled down to warmer, flatter lands, hoping for a place to find company as Christmas was only two days away. But the next town didn't stop me, and a guest house the gay Aussies had suggested was only another 24 kilometres away. When I got there, I'd just completed my first triple-figure day: 111 kilometres. However, there was still no company to tell this to, and by then no whiskey to celebrate with either.

I was once again by a river that formed the Burmese border. I had thought it to be Chinese but that lay another 250 kilometres to the north –

tempting but inaccessible, or at least unattemptable. My Christmas holiday would begin here and the following day I would attempt to take a boat to Chiang Rai for a proper break and to rest my knee for the China leg of the journey. I wasn't going to book a boat; I figured I'd hang by the pier and hope to find some foreigners to charter one with, because I really needed some company now.

Sharing my time with someone was not really something I could control. However, it was becoming more obvious that the internet café was a good substitute, not to find new friends but to communicate via email with old ones. In this case, I got a mass mail from a couple of acquaintances who had taken a sabbatical from their medical career and were travelling New Zealand together. I got the gist he was coming back and she was going on to Australia, so I emailed the doctor dude and suggested that, should we co-ordinate our return to the UK, he might like to come and live with me (and have my babies). I was already calculating the benefits of the additional income that a lodger would bring. *Extra money*, I thought, *will be welcome after China when spring rolls round once more.*

At 8.30 p.m. the train pulls into a Goan station and I take my feeling of well-being with me as I disembark, but impermanence is omnipresent, and the feeling fades as I walk the dark platform to unload my bike and then load my luggage onto it. I'm encouraged to follow a man on a moped to a squalid little fleapit of a room which, tonight, just like my first night on the road, will do just fine. I go find food. The town feels rough and I fit right in, I've got knots in my hair from hanging out the door of the train, a room with a one-inch-thick mattress and I've just cycled some of India independently, and I'm happy, happy with my decision. Cheated, cut short, copped out – yeah, you might say all those things. What, you hadn't heard enough hardships yet? Wanted to torture me vicariously? See how low I could go? Well, I didn't, I bailed, because I'm doing this for me, not for endurance, not for charity, not for notoriety or record holding, not to

break new ground and inform future followers but to give myself a new experience. Newspaper under the door; adopted by a family in an air-con carriage; falling into a failed town; following a local to less-than-illustrious accommodation; leaving it again to re-enter some tough streets without a chaperone; feeling like I'm found somewhere in time.

Join the company

The journey never really stops, and there is an important one on my mind, I simply won't accept there are no seats available on any train to Delhi. So it's without breakfast or even chai that I'm back at the station. Today I'm told the only available seat is on Christmas day. However, if I head on to Vasco there might be more availability. As I ride my first Goan road, it turns out that Vasco is on a peninsula 16 kilometres out of my way and signs for Panaji show that, although twice the distance, it is in the direction I want to be heading, along with Bombay 600 kilometres away. All billboards are in English now and most of them advertise alcohol. I annoy myself as I'm reading every one. They don't pass quickly on a bike and grab my attention, just like they are designed to. My attention, however, is easily distracted and I read them again before I pass to the next one. I can't help myself reading, because I can, I've been gifted back literacy, albeit limited, if it's not the same bus overtaking me it's the same advert striking me.

I'm running strong after a train day, and perhaps also because I know I've got company at the end of the road, or cliff, if I'm to believe the directions I've been given. Apparently, there are no roads where I'm going, which might make it a bit tricky getting there. Then all thoughts of alcohol adverts, overbearing buses and inaccessible beach retreats are put on hold. Coming the other way is a white-faced cyclist, safety helmet, yellow branded jersey and Lycra cycling shorts. He blends in like McDonald's in a mandir, as inappropriate as a billboard for bikinis, he crosses two lanes for traffic to meet me head on. Glistening teeth, clean-shaven and muscular, he's got perfect poise and matching panniers, slick, streamlined, and with skinny tyres. I'm like a tractor compared to him.

'How ya doin', buddy?'

Oh, you're American then, I instantly surmise, but before I get a chance to answer his question and tell him how I am actually doing he continues.

'I've just ridden down from Bombay.'

What, this morning? It's almost feasible. I've already got a sweat on and have only come from the train station. I don't tell him that, of course. 'I've come up from Kerala,' I say, and before I add, *Well, after I did Sri Lanka, obviously,* he fires another question at me.

'Where ya from, buddy?'

'England, and you?' I say, sounding more English than I have since I left his country.

'The States,' he enthuses. Why do they always say that? It's so bleeding obvious, be specific, I was, I didn't say the United Kingdom of Great Britain and Northern Ireland. From all the states? You're from fifty different places, are you?

'Anything I should know about the road ahead?' I ask, thinking to myself, *So I can lie about riding that too?*

He talks like he looks: fast, clean, efficient, like he's been doing it for a while. I'm out of practice, and swear for punctuation, a breather for my thoughts to catch up with my mouth. He's Lance, I'm puncture, he's Armstrong, I'm bum-sore, he's vitality, I'm fucked. The conversation doesn't go far, certainly not as far as he has seemingly already travelled today. And then with a 'Good luck, buddy', the yellow streak vanishes into the traffic, as undetectable as a performance-enhancing drug. Well, that was a brief encounter with a strange kind. I go to the station and have another.

A rather forceful man takes my seat application form and takes over. Again, there is only one seat available and it's on the 17th. 'Next week? No, forget it.' But he'll do anything but, and makes a call, then insists I stash my bike with a luggage depository, get on the back of his moped and we're off before I can say, 'Is it safe?' It seems like a long ride but then I'm not used to things passing by so fast. I feel I've got myself into a weak negotiating position, what with not exactly knowing where we are and unable to get back to my bike. We stop at the side of the road, there is nothing here, why have we stopped? He gets on his knees and prays. *Oh, right, mind if I just stand around awkwardly for a bit? I'll adopt the stance of the confused and vulnerable foreigner who has suddenly found himself in an uncomfortable situation, how do I look? Convincing?*

Prayer offered, we reconvene our journey to see if it's been answered. We arrive at a booking office, and whatta ya know? Either the phone call or the spiritual plea worked, I get a second-class sleeper for the 29th December, the exact date I wanted, and he demands 150 rupees, the exact fee he wanted. It's actually worth it, for the experience – *now take me to the station, my man, I've got a road to ride.* But no, first he must buy me an ice cream, and now it would seem the transaction is complete, so can we go back to my bike now? Other than some road dust the ice cream is the first solid to pass my lips this morning and it's already gone midday what with the tour de force of the morning.

Back on the bike I manage to find a few more hills. However, all the town signs are familiar names to me, they all represent something from being here back in '96. The paedophile beach, the hippy hang-out, the full moon party, the night market and the car ferry –*hmm, do I want to chance the ferry?* It's a long way to go if it's not there. No, I think I'll go the long way round.

My Thai Christmas break was also a ferry ride away but after a day of record-breaking mileage I was rewarded with a puncture and a sheared bolt on my pannier rack. That would have been the weight reduction caused by the discarded whiskey bottle – without it, there was room to vibrate.

So I replaced the tube and headed to town looking for prospective passengers to charter a boat with. I even went to a backpackers' hostel for breakfast to see what was cooking. I was offered a passenger ticket upriver and half as much again for my bike by a boat owner trawling for tourists. It wasn't my preferred way to go but I didn't want to be alone for Christmas either so I accepted. Then I found someone who could repair my pannier rack, or at least supply a bolt and fit it without finesse. I went back to my room and repaired it myself properly, packed up and headed for the pier where I left my bike and watched the foreigners congregate.

Despite the imminent chance of company, I was keen to see what the future may hold, but rather than find a fortune teller I went to an internet café and checked my emails: the doctor had said yes – well, to lodging if not having my babies. Reading this, I physically felt the financial relief, my permanent budget awareness was a knot in my shoulders and I felt it had just loosened. I didn't even consider how we would get on. He'd always been around but we had never had much to say to each other. We had motorcycles in common, and when we spoke he'd usually say something to me along the lines of:

'So is ya Harley on the road this year?'

My typical response to this was: 'No.'

And then we'd shuffle awkwardly to a more preferred part of the party. Anyway, having a doctor living in the house would basically be a permit to being totally irresponsible – if I broke myself he'd be able to fix me.

I met a guy from Italy and two Scandinavian girls, one of whose birthday it was. The bike broke the ice and was then loaded so sloppily it could easily have broken free of the skinny boat. I decided to take control and stack backpacks in a way that wedged it in. The backpackers and I were secured with more precision. Twelve bodies seemed to be the boat's passenger capacity if we were neatly laid head to toe from bow to stern as if Evel Knievel were about to jump over us. I was at the front with two Thais, so unlike the other passengers I had more than feet to talk to, however the conversation was still near impossible over the noise of the engine. I rested my head watching clouds and scenery pass by, effortlessly transiting through hilly terrain, it was such a luxury. We docked for a rip-off stop: five bhat to piss and a pay-to-pat elephant or to take photos with a snake hung round your neck. That one was definitely alive – I had become quite the expert by now. It was all quite horrendous but it was exactly what I had expected, and I got away with a wee for three bhat so felt like I had beat the system.

The inevitable touts and taxis awaited the boat's arrival, and I let them prey on the vulnerable and cycled off regardless, able to pick and choose from the guest houses I passed. I may not have spoken to many but

I was part of the trip and it was a small town, so I soon bumped into the Italian and we called for the Swedish sisters to see if they had considered celebrating that night. The boat trip had had the desired effect, I'd drifted into company. This little crowd would do just fine for the current time, and when Yuletide festivities ebbed I'd drift away. The night was unremarkable but easy company: pizza, beer, blew my budget, night bazaar for whiskey and coke. Some Christian evangelists told us 'Jesus is born!', some Thai Rastas invited us to their table and then to a party, but I slipped away, glad, like the Bushmills, to have had company and equally eager to be rid of it. It was almost like paying for companionship: I got what I needed and left what I didn't, just what the doctor ordered. I decided to stick around and have the leftovers for Christmas.

Passing up the ferry crossing means heading east to go west. Indirection as a trucker driver is a waste, but when you are cycling it's just wearisome. I could go all the way to the main road, over a bridge and then head back to the coast, but I'm told of a shortcut. *Only short if you know the way*, I think, but take it anyway. Through burned, parched, barren land, it goes on and on. I've underestimated the size of Goa. The smallest state in the country but I am going to the northernmost reaches and this so-called shortcut seems never-ending, more so with no distinguishing features to plot progress by. Monotonous to the very end, one might say, but I won't. There is variety in thought if not scenery. Eventually, there is life and I stop for a lassi and am given directions inland again and uphill. That can't be right. But I see a sign. Arambol is another 10 kilometres. I'm sure there must have been a shorter route but I'm powered by the anticipation. It may only be a beach, a place of western freaks, but it's a place I knew I'd be coming to before I left the UK, and now I'm less than an hour away. So I cheated, caught a train, but I'm still entering under my own steam and no one can take that away. And finally I see the beach – well, a beach, the wrong beach, and I'm directed back inland.

Oh come on, there is delayed gratification but let's not drag it into the dusk. And then there is clarification beyond doubt, the shacks of hippy shit appear, catering to roamers with aroma, everything a crusty needs is sold along this dusty track: baggy trousers, tie-dye shirts, fragrant air, the taste of dirt. Souvenir Hindu gods are displayed next to carved chillums and decorative stash tins. Hanging above are embroidered bags to carry the keepsakes home and henna tattoos for those who don't want excess baggage. If Goa is India-lite, then Arambol is Goa-lite. No two-week tourists here, this is a lifestyle. Hammock and hang out, chillum and chill out, yoga and yoghurt, the long-term lethargic. It would appear I'm expected. My long hair may give me tribal alliance but my bicycle stands me out, strange how my usual distinguishing feature here is part of the uniform. Still, at least my mane is brushed, last night's knots released, not locked into dreaded braids. Shopkeepers point, not at me, at where to go and sure enough a clifftop path takes me through a high-density parade of shade and hard selling. And there they are, my prearranged midway-meet-up companions, the invite honoured, back in the company of the two guys I last saw in China just under a year ago, video camera still in hand; my Indian arrival, like my Chinese departure, is recorded. It's as if I've been on the road the whole time and in a way I have, but mostly in a truck delivering lettuce to pay for this break as no tenant was ever found to fund this foray. They bravely hug my sweaty torso. 'You made it!' *Made it*, I think to myself, well, in a way, yes, made it up, made it too easy and lost the point, still a journey of endurance but not in the way the China trip was. Well, regardless of what I or anyone else made of it, the struggle is over. Made it? Yeah, made a hash of it.

Hash, you want hash? I have hash, good hash, good price.

Predictably, I'm ravenous and at 3 p.m. I have breakfast and then go to a freshwater thermal lake to cleanse and baptise my body. Submersed, I dunk my head, leaving nothing on the surface but warm, wet circles. From my friends' balcony we watch the sun set into the Indian Ocean, happy hour they call it, and drinks are poured, then to a pizza restaurant and beer flows. I feel my waistband tighten, my jaw loosen, my loneliness lost out to sea, and push my bare feet into the sand, as my sporadic tan is toned by a moonlight shadow.

They have made arrangements, there will be a room coming free tomorrow, sounds expensive but I'm told how fortunate I am, from now until Christmas this place will fill up and prices will go up, I should feel very lucky. OK, I think I can feel lucky, it's actually quite easy to here. For tonight though, I will be sleeping on the happy-hour balcony, a converted bed, star canopy, sea breeze, crashing waves beneath me and no traffic to be heard. My bike on one side and infinite possibilities on the other – once, that is, we've had a nightcap. So many words, several weeks' worth tumble out of my messy mouth but they get the gist – mainly, that is, due to my mass mails. They enthuse about how entertaining they find my tales, and I tell of my confidence-shattering creative writing course and how now I'll never write a book. They say you have to know the rules to break them. What inspirational words. I should write them down before I forget.

It's not a beach, man, it's a way of life

I open my eyes to pastel skies, held up by scruffy palms, that appear to tremble under the weight, or in the breeze, it's hard to tell. The sea throws up the froth, breakers broken on mauve volcanic-looking rocks. The first land since the waves were formed and flowed out of the Red Sea, through the Gulf of Aden to gain momentum across the Arabian Sea and crash in a grand finale right here in front of me. These sights and sounds have so much more appeal than the red LED numbers of a bedside clock burning into my retinas like lasers, or an electronic alarm of alert ringing in my ears. I keep my eyes open, not wanting to snooze and lose this morning. I could live here, on this terrace; I think the Kiwi in the room can read my thoughts and is keen to show this squatter to his own squat-toilet accommodation.

This whitewashed concrete two-storey accommodation is three rooms long, there's less desirable lodgings beneath. On the north end is a palm-thatch-covered restaurant where I get muesli with curd, fruit and honey, chai and toast as the rising sun shines on the surf. Where there is beauty there is attraction and this place has attracted some eyesores. The walk to the sweet-water lake takes me past the passed-out naked and dreadlocked, intertwined with heat-seeking stray dogs, both equally ugly. Is it like this every day? For them yes, so can I use this as a landmark, a point of reference? Head for the crusty, just follow your nose then fork right and ahead is the thermal cleansing lake.

My room is ready. It's the wrong side of the path, I can see the sea but can't hear it, I'm not sure it will drown out the unruly Israelis above. For the first time this trip I unpack, then I'm taken to order a hammock from a recommended Austrian artisan who works the season here. I stretch out on his samples; they seem supportive and well hung. Then back to the beach for a swim. 'You should bring Sofia here.' It's suggested, we'll see.

I rejoin my terrace chums for happy hour and then to a reserved table positioned on a plateau, clifftop dining, moonshine, shark steak and mash. I enjoy the company although I've not always got anything to contribute to the conversation. The chatter is all a bit full-on. I'm not used to such input, such all-consuming interaction. I'm persuaded to walk for miles along the beach to a nightclub/bar/disco. I'm knackered by the time I get there; I have a token beer but hear my bed calling over the sound system. It's a strange transformation, I'm not really in India any more. Head under the pillow, the calling bed can no longer be heard over Hebrew chatter from the high-volume occupancy above. At 3 a.m. I take out my earplugs and the sound of the sea floods my audible senses.

Other levels of life

I think I feel a routine forming, I want that fresh-fruit breakfast again. Then I get the tour. We walk north all the way to the river that divides Goa and Maharashtra and get a bus back. After the hundreds of people-carrying projectiles that have passed me, it's good to see life from the other side, and somewhat concerning to see what little respect the driver has for all life on the road other than potential passengers.

The bicycle wheels may have stopped turning but the appetite has not subsided. It's ferocious, in fact. Meals have ceased to have names. After breakfast behind wave-breaking rocks, I munch my way through the rest of the day, my stomach is bloating and blowing my budget in a blur of beach-shack restaurants. Enjoying the first beer of the day, the Kiwi commandeers a family from Brighton to our table. Endless, aimless travellers, with their two homeschooled kids. The Kiwi had an expensive education and is rich in experience, annoyingly he has the ability to retain every fact he ever learned and can find where he stored it. He speaks with an assertive, unquestionable knowledge. In this bohemian beach resort there is little opportunity to fact-check, which gives him the benefit of doubt. The conversation turns to the stock market, I have nothing to invest in that topic, then to computers, all I have is a Hotmail account, I can't communicate, then to books I've never read, even the kid offers his critical assessment and I can't get a word in. No point in asking if anyone's read *I'm with the Band,* my knowledge of a groupie's confessions will fall flat in this Hemingway hierarchy. Incidentally, the family rent out their Brighton house for £1,000 a month, keeping them on the road and their table full of food and beer. I'm bored and head off to see if my hammock is ready for collection. It's not, apparently, it's the weekend. So?

'Come back in an hour,' I'm told, so I grab a snack and return to be handed a stinking bundle of cloth.

'This is it?' I ask. 'Where's the ropes?'

Suddenly, the hammock-maker doesn't speak English. Some recommendation that was. I paid upfront for this shit. Fuck him, let him keep his rope, when he's given enough, he'll get his proverbial comeuppance. I find a shop that sells support by the metre on the way home and hang my stinking hammock on my noisy balcony. There is no respite in my room.

Respect appears to be a trait my neighbours seem to have had conscripted out of them. Music plays, the bass pounds until the early hours. It beats me, their blatant inconsiderate behaviour. I mean have they got a chip on their shoulder, or after three years of compulsory military service do they feel now that they will not be told what to do by anyone? I despise them, not integrating and isolating themselves with this conduct. My earplugs nearly meet in the middle, my wrist aches from pushing the pillow so hard against my head. They beat me, I have to isolate myself, at 1 a.m. the noise shows no sign of dying down, I go back to the balcony I spent my first night on, taking with me my resentment and a comfort blanket. Why am I paying for a room?

It's my budget that is taking the pleasure out of being here, champagne taste and beer money, or in this case seaside dreams and pigsty reality. I'm beginning to see the appeal of cuddling up to a stray on the beach.

Simply delightful

At 4.45 a.m. I go back to my part-time accommodation; I've got to move to a place of pleasurable permanency. It's true, the place is filling up, and I'm clearly at the bottom of the budget clientele here in Little Tel Aviv. Thankfully, the mornings are peaceful, I'd happily swap the all-night invasive Israelis for a morning mosque. I'd stomp around to state my displeasure but petty paybacks and reciprocating thoughtlessness don't come any easier than sleep did last night.

Life seems better after a muesli breakfast and being Sunday there is a concert to attend. A Dutch-owned oasis of palms and shade hosts musicians once a week and today a sitar and tabla duet play on a reed mat. Earl Grey is served in china cups and avocado salad arrives on plates without chips, even the dirt is cleaner. A kitten dozes on my lap and I actually drift off a few times. This place is everything my room is not. There is an air of hoity-toity, gracefully receding hair and years, loose-fitting linen and muslin, polite applause, silver service from white waiters, the only natives are here to perform, but they seem elated to. Particularly the tabla player, who is all white powder and clenched fists, the lucky student who got this gig with a sitar guru who has Ravi Shankar group connections. When the musicians and my acquaintances leave, I stick around as this is Eden to me. I hear an old British couple complain about being kept awake by Israelis last night. I don't join in, it's not a competition but I'm fucking winning. In fact, my thoughts are turning to the road again, because every night somewhere else has no expectations, and here I'm just lying awake waiting for the inevitable irritations, disturbance-inducing insomnia.

I'm supposed to play Frisbee in the afternoon but I find an Aerosmith autobiography in the book exchange and spend time reading in my hammock, happy to miss everything. I work out my finances and it does nothing to lift my spirits. The Kiwi has a friend arriving tomorrow, imported important social life, and I'm not really part of anything here on the wrong side of the path. Our meeting on the road last year had no obligation and lasted until the departure, but to reunite is forced, recycled, and for me it's failing the expectations I cycled here with. My neighbours don't wake me in the night. Still, best to think the worst of them, to avoid being let down.

Back to where it all began

The Indian breakfast, be it on the road or on the rocks, is my favourite part of the day. Someone turns a dial on a short-wave radio, I hear that Saddam Hussein has been caught. George Bush is quoted as saying: 'He won't be having a good Christmas this year.' But, being a Sunni Muslim, I can't imagine a Christian holiday featured highly on his social calendar anyway, although his capture is no doubt still an inconvenience to him.

I need to cycle again, just to remind myself I have the ability of independent movement. Without panniers I push the bike along the path to the track and head out, back to my first introduction to India almost seven years ago to the day. In life, I generally like to go forward not back, but I am hoping for some nostalgic wistfulness. Typically, the place has changed: lots of topless Western women on the beach, probably the same types who complain about niqāb-wearing Muslim women in the UK. I have a lassi, send a text and get the hell out, stopping to buy a 36-exposure film for the cheapest price I've seen. I suppose with so much exposure there is a high demand from the masses of men who come down on the Bombay bus boob tours. When I stop for water, I see an Indian newspaper and on the cover is a picture of Saddam not looking his best. I'm glad I can't read the text. What a mess the world has been in lately, I'll be glad when it gets back to normal.

I ride back along the beach, at between 3–5kph I can just keep balance and not sink into the sand. I see my guest house owner; he says I have a new neighbour. Wow, you go away for the day and everything changes. He also says if I still don't like it, I can move. Turns out she's from Holland and I really can't recall ever meeting an offensive Dutch person. It's a pleasure to be in my hammock now, I'm not coiled with tension waiting for disruption.

The Kiwi's friend arrived today; I meet him at happy hour. He's an expert on wine, collects, buys, sells, writes articles and photographs chilled bottles and glistening-rim glasses in seductive and alluring light. Basically he catalogues alcohol, makes alcohol lists, making him a functioning alcoholist. He seems OK but gets too drunk too quickly, as I suppose you would on your first night here: jet-lagged, excited, intoxicated. I leave them to escalate the intensity of tomorrow's hangover and chat to my Dutch neighbour from my balcony. She is the captain of her own boat, which is a coincidence as I'm the navigator of my own destiny. She has peaceful end-of-day wind-down wisdom in manner, the inevitable insights she gained alone at the helm viewing a sunset that no other human got to see. Her company has tranquillity and I take her inner peace to my bed and go to sleep at 10.30.

I'm woken by the Israelis above bouncing a ball around their room at 1 a.m. It's bounced intermittently on their floor, my ceiling, causing anger-boiling irritation. I get dressed and storm out of my room up the stairs to their door, then catch myself. A defenceless, skinny ball of fury about to scream at a bunch of ex-military fuckheads. I use cunning, scheming and vindictive slyness, simply sliding the bolt across their door on the outside. It's a silent victory, I wanted to tell them to shut up, I actually just shut them up, and go back to the Kiwi terrace of empty bottles and forgotten conversations, or perhaps it was empty conversations and forgotten bottles. I'm the after-party secret night sleeper.

No movement due to the bowels

Well, it took eighteen days to come down from the capital but it found me, I've got Delhi belly. I don't want to be out of clenched-cheek, bent-knee, lurching, rambling reach of my squat toilet. It's a great excuse to be antisocial. I cancel my appointment for a backgammon tournament and forgo the chance to see 'dancing girls', I don't even bother to watch the sunset. My landlord calls in and says I can move tomorrow to the rooms below the terrace I generally end up sleeping on. I haven't seen the room and just accept it, like getting the shits, and in that location I'll probably be able to watch the sun set into the sea from my toilet so it's an upgrade for sure. For today there is nothing more than hammock, book, squat and squits. Ho hum-runny bum.

The movement

It's getting worse, now it's not just inconvenient, it's painful, hurts to lie still, hurts to move. Sweaty shiver, hyperventilate, barely got the strength to hold myself up over the hole in the floor. These squat toilets may be ergonomically more efficient but when your legs lack support you are really in the shit. The Kiwi and his companion come round; my new room is available but I'm too weak to move. So they carry my stuff and I drag my sorry self down the path, to the room, fall through the door and collapse on the bed. That would be me accepting my new accommodation and testing the mattress, I'll take it.

I find that by controlling my breathing and focusing on extracting the pain with each exhale I can fall asleep. Limbs ache, head throbs, and my stomach is in knots. At 3 p.m. I feel a little better, at 6 p.m. I'm able to get up for sunset and discover I have a table and chair on my terrace.

My neighbour, who has checked in on me as she and the day passed, comes out of her room. She's an older hippy chick. English and kindly, motherly almost, with a slight air of seduction. We chatter easily for an hour, she offers me a chip off her plate, I'm tempted but think I'd prefer to starve this thing out of me.

It's not out yet, back to my room with a glaze of moisture on my quivering skin, warm clothes with the window open, then closed and naked, there is no comfort in any position. I think I may have caught something off that stinking hammock or perhaps it was the chicken I had two nights ago, ironic to think I ordered it to save money and I've spent nothing in the last two days, not really the economy I had in mind.

It's passed

At first light I'm very awake and feeling like it's passed. That was a tantrum of fury; explosive expulsion. I unpack and have a much-needed and desperately overdue shower, brush hair and teeth and am pleased to see I still have some energy left. So I go for a tentative breakfast, eating slowly, chewing meticulously, swallowing carefully and tasting fully. Hard-boiled eggs, dry toast and black tea, my tactical post-poop plan, nutrition and non-dairy; then back to my hammock to see what my tummy will make of it. It accepts my choice of food and I accept its decision. I walk to the internet café and, as I round the corner of the cliff, I get reception and my phone bleeps like a reversing truck. I look again at hotels in Delhi, there seems to be some availability and, extravagantly and romantically, I book what is described as an executive suite for $25. It even has a swimming pool on the roof. I'll ease Sofia gently into my level of living. I'm also trying to up my level of interest in her arrival – perhaps I've been gone for too long, too soon into the relationship and I'm not feeling the love.

My neighbours and the Brighton family are playing paddleball on the beach. I don't have the will or the energy and, even if I did, I don't have the hand-to-eye co-ordination. It's not my thing. Frisbee, hacky-sack, beach volleyball, any of those team-bonding pastimes, they just show my shortcomings and the game goes better when I exclude myself. Happy hour lacks the sentiment when I don't drink but I follow on to a restaurant, the entourage increasing in size daily. The Kiwi introduces me to a German girl as 'having an infectious disease' … thanks for that. The conversation is very money-orientated; my lack of it is often on my mind but their monopoly of it doesn't impress me, minted they may be but seemingly no happier for it. In fact they are guarded, volatile and nervous, global uncertainties influencing the value of dividends, advocating a safe investment in a Thai coastline development. Won't catch them sleeping on the beach naked with a stray. Somewhere between these extremes there has to be someone I can relate to. It's a place of reverse-snobbery nihilism, intellectual academics and ex-military. The potential is here, I just can't find a convivial crowd.

The conversation turns to which wine tastes best at altitude, what to order with your in-flight meal, 'Oh, dharrlin's … *you don't sound pretentious at all*'. The chatter turns to 9/11 and who was to blame. Thankfully, due to my sobriety I don't voice the connection I drew and ask which wine, blood-red or surrender-white, is best drank before your plane flies into a skyscraper. I don't order a main, and leave after my soup. How the fuck will Sofia handle this and if she can where does that leave me? I feel a disaster looming and a growing urge to rebuild the Harley in the shed, shut away with something I love and understand, created from scratch and that brings fulfilment. On the plus side they are only waking thoughts, the night is tranquil, the sea is soft and nothing much of anything takes precedence.

Further

I wake with a grand plan of a dawn bicycle beach ride. I put on my cycling shorts, prepare my bike, fart, consider having a dump, decide yes, and discover I already have. So I take off my cycling shorts, wash them and carry the bike to the beach, however the tide is high and I'm not moving on this soft sand. So I go inland and find a road but the traffic seems ghastly. I've been desensitised. God, wherever I am, squalid guest house, obnoxious neighbours, intellectual chatter, down-and-out freaks – I see hideousness in everything. I feel contentment is so close, it's there, it's here, it's not that far away, and that's the frustration. I don't want to give up on this place as I'm sure there is somewhere I fit but I'm fucked if I can find it. I realise as I push my bike back home along the path that I recognise a lot of faces now in the week I've been here. I can nod and say hello but that's as far as the conversation goes, maybe they think I have somewhere better to be – *no, I'm just looking for it.*

My hippy next-door neighbour is going to the banyan tree, a fabled place, mentioned in hushed respect by those who know, deprecating tones by intellectuals who don't, possibly of no interest to the Israelis and revered by the dreadlocked. I willingly agree to accompany her. Past the thermal steamy lagoon, and along a jungle track that runs by a river that feeds the lake. Fresh water springs out of a crack in a rock to fill a pool where mud-covered and indistinguishable humans sit and harden. Caked and baked the dried earth apparently has some kinds of qualities. They then crack and crunch down to the sea to return to their characterising skin colour but now penetrated by nutrients.

I've read that in California the greater your success the further you can afford to ascend in price of property perched on the Hollywood hills. The more prestigious the house you inhabit the higher your social standing, the greater your achievements, your fame spread further from this elevated vantage point. Paradoxically, there is some correlation as we climb to the banyan tree. Things are getting freakier, the locks are more credible, the dread more palpable. Reality less evident, escapism more prevalent. I hear music, pipe and drum, I smell chillums burning with Dutch tobacco. There are people coming down, but only in altitude, they are far, far away. The path leads us beyond before it doubles back into a clearing. The tree is truly stunning but that's not what is noticed first. I hear monkeys screeching from the canopy and in the lower branches a feral human of female gender is imitating them so convincingly I half expect to see David Attenborough in the undergrowth, describing this rare and unhinged life form in whispered awe to a camouflaged camera. On ground level are more recognised life forms, they have shined their coconut shells and mixed their medicine in them. Carrot-sized chillums are passed around, I pass, they must be absurdly high. I don't sing and I don't play but my neighbour has a flute and toots along with some other instruments. It's a peaceful place, has the vibe of a commune, a few possessions scattered around, blankets, bottles, some wood smoulders within a stone circle. I'm not quite comfortable, this is extreme and I'm living on the edge of it. I do not want to go any deeper. Not afraid, I simply feel that immersion is permanent and I like the variation my life offers. I've never worn a patch on my leather jacket, nor dreaded my hair, my tattoos are seen at my discretion, not fully committed to any one thing. Perhaps it's a middle path but it allows me access to many directions. That American cyclist was only a cyclist, the commitment lacks options. I float, not to the surface of high-intellect chatter but just around, driftwood, not much use but unobtrusive, won't provide much heat or light for very long. Can't be carved into anything of real value but there is a beauty in the freedom, a liberation in the inconspicuous, an acceptance in the undefined, not fanatical in any thought, faith, or following. Work a bit, travel a bit, drink, party, socialise; love, cycle, hike, hang out and hammock all in moderate and unrestrained amounts, as and when, wild and willing. Here is a place of dedicated hardcore obsession to the point of possession. I respect but don't envy the lifestyle, it must come with some severe hardships. I appreciate the insight, the highest of the high up here by the banyan tree.

We go back to our more familiar level, passing a film crew heading up, I don't see David Attenborough though. I buy my chaperone a juice. Thanks for taking me, I'd not have gone alone.

Later I sit alone at a table with an English couple directly behind me. They are in deep and desperate conversation about his inadequacies. It's conducted totally within my earshot and I have to concentrate to make sure my body language doesn't betray my eavesdropping, mustn't nod and certainly not laugh.

I head to the terrace for happy hour, which is more like happy ten minutes before the intense, educated, informed, heated, drunken discussion ensues. I try to keep it light, mentioning Sofia and saying that before leaving to come here our relationship had just reached the point where we could comfortably fart in front of each other. It gets a giggle but the topic moves on to religion, then back to 9/11, still a popular subject two years on. I can't follow the conversation but I still follow my fellow drinkers, the Kiwi and the alcoholist, to dinner, more to observe than participate. Acting like a couple of intoxicated, public-school-educated, obnoxious, vacationing embarrassments. The menu has as little variety as their conversation so I leave them to repeat their outlooks with the same views and food. In a beach shack with spinach curry and again in earshot, this time of a couple arguing, I avert my eyes to see other couples sitting in absolute silence. This is hardly a good omen for what's to come. I go deep into my own thoughts. I witnessed much today, but all of it felt like it was from the perimeter, I'm not sure where I stand. I lie in my hammock and my next-door neighbour brings home company after midnight, I'm just the voyeur.

Piña Colada Syndrome

I can't help but wake at dawn, and am drawn to my hammock to watch who wakes up next. It's high tide directly beneath me, thunderous and exhilarating. The palms aren't bowing, the sky is clear, something stormy happened out at sea somewhere and the ripple effect has just arrived. I walk the ten paces to the restaurant, I'm the first diner and await the sweet chai patiently. There is no urgency or boredom, just the well-being of being in the moment this morning and slowly I'm joined by my closest neighbours. They are far more tolerable first thing, or perhaps I'm more tolerant.

'Exactly how long is it before you can comfortably fart in a woman's company?' asks the Kiwi. I feel he has given this an awful lot of consideration.

This inquiry notwithstanding, there is an ease to the morning's proceedings – in fact, it doesn't look like progressing far beyond breakfast. This company has reached a higher level of relaxation that is only obtained during prolonged stretches of absolute inactivity. The seats around the breakfast table have become a metaphorical talk show couch and we are joined by one guest after another. As muesli and porridge plates are cleared, a space of temptation and opportunity appears on the table. It would seem like a waste of a perfect morning if this gathering were disbanded prematurely. It has to be said and, eventually, predictably, it is. Piña coladas are ordered, they hardly count as alcohol, and the alcoholist who ordered them should know. Some self-righteous types might see this as a wasted morning but every day's a school day if you care to be aware. If I had to restage this scenario there is nothing I would change. Open-air restaurant, the sea beneath providing a cooling breeze and background serenity, barefooted, wrapped in a sarong and fluttering thin cotton coverings. Diverse company but with common ground, no agenda, utter spontaneity, and those ingredients have always instigated the most sensational of sessions, the round comes around again, and everyone gets funnier with every sip. Put it on the tab, I'll feel the pain later.

Somewhere down my tall glass lurks today's lesson – as I idly rotate my cocktail stick in the concoction of coconut cream and white rum a tragedy occurs. A pineapple chunk falls off my little wooden spike and retrieval is futile, like a playful dolphin it dips out of reach only to bob up again in defiance. Feeling the need to voice the misfortune, share my grief and draw attention to the horrific luck I'm suffering, I say, 'Oh no, my pineapple has fallen into my drink.' Then I pause as I hear what I have just said. 'If that's the worst thing that happens today, it's a pretty good day, isn't it?' Piña Colada Syndrome. There will always be something to moan about if you choose to, and that philosophy has stuck with a bond stronger than said pineapple chunk to cocktail stick.

I spend the rest of the day waiting for the night market, and avoid anything too strenuous.

For people whose finances feature so frequently in their conversation, my acquaintances' capital doesn't stretch to leg room. I'm crammed into a tuk-tuk with two other grown men, keener to get out than get there. Anjuna market is where east meets west and takes all their money. The package tourists barely cover themselves and get ripped off. Paying the asking price and asking for it. The place still has a little atmosphere, but belligerent Brits dominate the night. A labyrinth of stalls delicately lit and selling every accessory your Indian holiday needs. Some really intricate jewellery and craftsmanship, not much in the way of plastic shite but carved, embroidered, silver-soldered, woven, sculpted, fashioned, and painted, not imported. It's got the charm of an exotic bazaar but diluted with the uncouth car-boot brigade. Fat Essex girls with muffin bellies and ॐ symbol T-shirts, the omnipresent sound of Estuary. Most that entices me is weight I don't want to carry and money I don't have to spend. I'm haggling hard on a claw earring when a flabby, burned and sweating slapper pays the asking price. 'It's only the cost of a tube ticket that I am asking, sir.' *Yeah but I've got a bicycle, I'm not a fat-bottomed girl.* A rumour is circulating that Tom Cruise is among the crowd wearing a red baseball cap; trying to spot him is an impossible mission. I believe it for a second and then see a free gin and tonic promotion stall which is equally unbelievable, but it's true, I get one, and then another. Individually, my neighbours are all right, much like a G & T, and as our paths cross intermittently, we have a laugh, but like whiskey and coke they are better when not together. Like back-to-back cocktails they take the conversation to a level I can't reach. The funny thing is I only hear them laugh when they are apart. Me and the alcoholist crack ourselves up putting down the easy Essex girls. 'Naa, tits first, innit? Um notta slut.'

I'm in with the band

It's Sunday again which means sitar and tabla in refined but affordable surroundings. I can't wait and remind my happy hippy neighbour. She's still keen and we walk that way at 10.30, ecstatic to find an available table in the shade. Today there is mantra-chanting and acoustic guitar as support. When Mr. Sitar takes the stage, he recognises me and we exchange smiles. I think my hippy date is impressed, hanging with the musicians, I must confess we've met before but not in a groupie kind of way. My other neighbours are the other side of the gathering, I acknowledge them from afar. I've found a good spot here, and I don't want to lose it. This is definitely the high point of my being here and, best of all, despite my hype to the hippy, the event still lives up to expectations. We go get lunch together, there's nothing going on but we don't seem to have anything better to do or anyone better to do it with. I don't think she has an agenda, says she's got a daughter somewhere, so we have that in common. She's not clingy, we just keep crossing each other's paths. Hardly surprising when she has to walk past my room to get to hers. I smell her joss sticks and hear the hippy bells on her clothes. Wondering with worry what comes through her window from my room. Especially thinking back to the state I was in when I arrived. Still no judgement on this terrace, happily on the same level.

I hear the boys above at happy hour and decide to remain in my hammock and give the sunset my full attention. Some kind of super sun, deep red imposing as it hangs above the horizon and then melts with distortion into the Indian Ocean. Stone-cold sober and undistracted, it's a stunning sight – see you tomorrow for your shortest shift of the year.

As the light of the day dims the tide comes in and pounds the rocks below. I wonder if my neighbour is home, I wonder if she is in her own thoughts. What demons do the pounding waves unleash in her guarded heart?

A revelation

It doesn't matter where I am or how I try to escape it. This will be my seventh consecutive Christmas out of England and still it looks like desperation, an unavoidable acknowledgement: put my head in the sand and that holiday will come up from behind. You were christened, motherfucker, you should be playing happy families, turkey stains on ya once-a-year jumper, Queen's speech and port. I've hated it ever since I stopped believing, not in the baby Jesus, or the other fairy tale that all material needs will be met by a mythical merchant who delivers to the good as they sleep, but the superficial pretence and emphasis that just for today everything – family unity, food, future and world predicament – will be better than yesterday. No other part of my life, day, year or belief, revolves around Christian dogma, but at the end of December it encircles me, entraps me and ignoring it so vehemently is an acceptance that I'm acknowledging it. Hypocrisy rains down on me, because I accept no other aspect of the faith.

However, I've found a compromise. The solstice is undeniable, and the more extreme your latitude the more significant it is. I have a devotion to planetary change because it's real and, sometimes with the right awareness, I can physically feel it. The peak of the axis, the crossover of a timeline – today things change, beyond human beliefs, beyond a calendar. This is rotation, this is orbital, this is momentous and like a heretic in a place of worship I may not voice it, but I know it, I sense it, I count down to it and I happen to love it. Whether it's witnessing the daily increase in light as we leave the darkest of days, or a slight sadness that the pinnacle of summer has passed as we are falling back to earlier shadows and shivering shade. It is all remarkable and always worthy of recognition, it keeps me in line with the planets, keeps me aware that something is greater than anything and everything I do. Be it stoned on the couch or driven to goal scoring and growth, the rock we exist on has just completed a rotation that is beyond any means, ability, agenda or manipulation of the numbers we choose to put on time. Whether we divide an orbit by 24 units and that by 60, multiply it all by 365 and subdivide it by 52 and then 7. The numerals are irrelevant, the fractions unimportant, the counting conditioned, the names superficial and superfluous. But every six of our man-made months, give or take a night or two, something happens that represents the repetition of seasons, the revolution of our existence. Something has ended, something is beginning, and be you flat-earther, pagan, Hindu, Muslim, Jew or any other ethnic colour, creed or race, you can deny all you like but today something changes and it's bigger than all of us. So I silently worship it because this will bring irrigation to the parched, crops to fruition, food to tummy, sustenance of life, and while it works in that fashion I'm indebted to it, reliant on it, conditioned because of it. Seasons, man, they blow my fuckin' mind.

I can't help but wonder what wine is best suited to such planetary change and travels best at the speed of time and doesn't stain white linen if dropped from a jolt in the time-and-space continuum. I opt for the support of my hammock suspended above a moon-controlled tide, undulating from faraway winds and hitting protrusions caused by moving tectonic plates. And after all that grandeur I go for breakfast – banana porridge, I think, should be the order of the morning.

I don't make promises easily, the word implicates honour and if I say I will, then I will, at all cost and inconvenience to me. If I say I promise then barring alien invasion I will endeavour to honour it. Somehow a beach hawker prised a promise out of me to visit her stall. I do, and part with an appropriate amount of rupees worthy of my guaranteed assurance.

My neighbour has scored some smoke, the second-easiest thing to get here after sunburn. I don't want either and she doesn't want to get high alone. If she only knew what spaced-out thoughts I'd already had this morning she wouldn't press me. *I'll tell ya what, I'll order a beer and we can share a buzz and chips on our balcony. Oh wait, cocktails are two for one today, oh, OK, I'll drink the other one for you.*

Misjudgement is my mistress and I follow her misguidance to an overrated restaurant with those who reside above me. By some miraculous accident I manage to direct the conversation and attention to myself, my needs, my future – must be a slow news day. My announcement that I want to leave the haulage trade for good is met with whispers as hushed as that of a foray to the banyan tree but considered in far greater depth. There is envy at walking away from a livelihood of twenty years, admiration at the bravery and advice as for the continuation of belief in my direction. This turns into encouragement, reassurance of ability, a testimonial to my talent. I've become the topic of conversation and the centre of attention, I've become earthed and everything is revolving around me. It's the ultimate pep talk, participants reveal their pasts, column writers, article submitters, in-flight magazine providers, all agree my submissions would be above average, don't submit, give it to 'em. 'You have something to say,' I'm told. 'Tell 'em, say it.' I'm speechless, my reaction is confidence, but beneath is cynical doubt.

Having hijacked the dinner conversation I leave them to go for cocktails and walk the path back with a German I've been in the company of a few times but not really spoken to. Like me, he shines brightest with his light concentrated, not dilated in a crowd, and with that personal touch I see what failed to shine on me in the presence of the pretentious.

A dawn patrol

The tide has moved on and left hard sand in its wake, I wake early to ride it. I cycle south past the stretch of beach dedicated to yoga classes, towards the river where tai chi flows beyond the merchants of chai tea infusion. Past the dreadlocked and wasted, the washed-up on the tideline, a lifeless jellyfish and even a decomposing sea snake. I find a hidden resort of bamboo walls and palm thatch at a dead-end backwater, cut off by a river running into the sea. Fortified with prayer flags, ॐ and peace symbols, and the odd yin and yang. It's a bit too far out for me. I head back to the road, my intention was to find the train station and work out how I was going to cycle there for my 4.30 a.m. departure next week. It soon becomes obvious I won't be. Bugger that, a 40-kilometre ride through the night to arrive all sweaty for a forty-hour train journey to Delhi, some savings are not worth the hardships, I'll be booking a taxi.

So I return to my enclave on the cliff, and have a well-earned breakfast as my neighbours drag themselves from bed to bench, with bleary eyes and nothing to recount from their morning but dreams and intentions. But this place has affected me too, despite my dawn tour of discovery, my pace has slowed, I find the roads beyond here a harsh reality, the traffic a brutal invasion, the noise an irritating distraction. This place is far from silent but the waves have a tranquil repetition like meditation, and I've inevitably tuned into it and adjusted my pace accordingly, moving with the tide, tied in with the motion, tired of turmoil beyond the sandy surface. Although, the beach is getting busier and louder every day, the hammock has more appeal and anyway my neighbour is ill, time to reciprocate and I hang on the terrace like a guardian angel should she need anything. An avocado salad and multiple siestas make the hardships of being a hovering carer quite bearable.

203

In the evening after happy hour I take on porter duties as a German mother-and-daughter combo arrive and I carry their bags to what little rentable space is left. Their arrival is met with charm and smarm depending on how practised you are in the art of compliments and seduction. The delicate assumptions of availability, access into knickers, is a rite of passage to some. I wouldn't consider myself a womaniser, I don't know what to say, but I certainly know what not to say. The Kiwi clearly doesn't have this filter and blurts out, 'Which one is the daughter?' and all access is blocked, barriers come down, the alcoholist and I hold our heads in our hands as embarrassment radiates out like shock waves. A night in the hammock, I think.

If I didn't drink?

The waiters and cooks sleep on the table tops like Snoopy on his kennel roof. I leave my hammock to see if their bed has turned to breakfast. I'm too early, if only I had a kettle, or they an alarm. I seem to be the most morning person in the vicinity, it's a secret. The best of the day is all mine and I don't like to share it as generally I find that makes it half as good. However, when company comes to the table, I'm happy to leave my dawn single-dining daydreams and engage in what little reality is available. The alcoholist is up and about, my neighbour is feeling better and philosophical, asking us this morning, 'What would you do if you didn't drink?'

Well, as long as there was still sex, drugs and rock 'n' roll … I decide not to say. 'I'd probably join an interest group or organisation … AA, for example.' *Yep, sorry, can't keep it serious.* 'Piña colada anyone? It's got two of your five a day. It's what the baby Jesus would have wanted. Oh wait, is tomorrow his birthday? I got my days muddled.'

It's suggested the Kiwi is afraid of women. The evidence is overwhelming, his misogynist jokes, devotion to Eminem lyrics, chauvinistic philosophies. Quite possible, I suppose, I'd not considered it, now I do I don't know what to do with it. Unfortunately, this conversation is overheard as he approaches from behind and the sudden and censored silence confirms beyond any doubt that we were talking about him. Awkward! Piña colada time yet?

The merry gathering disperses to go about their daily duties, a swim in the sea, a rinse in the lake, a tan top-up on the beach, a snooze in the hammock. I opt for a little snack en route to the internet café and see the introspective German, he's lost his passport. I see him again on my way back, he calls out my name, twice, so I decide I'd better acknowledge him and he invites me over for a beer. That's not going to get him his passport back, but he's undeterred and orders a second and then a third. He reminds me a lot of myself, other than I haven't lost my identity, he's introspective, over-sensitive, isolated, wants to belong but not for long. After the fourth beer his friend comes and I wander off feeling the positive effects of afternoon drinking. What last week was a nod of acknowledgement is now a brief exchange of pleasantries, more intoxicated, less inhibited and hopefully more sincere than, 'I fuckin' love you, you're my best friend.' In fact, when I get back to my room I even share a smoke with my neighbour, she has to finish it, she leaves tomorrow. Tomorrow? On Christmas Day? No one leaves on Christmas Day, even the most fraught of relationships, the biggest of issues can be put aside on that day. Boxing Day is a far more auspicious day to pack up and part ways, that's generally when the second wave of tenancy begins, the second chance to rent out my house. Couples bite their tongues, fill their mouths with turkey, and quietly contemplate moving on with new resolutions the following week. I'm hoping for a call from Barry, desperately seeking housing for the recently separated that will put an end to this horrid middle-class poverty that restricts my cocktail intake that I've been enduring like a bad romance.

However, under the circumstances I'll settle for what I can get, and I get stoned. Inevitably, the conversation goes into observations, suspicions, deliberations, sensations and infinities. My neighbour points out the five of us residing in this guest house are all without partners, even if we have them. Different nationalities, a common language, and brought together really only by our accommodation, an unlikely combination that will never come together again, here and now, me and her. 'Fancy a farewell cocktail?'

We go to the terrace above for happy hour, and due to my naivety I don't realise the discomfort this causes the Kiwi. He says, 'No women on thc balcony.'

I reply, 'Well, not till now and not through choice surely.' So me and me bitch go to a beach bar where fire jugglers perform for the drinkers and diners as a slither of a Shiva moon shines discreetly in a purple western sky, all viewed through glassy eyes. Why does this shit only happen when ya stoned? It's bloody brilliant. We have connected, an afternoon of alcohol and a week or more of living next door. Meals, drinks, terrace and conversations shared, our chatter is now as relaxed as a sunset, still nothing sexual, just neighbours becoming good friends, convivial company, and little want or need to look elsewhere. The Kiwi walks past on his way to the pizza place, I say I'll be bringing my neighbour tonight. 'Can she grow a dick in twenty minutes?'

About as likely as you not being one for twenty minutes, I think.

The secret to a good dining experience is one's position at the table, that's why wedding planers agonise over the Tetris of seating arrangements. The table is large and the Brighton family are there too, the only available seat is in an unfortunate position and I'm out at the end on my own. Once again I realise I much prefer a smaller and more socially selective group, as opposed to dealing with the politics of preconceptions and the uncompromising preferences of various individuals. Give me belonging and I'll soon be leaving. Disputes arise, feelings get considered, perspectives are assumed, issues come to the surface like dead fish. People are strange, what would they be like if they didn't drink? I don't know, it's hard to say, I'm quite drunk.

It all feels forced

I'm woken by the sound of activity, my neighbour is packing up and taking off, so I pack up too. I'm taking her room: the end-of-terrace location will come with privacy. I don't mind her walking by but new neighbours and new noses poking past my billowing sarong of seclusion is not welcome. She leaves her pegs, joss sticks and mozzie repellent for me, like Christmas presents.

This morning breakfast is prepared with extra diligence and artistic flare, no doubt in lieu of a seasonal bonus, a Hindu interpretation of the concept of the mass of Christ and the extra income from the influx of tourists it brings. A lifelong traveller I may be, but for all that experience, goodbyes have never got easier. They loom, they are drawn out, they are more often than not forever, and even if they aren't, the reunion seldom recreates the magic of spontaneity and serendipity. The more genuine the meeting, the more forced and insincere the parting words sound. Be it a holiday romance, or beach freak friendship, a road shared for a few miles or a few days, when the parting comes, it has never brought with it words that flowed as easy as the moments that were spent together. Maybe we'll send a few emails, smoke signals from the dying embers, the ashes will be kept in a mental urn, selective memories, occasional recollection with wistful inaccuracy, that no one can correct. That's what we will always have, impressions from a failing mind, where no one ever ages and the recounting and revisiting of those days will be all the better for it.

And she's gone.

Back to lone observations, I sit shrouded in the shade at the back of a beach shack. I see my neighbour from above perusing the mother and daughter, the German of lost identity, the alcoholist all pass by and I slink into the shadows with no want to engage. I make the obligatory Christmas Day phone call to the parents. It's a bad line and I've got nothing to say anyway. Beer, hammock, read and finish my Aerosmith book. Now I have absolutely nothing to do. I'm waiting again, for my departure, for Sofia to arrive.

The previous Christmas in northern Thailand was a forced acceptance of the day too as I awaited my departure to China. I'd taken the insulated water container from my bicycle bottle holder and filled it with a chilled and concealed morning beer. It was another day off the bike but like a fool I let myself become a shorts-and-sandals pillion to an Italian teen on a rental moped. We rode to a beach formed by a bend in the Kok River. We came to no harm, suffering only depressing dampness as grey skies rained down and dripped off cabanas thatched with banana leaves. The day was moist and miserable, roads were slick and clammy clothing added to the windchill.

As I drip-dried and drank more back in my guest house, I met another cyclist, who, like every other Westerner, was on her way to Laos. She was Hawaiian and her experience of cycling Asia had granted her an encyclopaedic knowledge of how to take her bicycle on public transport. We all, I suppose, have our limits of endurance, although I wasn't sure she had been introduced to hers. I wasn't exactly committed to riding every mile regardless, but her tyres had barely trod any road from there to here, and I felt quite achieved next to her avoidance of any energetic hardships and ethnic experiences.

Not that there was much in the way of Thai life to be had as I strung out my clothing in the room and the day into the night market. The expats were out, more dedicated to expanding their beer bellies than their cultural immersion. I had my first banana pancake of the trip to try and blend in. Cycling in the rain never seemed so appealing, as I counted down the last four days, when I would leave my place in the procession to Laos and fly north to China.

The day feels forced whatever is done with it. Sunset happy hour has been deemed worthy of an overrated bottle of wine. A table has been booked for the fish dinner special. The alcoholist gets very drunk, I cringe as the German mother and daughter combo join our table, the teenage girl sits next to me. She's chatty but I'm on edge, beyond our pleasant interaction is the volatile vibe of a drunk Brit abroad in German company. It's gonna kick off further down the table, at best it will be football but I'm thinking more likely the war, the possibility of a threesome or defensive chauvinism. It's a time bomb and I pay up and get out before it blows up.

The more I've got to know them, the early retiree, the minted, the successful professional, the more the initial envy of their status has worn off. Their personalities grate like sand in sandals, there appears to be a lack of fulfilment in their actions, and an air of the superficial, an emphasis in finding entertainment that fails to reward. There is a search, a need, all endeavours are vapid substitutes for happiness. Nothing quite seems to fill their void; I generally avoid that vacuum by filling mine with miles.

I have new neighbours, not sure how many, I hope one with three pairs of shoes, although it could be a family of four and one is barefoot.

Friday 26th December
Arambol

Offhand accuracy

It's time to revisit the book exchange, I've deliberated less over accommodation and location than what I will choose to read and carry around with me from now until next year. I eventually settle for *The Wind in My Wheels*, the tales of an overland cyclist, paradoxically unsure if I want captivating or crap. Either way, I suppose it's research.

Despite my better judgement I return to the place for dinner that could well have been where I got a dose of runny bum ten days ago. I order a vegetarian dish – *ya not gonna get me again, ya bastards*. Accompanied once more by the mother-and-daughter combo who remain at the top of some of the diners' menu. No potentially explosive conversational topics tonight, instead there is a firework display above the bay, entertainment for the unstoned, I preferred the fire jugglers. The mother wants to read my palm. I don't believe but not as vehemently as my opposition to Christmas, so I happily let her look at my lines. It starts off with vague off-hand sentiment: single-minded, achiever, no wish to be leader, and then she stops in my tracks. 'Oh god, I'm not going to die, am I? Just when I was becoming convinced that I was immortal.'

There is conflict, I'm told, it's immense, so big she shows my palm to her student daughter, there are gasps at the level of prominence and pronounced prediction. They scrutinise the evidence. 'It's with family, they say.' Well, that's a load of bollocks then, as all is well with Mum and Dad, I just called them earlier today. Interesting how the Kiwi puts their practices down but is too unsettled to show his hand or unclench his fist. His womanising mate feels excluded, tries to keep a hand in, interferes, comes on too strong, and the atmosphere becomes tense.

Once again, predictably, I'm first to leave, not wanting to be part of the complications. Not peacekeeper or instigator, not that interested at all really. I leave them all to make their immediate futures and go to my hammock.

211

Boxing day in Thailand, and my future was on pause. I was awake, ready and willing to move on, but the weather remained the same. Rain hammered on the metal roof and cascaded off the canopy, keeping my door shut. The bike was packed but despite my will the rain would not relent. It was the first time weather had affected my plans. It was cold, by Thai standards, and my clothes were still damp from the day before. I stayed under my duvet and read, maddened that I couldn't leave the crowded guest house.

I convinced myself the pages were brightening, the day lightening and the clouds lifting, but for all my urgency and optimism it really wasn't riding weather. I deemed it a research day, and revised my Chinese phrase book, looked at my map and read my guidebook.

When time zones became compatible, I called my father to wish him happy birthday, a long-distance call being significantly easier than coming up with a Boxing Day birthday present. No Capricorn wants to hear the words: 'This is for Christmas and your birthday.' I was glad I had made the call; he was chuffed to hear from me and the effort made gave meaning to an otherwise wasted day. He told me not to skimp on the opportunities open to me purely for financial reasons. So I took his advice and bought a beer on the way back from the international phone call shop.

Maybe it was the birthday banter, the beer, the goodwill or the guidebook, possibly a combination, but I couldn't recall ever being so excited to go to a new country. It'd been a long process from planted seed to fruition, and now only three days from picking, ripe and ready to ride. I was not nervous in the least, keen to put eighteen months of learning the language into practise and a month of cycling preparation into momentum. Maybe it was the humidity or perhaps dreams of the Himalayan exertion that lay ahead, but the night was long, sweaty and restless.

Family conflict? The words come back in the blackness, so loud they wake me. I didn't think beyond my parents. Of course there is family conflict, conflict that I even have family. And it's had nearly two years to harden into my hand, blister into a palm. Well, that reading was beyond perceptive, inventive, even acceptance. She knew it like the front of my hand, and I hadn't even considered beyond my relatively small family tree trunk of predecessors. I only looked down to ancestral roots, forgetting the possible new growth of descendants. And she said *family* conflict, not implied impregnation, or accusation by association, but *family*. That implies blood. It's not quite got the evidence of a DNA test but there is an uncanny accuracy. And although the reading was not requested I have now to accept that it clearly contained some truths. I need to have some faith because acceptance is in my hands.

Various departures

There also seems to be little doubt that last night's restaurant doses out rancid food like a leaking dustbin bag. You've got to be pretty stupid to eat again in a place that made you sick, but I am, and I did. At 7 a.m. my bloated tummy tells me it's toilet time and there will be little of any other exploits today. I go to the restaurant for a black chai, just in time to see the Kiwi cover his mouth and run from the table to throw up. The second consecutive day of conclusive evidence, you don't need to be a gifted mystic to see his palm displays what he's recently eaten.

Today the alcoholist leaves, I enjoyed his company and will miss his influence. He found a septic dog on the beach, an abscess blown with maggots, about the third easiest thing to pick up after sunburn and weed. However, his heart went out and he took the rotting mutt to a vet so as its miserable, hopeless life could be prolonged. We all have our causes, I suppose. Animal lovers, they can get a bit extreme. I don't want to see cruelty or suffering, I quite like animals, several varieties are particularly tasty. But this is a country of over a billion people and there's such poverty among our own human species. The money spent on supporting a vet to fix a stray could put food in the tummy of a street child, clean clothing on an emaciated body, a pair of flip-flops for hardened soles. But then I suppose in a place of no roads you don't see people living on the streets. You can't fix India with your holiday spending money, and even if you could, your interpretation of living standards won't cross culture and climate. So I reason, you find your cause and fund the foundation that can fix it, so as to console your conscience as you order another cocktail. A little volunteering, a little charity, is at least a tangible action. It's all too easy to be daunted by the discovery that the chaos of the country is unfathomably complicated and beyond correction. Charity begins at home and a scabby dog on ya doorstep has feelings too. Possibly stitched up and sterilised, it will have reason to wag its tail and that vibration could have a butterfly effect. At least the alcoholist did something, seems like a waste to me but perhaps his holiday would seem wasted if he hadn't left the place a little better than he found it. Still, throwing another $100 at the vet for the mutt's continued care when he's already been stitched up once seems a bit excessive. Funding the ongoing treatment of a growing abscess in his absence with more money than I spend in a week seems obscene. However, a local labourer might toil all day to earn what I spend on a piña colada so who am I to judge?

Anyway, like so many things I've witnessed these last few weeks, I keep my mouth shut, pry my mind open and keep my opinions to myself. I don't think I have the capacity, insight or right to change any mindset but my own, any more than I can halt the morning ritual of the burning of plastic bottles. And who knows, maybe indirectly, stray dog rehabilitation, cleansing via palm reading and rubbish cleaning by incineration prevents food poisoning and that's why I've got the shits again. It was written in a way I couldn't see, existed somewhere beyond my beliefs.

So I pucker up and walk the path to the taxi stand to wave off the alcoholist. It's not an entirely selfless act as I want to arrange my transportation to the station tomorrow night, even though my train doesn't leave until 4.30 a.m. the following morning.

With the end in sight I decide to see what this beach break has cost me. I've now got less than $16 a day to live on as I've pretty much overspent every day during the six weeks of this trip so far. I think I'd better spend the afternoon in my hammock and stop spending. So I make a start on the bicycle book, a girl who cycled alone in India. Coincidentally, this author, Josie Dew, also read *Far from the Madding Crowd* on her trip. What are the chances, is it the slender spine and light reading, the low cost of reprinted classics that attracts the insolvent cyclist to this literature, or perhaps the lure that the prose will rub off on our own offerings? I wonder what book exchange she left it at, maybe I read her copy.

I finished my copy through a sweaty, restless night, my load was definitely lighter, firstly through dehydration and now with a redundant bookmark. I had even paid the day before for my three-night stay, so I could make an early start and carry less bhat. Noodle soup breakfast, 7-Eleven for supplies and a petrol station for air to harden my tyres. I left cloudy but dry Chiang Rai with forceful propulsion. I'd never had such strength and stamina, I was slicing through the humid air, no drag, no friction, no want or need to stop. The momentum was self-generating, the figures on my trip gauge were breaking new records and the calculations propelled me onwards. I adopted a new position, forearms on bars and bum pushed back against the seat. I caught less wind and my legs seemed to have more power to push at this angle. A lean, mean cycling machine. I reluctantly rested after 20 kilometres, whatever I was running on was high-octane. I stopped for crisps and coke after 50 kilometres, lunch at 85 kilometres, these felt like the scheduled stops of a bullet train. I was going to complete my first 1,000 kilometres that day and I saved my breath for a whooping victory fanfare of achievement. Then, for the first time since I'd ridden alone, I saw a Western cyclist coming the other way.

I was a bit full of myself, having had a day of personal bests, what I'd accomplished so far and was about to embark on. He was Irish, had cycled from Dublin 15,000 kilometres, a year on the road. *That takes the wind out of my sails.* Said he had dysentery as he passed through Eastern Turkey, barren red desert, no shade, no shelter, crouching behind his bike, thirsty, burned, shrunken and feeble. *Right, well I can see there is absolutely nothing I can bring to this meeting.* He wasn't bragging, not sobbing, just relaying, and there I was, less than a month since I'd bought the bike, not even crossed an international border yet. 'I'm not going to Laos, you know,' I said, but in his eyes I felt I was coming across like the Hawaiian I had cast my harsh judgement on came across to me.

It wasn't only my sails that hung like damp laundry. As he talked and I recoiled my front tyre went down. It was a wholly deflating experience.

He left me on an empty road and it was clear I wouldn't complete the 185 kilometres to Chiang Mai that day. As I passed my 1,000-kilometre achievement the moment was marred by the recent meeting. I continued to pass my personal daily best of 111 kilometres, but felt little consolation, like I'd got a leg up onto my own pedestal, but couldn't rest on broken records and scratched laurels.

Then came the second unwanted meeting of the day: the hills approached. It was a steady gradient and coincided with the sun breaking through the clouds, activating moisture to break through my skin: automatic air-conditioning. Automated temptation came from behind in the form of a pickup truck. It slowed and as it passed I got the obligatory: 'Where you go?'

'Up,' I gasped in sarcastic despondency.

That brief interaction soon had the wind cooling me because my progress was increasing dramatically, from the bed of the truck. Well, fuck it, why not, I'd beaten my bests, and they'd not compared to the Dubliner's. My half-cup of single-currency kilometres from a free spin on the slots showed their true value against his accumulated wealth of travel, the long-distance high roller at the roulette wheel of fortune.

Without the sweat of effort or thrill of achievement the summit was reached. *I can make my own way from here, thank you*, but he didn't stop to drop me off, because I didn't actually say that. And as I freeloaded along what would have been tomorrow's ride, I saw no guest house, no accommodation at all, and I was quietly pleased that I had taken the hardships out of my day of premature accomplishment. The road dropped down and I was dropped off 20 kilometres out of town. We swapped addresses and I freewheeled on, deep in a daydream and planning my packing crate as I descended. With a cheeky hoot I was pulled from my thoughts, he was back again, offering another lift, but I was on the downhill stretch now so declined with lungs full of breath to spare. I glided into town, and got my bearings. It was rush hour; fumes hung in the humid air. I weaved carefully and confidently through the stop-and-go traffic, and found my guest house, same room as last time, my box awaited. Legs ached, forearms were burned, body felt like it'd been punished. Days like those I was so glad I travelled alone. I couldn't imagine many would have put up with such a sporadic day: a high-speed start, a 40-kilometre ride in the back of a pickup (which probably wouldn't even have stopped if I weren't solo), and a brutal finish completing 146 kilometres of cycling. My leg had held up, I was recovering. Lying on the bed I had left six days ago, I had no doubt I had made the right decision to leave. OK, I hadn't met any amazing people, seen unforgettable scenery or had any life-changing experiences. In fact, the brief exchange with the Irish cyclist was all that would probably stick with me. But, ultimately, this circuit had assured me with absolute certainty that I didn't want to ever go back to Laos. Everyone and their friends were heading there, even the Dubliner was. It must have been full, and I didn't want my memories of getting there before the hordes tainted. That well-timed trip of bumbling bewilderment was embedded in a diary from the previous millennium. And in the last pages of my current diary, by the last of the day's light, I entered the stats, which spoke for themselves: a portfolio of personal achievement that no one could take away.

Annoyingly, with every page the cycling book gets better and better, perhaps because I can relate with muscle-aching empathy to the overwhelming multitudes and enchanting interludes. I'm not sure if her account has captured the feeling of India, or simply reading this book mid-trip evokes reflections from the road I took to get here. Either way, I can't compete with this, not yet. I will need another twenty years of travel and five accredited books behind me before I'm able to recount this trip with any credibility.

I take a ginger tea up to the terrace for happy hour. First my neighbour, then the alcoholist, tomorrow it will be me, feels like an ending. The conversation is back to assets and investments. The instigator seems to be the most interested and impressed with his sterling and dollar verbal portfolio. I go back to my hammock, the sea pounds loudly beneath me, now that's a repetitive noise I *will* miss, but I'm looking forward to the next chapter.

I don't think I really got it

It turns out it's Sunday again, what are the chances? So I head for my final performance, a sedate and subdued morning of live Indian music. I have no strength from all that's passed through me and sip an equally weak Earl Grey in palm tree shade darker than my drink. I've got packing on my mind and eviction is imminent. I have to vacate my room and can't relax here knowing my hammock is about to become unhung.

It was Boxing Day – defined by my activity rather than the date – the last day of my Thai trip which, from day one, was always going to be the place where I had launched my Chinese cycling tour from. I mended the previous day's puncture and cycled off to the Thai string and tape shop, stopping for a beef noodle soup en route back to my room to begin the much-anticipated conversion of fridge box to bicycle flight case. The job stopped before it started when a pedal refused to come undone. Left-hand thread or right-hand thread, it was steadfast and stubborn against an unfitting tool. I walked to the 15mm spanner shop and got what I needed. I was glad I had cheated and arrived here last night – as I was under no pressure to get this box just right. I made a pile of things I would be leaving behind: my big fat Thai guidebook; some ripped and holey clothing; and a 17mm spanner. The panniers fit into my *Ghana must go*: the universal check woven bag with a one-time-use zipper that said: 'More contents than quality'.

As the operation came to a close, precision and perception became paramount. Before the box became impenetrable, the Swiss army knife that had shaped it thus far had to be stashed for easy retrieval. Last in, first out. The following day, my bike would be reassembled in China.

Which reminded me – I headed out again and collected my passport with a Chinese visa stamped inside it. I was glad I had remembered that, the last part of the plan, perhaps it should have been higher up the priority list, still, all was done now. And with that, for the first time the excitement and anticipation turned to nervousness. Nothing more to think about other than getting this big box and all my luggage onto the plane. I needed a distraction and headed for the book exchange. There are certain Asian countries that have obligatory reading for the traveller. Thailand: *The Beach*. India: *City of Joy*. Cambodia: *The Killing Fields*. Mongolia: *In Search of Greener Grass*. And for China it's not a little red book but a big green one: *Wild Swans*. About three generations of women, it's big, heavy and enlightening. I added it to my load happily.

I'd gone completely over budget, and it wasn't from what tempted most tourists here to blow their wad on. Not the jungle trekking, the cookery courses, the sex industry, it wasn't even public transport. I had just eaten a lot, I had lived for food, from dawn to dusk I had stuffed my mouth. I had burned it all off, I wasn't gaining weight, but my running costs were crippling me. I supposed I could cut down on the drinking and, for all the tea in China, I decided to try. That night, however, there was a party in my guest house, although it was not to celebrate my triumphant return, nor to wish me well on the next leg. I was invited, and it had probably been a case of *ask him to come so he doesn't complain about the noise*. Perhaps my 10 a.m. drinking the week before had given them the wrong impression of me. I sat at a table of twenty. It turned out they had whiskey and my glass did runneth over beyond necessity. It was hard to get the liquid to a level where I could leave it and politely say goodnight. One has to have an air of responsibility and decorum. After all, I did have a flight to China in the morning.

Packed up, vacated and back on the balcony above, where I began my sabbatical from the bicycle seventeen days ago. I've watched the tide, moon and sun rise and fall, and the number of tourists swell and engulf the beach. I think for the regular winter Western disciples who return to this place every year, the beach is merely a by-product. For the select few there is community here, under the skin, beneath the surface. It's exclusive but somewhat diluted. There are tourists with other traits too, the Israelis and middle-class Indians, the Russians are coming too with new money, travellers with their own attributes. But at the hub, perhaps before the minions arrived en masse, there was a hardcore elite who shaped this place into a retreat with unwritten rules and observed diplomacy. I didn't get it, wasn't part of it, didn't really want to be. I feel a bit sorry for the soul survivors who saw this place sell out, but who stay anyway to try and sustain the gentle vibrations that brought them together, back before internet interrupted and bass pounded all night.

I drag out my day much like those who live here long-term, searching the last of the unturned stones. I want to leave with a little more information, and instigate a conversation with the mother of the Brighton family who homeschools her kids. Based on their intellect and general knowledge she appears to do a good job. She may have the antidote to Sofia's insatiable need to procreate, and mine to be free of the confines of catchment areas and trips dictated by terms. Homeschooling is the only compromise I can see that has a hope of keeping us together. I listen to her schedule and syllabus, it's all there, of course, online, log in and learn, *but what is this internet you speak of?* Apparently, there are even accredited courses for the nomadic progenies, get the academic qualifications via the computer and a worldview first-hand, gonzo education. It gives me hope, not so much for the kids without union or uniform but that Sofia might settle for this. Something beyond the pilgrimage to Mothercare and 4x4 kerb-mounting school runs, the school of life is accessible worldwide without restrictions.

The party of Brits has swelled to dominating proportions now, over twenty of them round the table at the pizza restaurant, where the service is shite and the beer is warm. Goodbyes are swift, easy and genuine. Enough! I've seen enough, I've been here long enough, I've waited long enough. I put on my panniers and push my bike along the dark cliff path, past the locked-up shacks of hippy shit, baggy trousers, tie-dye shirts, fragrant air, the taste of dirt. Leftover Hindu gods souvenirs, dust-coated carved chillums and dented stash tins. I have no embroidered bag to carry as I bought no keepsakes and have no need for henna tattoos. My ink is permanent, my status impermanent, and this will be the last journey with my excess baggage. Too much on my mind to take it all in, too much on my bike to get it in the taxi. It hangs out the boot, I hang out the window. Paths become roads, the transient reappears, horns sound, cows stand on blind corners, the unknown is everywhere again. I'm back in India, it hasn't changed a bit.

I'm confused, oh wait, I might not be

Down to the train station at midnight, I'm four and a half hours early and the train is an hour late. It's only time and it doesn't really matter. The tiled floor of the tiny terminal is covered with snoring Indians, lying under blankets, the obligatory *Ghana must go* bags by their sides. But this trip I don't have luggage to match, I'm not blending in, which is perhaps why I'm instantly befriended by a Kashmiri. His company is so intense I'm wondering if deliberate distractions are afoot to part me from my excessive luggage. Perhaps I'm being overcautious but his over-courteous companionship refuses to let me sleep. This in turn attracts the attention of the station attendant who apprehends me saying, 'No bicycles,' which is a worry to keep me awake. It's explained to me that it's not the bicycle that's the problem, it's just that the station is too short.

'Right, yes, of course,' I say. How did I get myself into this situation? *I've not been here fifteen minutes, what are you talking about?* Typically, I'm not getting it, there is no logic in the explanation, not at first, not to my Western mind, but actually it all makes perfect sense. This is a substation, a short stop, and the luggage car being at the end of the train will not be accessible. The guardsman will not be expecting anybody's belongings and no amount of paperwork or baksheesh will pre-alert him or change this fact. I will have to take the bike to my bunk. Bugger. Of course there are options, I could get a taxi to a longer station …

'But my taxi has left.'

'Then why don't you cycle, sir?'

I could, I suppose, but in the middle of the night, with no lights, no map, no clue, the only sure way of finding a longer station would be to ride along the railway tracks. I take matters into my own hands and strip the bike, putting it into its carry bag. Happy now to have this option, it's mostly a pain in the area I sit on but, there being a distinct lack of discarded fridge boxes about, I'm damn pleased that the disproportionately heavy bag I've dragged this far is becoming worth its weight.

With the dismantling done, the bike disguised as just luggage that's oversized, protocol is met, and I try to get some sleep. It's probably about 2 a.m. when I take my place for a night on the tiles. Ants crawl on my moist, exposed skin, there is an omnipresent vibration of snoring and police prowl with guns and heavy boots that come close to my covered head and open eyes. I get a text from a coked-up mate in the UK, he's full of chemical-induced Christmas sentiment. I can't begin to explain my current predicament in 160 characters. It reminds me of a quote from John Cooper Clarke: 'To convey one's mood in seventeen syllables is very diffic.'

A resonating bing is followed by an amplified unintelligible announcement, which I interpret as 'Hey hey, rise up' because the assembled congregation pick up their beds and move to the platform. I find a bench to continue my dozing, now getting bitten by outside insects. My head is rested on my bike bag, to prevent theft more than for comfort. I notice a praying mantis perched on the handle. *Say a little prayer for me, I really don't want to be refused boarding with all this baggage.*

You could get on a train without a ticket but you wouldn't stay on it for long. Everyone has an allotted seat and the ticket collector will get ya if you try for a free ride. This is the way it works, and everybody knows, so no one tries it on. Why then, the need to push and bundle when the train arrives? Another facet to the India psyche that is beyond logic, and when you have a bicycle in a bag along with your other luggage, being shoved up the aisle is more than an irritation. Proving once again that when you are not riding it a bicycle goes from a physical to metaphorical pain in the arse. When I do pant and push my way to my assigned bunk I find someone is sleeping in my bed.

'Oi, Goldilocks, get up and get out of me bunk.' I have not the slightest remorse at waking the intruder. I paid for this place, I waited two weeks, fuck, I've been waiting since I left to get this train to meet me bird. I'm looking forward to sharing a bed but not this bed and not with him. He offers no resistance, knew he was taking the piss, knew his hours were numbered, just didn't know at what station and what time the rightful renter of the space he's horizontally occupied would come and claim it.

There is no option but to leave the bike on the floor, encroaching into the stampede zone, and undefined in its carry bag there are trample possibilities. Although its allure not being on display makes it less stealable.

Last time I was in India I perfected the second-class-sleeper sleeping poise. Zigzagged around my backpack, head on my daypack, covered by a sarong, tamper-proof, self-contained and concealed. I always opted for the top bunk. You can stay there all day. The middle bunk becomes a backrest when the bottom bunk becomes a bench seat, designed to accommodate one sleeping or three of you sitting upright during waking hours. However, in reality, you generally have double the number sharing your seat and you will never see an empty space where their assigned seat actually is. Yet another anomaly beyond logic. It's like asking, 'What did you do with the dirt you dug out for the tunnel?' And the answer: 'Dug another hole and buried it.' Overcrowded is the only way to travel, overloaded is the only baggage deemed worthy of taking, and oversleeping is never an option. The train may rock you into a slumber, but the permanent parade of passers-by will take away any but the deepest of sleep. I squeeze onto my bunk awake and alert, uneasy at the vulnerability of my bike. In the morning I'm going to have to fix this. Actually, it's already 6 a.m. And sure enough it starts to get light.

Indian Railways is one of the world's largest employers. In fact, Indian railways has just got online, the journey to booking a ticket is a round trip, round in circles, as you need to give your booking number to access the checkout and that information is unavailable until you pay. Consequently, we all clutch on to our station-issue tickets with their perforated edges, that not only state our seat number but name, age, sex and, of course, destination. The same details are also printed out and pasted on the side of the carriage you occupy, presumably to easily identify your allotted place. Making trains the least preferred method of undercover transit, probably not favoured by those escaping an arranged marriage or other forces of entrapment. With your name plastered on the side of the train it is not what you'd call anonymous travel.

Natives book up to three months in advance, making any journey quite the celebration and momentous event, therefore much mirth and merriment ensues for the entire journey. The waiter comes round and I place my breakfast order, now accepting that this is morning and there will no more attempts at sleeping, not that I have anywhere to sit other than up here on my bunk. Head inches away from a filthy fan that blows nothing worth breathing, offers no cooling but subtly and evenly coats you in every passing particle. It's going to be a long forty hours. I eat my omelette sandwich and drink my chai bent double on my bunk and so my food, like me, is also stuck mid-transit. We may reach our destination together.

With the light it's revealed I'm not the only foreigner on board. On the bunk below me is Shane, a Spaniard from Australia or perhaps it is the other way round – anyway, we make friends and make the bunks into a seat that we share with three other Indians, where do they come from? Now though I can stash my bike up above and out of reach of clumsy feet. Outside, the land is hot and arid. Emaciated buffalos attempt to plough the hardened soil and sun-bleached hills shimmer in the distorted distance. However I was to pass through it, bike or bunk, there was always going to be discomfort. The day gets hotter, the air thicker, the fans do little more than rattle. Food, hawkers, stations and stops define the time of day, and tunnels mean grabbing the handle of my bag so an opportunist can't steal it away in the darkness.

The Indian whose ticket entitles him to the bottom bed decides he wants to sleep, so we have no option but to return to our bunks. I'm squashed between the chains that support the bed and the grill that divides me from my neighbour. Up here I can feel the heat radiating through the roof. I'm above the open window and there is no air at all. In such predicaments I find solace in considering how much worse it could be. I have food and free will, I may be restricted and confined but it's my choice. I'm not incarcerated in a foreign prison, not entrapped, not being transported to a gulag or internment camp. It may sound morbid but it always works for me, and I feel better for knowing that, to some degree, I'm livin' the dream. I write my diary, it's a source of great interest and dark eyes are upon me, is it because I'm left-handed? I don't wipe my arse with this hand I hold my pen with, you know, I'm creative, I'm alternative, I'm inventive, I'm hygienic, I've adapted, I'll be famous one day but no one wants to shake my hand, which is fine, I'll fold my chapatti with it later.

Out of habit I hang out at happy hour – that is, I stand by the door to watch the sunset, no cocktails tonight, but the evening does seem to make my fellow passengers more convivial, perhaps it's the cooling temperature that instigates the chatter. A schoolteacher is taking a few select students on a field trip, he's got an air of authority and is equally proud to be able to converse with the foreigner in front of his pupils. Later he dozes off and snores so loud we all roll our eyes and laugh out loud at his expense. I imagine this won't be so amusing when the sound and vibrations of this characteristic echo through the night, keeping sleep the other side of my irritation. For now though he's doing us a massive favour as we are bonding over this and that makes the cramped conditions much more tolerable.

I left the gathering but the sound of festivities followed me.

'Pa-ree lar long time, all nigh', karaoke sing, really fucki' noyin'.'

'Righ', that' it, I goin', piss me off.'

There was no way, no amount of whiskey, not for all the tea in China would I be getting any sleep. Until, that is, it occurred to me I could utilise the metre-wide balcony at the back of my room. So I unpacked the *Ghana must go* and unrolled my sleeping bag, taking both pillows from the bed to sandwich my head. Thais outside murdered Kylie, mercilessly strangling her with a screeching feral cat. Even with distance and padding pushed against my ears I couldn't get it out of my head. It was too hot to be inside the sleeping bag and there were too many mozzies outside to lie on top. So back to the bag and I unpacked my mozzie net, which was strategically placed right at the bottom, hanging it with some packing string and taping it to the tiles with convenient leftovers from my box-making. I settled down, Sellotaped inside and thinking, *If I'd have paid as much attention to this operation as the bicycle packaging, I would have had a wee before I sealed myself in.*

'Righ', that' it, I no goin' now, no piss off.'

The day dawned on me. The cat had been suffocated, the karaoke terminated, the mozzies gone back to their stagnant water tank. Invited I was, so I hadn't complained about the noise – still, I tore off a strip of tape and got out of my makeshift shelter. Strong desires, weak stomach, light sleeper – the first keeps me travelling, the other two traits would be best left at home. I had a shower, I was so brown but only in certain places, you could tell I was a cyclist – well, you could when I was naked, it wasn't what you'd have called an even tan. I had a creative moment and wrote 自行车, the Chinese word for bicycle, on the box. Typically, two Aussie girls moved in next door just as I was leaving, I should be so lucky, g'day and goodbye. Unless they could read Chinese they would never have known I was a cyclist.

It was a short tuk-tuk ride to a very small airport, where I hoped the runway would be long enough to let me take my bike on board. There was a very long check-in line, which I naturally assumed was mine, but it was going to Laos, everyone was going to Laos, not me, been there, done that and literally had the T-shirt. I was going to the check-in less travelled where they didn't bat an eye at my excess, or notice I was hovering my foot under the box as it overhung the weighing belt. *I early, I wait long time*, so I treated myself to a Toblerone, justified by the useful duty-free bag it came in. The bag was what I would use to conceal the pillow pinched from the plane. I wasn't sure it would be any more comfortable than the Qatar Airways one I'd got on the way to Bangkok, but this was Thai Airways livery and therefore purple, which I much preferred.

It was a short flight over very mountainous terrain. Again, I was glad I wasn't cycling it. I looked eagerly out of the window as we came into land seeing the city-defining Dian Lake and then the endless high-rises. The place had a joyless look, no pride, just function, and they drove on the other side.

As I left the plane, it was instantly evident I wouldn't be missing the shorts I had thrown out the day before. Kunming was over a mile above sea level and, it seemed, closer to winter. Immigration was a short queue and a quick stamp, my bike was revolving on the carousel. Customs laughed at my attempt to write *bicycle* on the box: a label that may have been best avoided. The box clearly no longer contained a fridge. I had only studied the spoken language, not the characters, I remained illiterate and what I had written could have been very wrong – even if it wasn't, sometimes words have two meanings.

Welcome to China, no one said in any language, nor was it written in a way I could read. It felt like the most foreign place I'd ever been. The only similarities being that I was besieged by touts and taxi drivers as I exited the airport. I was, though, able to confidentially ask how much to my chosen hotel. He said 40, I said 30, he said no, I said OK. *Another ruthless bit of negotiating*, I thought to myself.

I had a wide-eyed smile on my face as we drove through the city. So many bicycles and appalling driving habits. Typically, the taxi took me to a different hotel and I had to assert myself, saying it was imperative we went to my requested lodging as I was meeting friends there: an arrival phrase that has worked the world over, as prevention from being coerced into the driver's commissioned accommodation. I felt quite chuffed with myself conveying this in Chinese. He took me to my requested place; it was very expensive and that was when I realised the first place he'd taken me to was in fact where I had asked to go. Their names were very similar, my guidebook was clear, as was now my inability to read what I could speak. Now I was defenceless, having revealed my tenuous grasp of the language. It had not helped me, the passenger had become prey, and the fare I'd failed to negotiate had gone up with this wild swan chase. Great start. I just sat there feeling stupid, keen to pay up and get out of the cab of confusion.

I took my baggage up five flights of stairs into the so-called hotel, it was not like anywhere I'd ever stayed before. It had concrete communist misery, no refinements and was barely functional. No reception, only regulation. A very fat, bolshy woman sat at a table on the landing, like a jailer jangling her keys she walked me down the corridor to my room, unlocked the door for me, and left, keeping the key.

The room looked OK: high ceiling, whiteish walls and light coming in from a large window by the single bed. There was a TV on the wall and chairs … err, on the floor. The room was bigger than it needed to be and didn't have an en suite toilet or even a basin. But the most noticeable thing in the room was the temperature. It was frigid. However, there was a blanket folded at the foot of the bed. As I completed my 360-degree assessment and near-freezing estimate, I noticed on the inside of my door someone had written in English: *There are cockroaches in here.* And underneath someone else had added: *and bed bugs too.*

This was my first impression of China, unless you counted the taxi ride and I really didn't want to put that expensive experience into the equation. I felt very alone, somewhat captive, unsure what to do. I needed something to focus on and decided to unpack my travel companion. The activity would warm me up, assembly would remind me why I was here, and being let out of the bag would cheer the place up a bit. I greased and oiled everything as I went, reassured to see it had travelled without incident, I'd made a good flight case. Then I unpacked my *Ghana must go,* sorting everything out methodically. The whole process didn't take as long as I'd wanted but well-being, if not flourishing, was at least germinating. It was 6 p.m. and still light, so I decided to go out and get a second impression of China before the first one embedded itself.

The door slammed shut behind me, committing me to continue. First I found the toilet across the corridor, there was a sign above the urinal for a pizza place and that seemed like a good place to head for. No point in getting a Chinese delivered. I was glad to have my fleece and trainers with me now, despite my seemingly excessive load, all I'd carried with me from Bangkok had been used, right now I wished I still had some whiskey.

Out on the streets, I was instantly enamoured, in awe. It had been one thing to view it from the taxi but here I was immersed, though not over my head. It felt like I'd taken a big pill – and though *this must be how Dutch people feel*: I was taller than everyone. Predictably, I was stared at but not looked down on. This was all very different ... to everything: bicycles with massive wicker panniers overflowed with vegetables, making my load and capacity for food look minuscule. A tricycle was pulled by a donkey. Some people said hello, like I was a stranger in the village square, but this was a vibrant city, the cycle lanes were busier than the streets, where archaic transportation lumbered along with a punctured lung, smoking like death row. The trees were bare and wintery. I took a side street where Chinese lanterns hung across the road and shopfronts were lit by neon lights. For all the visual distraction, I couldn't read one single thing. This was not a typical tourist city, there was no need to display a second language. It didn't feel unfriendly but I did feel uneasy. There were a lot of men in uniforms around, they didn't look like police and were too obvious to be secret police. Perhaps they were just some kind of peacekeeping, all-seeing security. But before I could think *repressed communism*, I saw everybody had the freedom and liberation of a mobile phone, the flip kind hanging from a lanyard around their necks.

There seemed to be a high demand for inner soles or at least hope for a high demand, as someone was selling them on every corner, perhaps emergency insulation for this penetrating cold. There was a definite juxtaposition of red repression and greenback capitalism. I looked in shop windows to gauge prices, a Budweiser was 42 cents, a pair of trainers was $10 and CDs were not much more than a beer. That couldn't be right. I had done the same in Buenos Aires: beer and shoes are my Rosetta Stone, and from those commodities I can define the value of everything else. People, lots and lots of people, like it was a republic dedicated to them, they were everywhere, presumably shut up and condensed in the high-rises, but also spilling out into the streets, most on bicycles, many walking, high-capacity crammed into buses, a few driving and a fair amount just standing around reading newspapers pinned to communal noticeboards.

I was not going unnoticed but nor was I harassed either. Other than the odd pleasantry, I wandered unheeded by all, but not overlooked. Which I supposed was more interaction than I would have got on a Western city street. I mean, I wouldn't bow to a Chinese tourist in London, or anywhere actually. Despite having no whiskey, I was finding it hard to walk in a straight line, my eyes were everywhere, overwhelmed with visual stimulation, the diversity was staggering, the numbers, the signs, the variety of what was carried on a bicycle. Also contrary to popular belief, everyone looked different. OK, I might not have recognised them again the following day, but I couldn't help but be in wonderment of nature's subtleties, a country of over a billion people and certainly in this city it seemed, despite the same colour skin, hair and eyes, they still had such visual individuality. *I bet their fingerprints are all different too*, I thought.

I found the pizza place effortlessly and was welcomed in English … how did they know? I spoke my Chinese too quietly to be heard due to inhibited uncertainty; my learnings went unnoticed. The restaurant was the same temperature as my room. I wondered if this was an unexpected cold snap. The inner-sole sellers suggested so. I scanned the menu: Chinese food was cheap, but there would be plenty of time for that later. I placed my pizza order and a tea – yes, a tea – it was time to put my money where my mouth was, or at least my budget where my beer addiction was. The pizza was massive and I devoured it effortlessly; flight, transition, excitement, cold, all those aspects added to my ferocious appetite. There were a few Western faces in the restaurant but I didn't talk to anyone. I was thinking, forming a plan for the following day. I would cycle to the dorm place for breakfast and see if they had single room accommodation, then to the camping shop. The excursion was bound to help me find my Chinese feet. In fact, just thinking about it made me feel a bit more comfortable with this really quite dramatic transition. There was no familiarity in anything. I hadn't been expecting it to be so cold, like winter. It was a busy city I'd been thrown into, and the hotel was really quite horrid, plus from what I'd read on the door I was itching to leave. Collectively, all these sensations were quite overwhelming.

The bolshy babushka seemed most perturbed that I'd returned and she again had to leave her rickety chair to open my door – which I thought was the only obligation of her employment. I didn't bother pointing out a key strategy that would lighten her workload.

The snoring doesn't stop but the train does and I jump out at a station to get a snack to keep me going until dinner arrives. It's dark now and much cooler, I'm looking forward to climbing into my cramped but padded blue vinyl bed, and patiently await the body language that says it's unanimously agreed we will change backrest to bunks and call it a day. Just before 9 p.m. that time comes. I climb up, wrap myself around my possessions, my hammock becomes a bed sheet and my daypack a pillow. Put in my earplugs, and as they swell in my ears the voices merge with metallic movement and the audible amalgam melts away into the night.

I don't like it up here, I want to go back down

It cools in the night, I put on my socks and the hammock rises from bed sheet to blanket. I assumed we'd pass through Bombay, I've never been there nor to Mumbai as it's called now, the biggest city in India by population. Viewing from a train would be slightly more insightful than a plane but hardly counts as a visit. Still, passing from southern suburbs to the northern outskirts would at the very least give a sense of proportion. But we seemed to have bypassed the place completely, perhaps the driver knew a shortcut. At some point in the night I misread my watch thinking it was 7 a.m. and the night dragged on from there. The light brought no warmth, my feet are really cold, how can it change this much, there's been no comfort zone. We went from sweltering and sheltering from the biting masses, missed room temperature completely, passed through nippy in the night to find penetrating cold light. I order a chai from my bunk, and a long-dormant nicotine craving stirs. When my bladder can hold no more I head for the stinking toilet. Seems to be a popular time, and I hadn't allowed for a queue, and certainly not for people pushing in. I'm not putting up with it, I'm bigger, smellier, older, and mostly more assertive, what's more I'm bursting now and anyway it's my turn next. So desperate to enter such a foul environment, it's not through consideration to my fellow waiting passengers that I forgo brushing my teeth, and running water on my hands is a futile act of hygiene that fails as soon as I touch the lock to leave.

The seats have been folded down when I get back and I wrap my hammock around me. Tomorrow Sofia will bring the fleece I left behind six weeks ago ... about thirty-six hours too late. The sun is out but it's not doing anything, breakfast comes, I'm not sure exactly what it is but eat it anyway, rice-based matter, I ascertain. I buy another chai: a very affordable addiction and I can't get enough of it. Along with the constant flow of spicy tea is a parade of beggars and sellers. Never a dull moment, never deterred, the shoe shiners will attempt to polish your sandals, the toy sellers will tempt the single to procreate, and ice cream? You must be joking. Limp bodies crawl, bony fingers poke and open hands plead, it's best to avoid the aisle seat. I get out at a station to stretch a little, a platform omelette maker entrances me, I don't notice the carriages pulling away. Shane, my buddy on the train, the Australian Spaniard, does, and calls to me. I grab my order and run to the moving door, now feeling obliged to share my food with him. He left Spain at the age of two to live with his granny in Melbourne, when he was seventeen she died, now he has no one. I would have given him some of my omelette anyway.

My hunger has become insatiable, must be the cold. There's no shortage of people catering to my needs, I munch the journey away and continue to consume copious amounts of chai. As we approach Agra the students strike up and sing loudly, clapping their hands and whistling. I put in my earplugs and look out of the window. Thankfully, they disembark at the hallowed stop, that must have been what all the merriment was about. They are replaced by a subdued family, although after that onslaught anything seems tranquil. I think I get a glimpse of the Taj Mahal after the train leaves the station, I tell myself that's what it is and believe it too, it looks smaller than I remember, but then I am further away. It's not exactly sightseeing, like watching an eclipse on TV, some sights deserve more devotion. Sofia sends me a text, she's at Heathrow, only twenty-eight hours to go, assuming they have a connection and she doesn't spend a week in Sri Lanka like I did – *unlikely*, I think.

The train passes railway-side slums, sagging tarpaulins cover shitty lives, I can see right inside, there appears to be some happiness despite the hopelessness. It's endless, kids play among piles of rubbish, mothers attempt to cook and sweep the dust and shit away. Mile after mile, what does that do to their spirit? You are one person in a line of desperation. Passed by varying wealth from third to first class. What do they dream of, what do they yearn for? Today, perhaps a thermal sari and some sticks to burn. Even if Prince Charming was to ride through, how would he spot you, what's your individuality, your personal talent? These single mothers, widows, runaways, drunks, disabled, dysfunctional, their stories surely differ but from here their lives all look hopelessly homogenised and inescapable. What difference would a donation make, would a wagging tail change anything? Even if these people condition their outlook to seek pleasure in the little things there still isn't enough to go round, this homeless poverty has no bounds. The man who has occupied the seat opposite me may perhaps have seen me fall into this despairing train of thought and engages me in chatter to get me back on track. He's from Hyderabad, says he works in IT. He's ahead of the game in his chosen field and won't be living like they do outside. The stops become more frequent than the movement, it appears even the train tracks are gridlocked as we approach the capital. However, our arrival is still earlier than I expected. That Bombay bypass was a bonus, we crawl into Delhi at 5 p.m.

I wait until most have disembarked but that doesn't work, the train is filling up again. When is there ever a chance to clean them, let alone do maintenance? It explains the state of the toilets. I fight through the crowds on the platform, up the steps, over the bridge. I then descend into the stagnant, piss-stinking, dusty lot of rickshaws and taxis. I happily pay for chauffeur-driven sanctuary – well, if not happily, at least with desperate need. He takes me to 'his' hotel. Jesus Christ, it makes the train look salubrious, and I've been contaminated to the point of impregnation on my thirty-six-hour journey. The room has no toilet, the walls are putrid, flaking, decomposing, a tumour of a bed and a festering blanket, but it is available, I won't be homeless, although those slums today had more pride in them than this shithole. I'll not be bathing yet.

Shitty accommodation on the first night in a big city seemed to be compulsory for me. It had happened when I arrived in Bangkok and now again here in Kunming.

I had two choices, as we generally do in life. Last night's had been: when I wanted a wee, I could either leave the door jammed ajar and take my valuables with me, or I could let it slam shut, which meant waking the warden to let me back in. Their system seemed dicking-refucules to me and was arse backwards, but it probably made sense to the Chinese, more so than the English do to them, a nationality who pay to go to a public school or park cars on driveways.

Equally unclear was the view from my bedside window this morning, it turned out to be condensation. As I readjusted my body to wipe away a night's liquified breathing, my next breath was taken away. A rat jumped out from under my blanket and escaped under the door with its written warning of cockroaches and bedbugs. It was a short and quiet scream, more a gasp. Again, I had two choices, and it was at this point I decided to exceed my daily budget and move to another hotel, spend a little more, get a little more, share the bed with a little less.

I turned on the TV, because I could, because I had one. On the single-channel state TV station it was revealed I wasn't the only one under a blanket. Most of the country, it seemed, was deep under snow, only this province of Yunnan was spared the freezing coverage. Ice storms had brought down power lines, and airports appeared to be closed, judging solely by the imagery. I assumed this was the news, not the history channel. With altitude and latitude the days had cooled as I had approached northern Thailand, but my hour-long flight had taken me close to freezing.

There was not a hint of anything hot in the hotel either, not in the form of food or tea, so I took my bike down the five floors to the street and, although it was not quite in keeping with the ritual I had visualised, I took my first bicycle ride in China. The cycle lanes were not, as is the case in Colchester, some sporadically coloured asphalt allotted to pedal pushers when it wasn't deemed inconvenient to more prevalent traffic. Here, the bicycle was king. We had our own road signs, traffic lights, and probably fines too, because we were the prevalent traffic. Everyone was cycling, they even had little number plates of identity hanging under the saddles. I joined the throng and instantly felt like I belonged – well, to a degree. There was safety in numbers and between the barriers of cycle lanes. Now all I had to do was navigate. Predictably, every other rider knew exactly where they were going so my apprehension was somewhat frustrating to the destination-driven cyclists. With numb fingers I found my way to a place that sounded quite appealing in the guidebook, possibly too appealing as it had been taken away, it was gone, only a broken sign on the wall dispersed any doubt that this was the place that once had been. Which only left me with one more choice: the other hotel the taxi had taken me to yesterday. I tried to get some noodle soup en route but failed. The Camellia Hotel was multi-star luxury but had a distant annex for people like me, it was over double the $5 I was paying for my rat, cockroach and bedbug infested room, and what did I get for that extra money apart from less company? Well, there was a breakfast buffet, I was told. Excellent, sold, for an extra $1, oh come on. Could I try it now? No, it was finished.

I wasn't having much luck in China. I asked to see a room and got to stand outside a closed door. While considering how lucky it was that I had bothered to learn the language, eventually it was opened for me. Yep, TV, toilet, bath, telephone and even a toothbrush. *Great, lovely, very nice, I'll take it.*

I met a Dutch cyclist as I was leaving the premises. He seemed like good company, as Dutch generally are. Things looked up briefly, better accommodation, interaction, and then on my third attempt to feed myself I managed to order chicken noodle soup. But it didn't come with a spoon, and the bones came without meat, catering for the vegetarian, I assumed. Slurping from a tilted bowl seemed to be the favoured way to consume the consommé, cutlery notwithstanding I made no bones about it.

So fed up, or perhaps watered down, it was hard to say, I sped back to my rat-infested hole, now sure of my direction. Up the stairs, pack in record time, check the panniers for stowaways, and get the fuck out, too hastily to add my vermin warning to the door of parasites. Then I took my first fully loaded ride in China. After a morning of good decisions another first occurred: the sun decided to shine, and everything brightened and warmed up. I felt so much better. The country didn't seem so bad from this new room. I felt myself unfurl, straighten and with that I decided a walk was in order. A slower pace, I wasn't ready for the speed of a bicycle, there was still too much to take in and I needed to do shopping. I bought gloves and a fleece, and was given a free local guidebook. It was full of enticing pictures, there was so much to see in this province alone. Another wave of well-being washed over me, I felt excitement levels rising, once again remembering why I had come, and my luxurious new room lost its appeal over the open road. I walked on to a bike shop. A man branded in

Mountain Hardwear clothing spoke excellent English, and I was shown that the shop was well stocked and the prices affordable. Accessorising could be coming, like the bike wasn't heavy enough. I wasn't quite sure of his association with the shop, turned out I'd assumed his nationality wrong too – he was a China-assigned Japanese expat and cycling enthusiast who hung here when he wasn't doing his important export work. Everything, he said, was available in this city, from outdoor clothing to performance cycle parts. It was all so tempting.

These little successes in finding, affording and communicating gave me confidence to enter a street café for lunch. As I sat at my table wondering if I should order at the counter, a man came in with a dog, a dead dog, it was skinned and gutted, he wanted to weigh it, it had a brown colour like it'd already been cooked, even the Chinese customers seemed perturbed, I wasn't sure if it was the meat or method or preparation, perhaps they were frowning that it wasn't sautéed with rat wine. The Japanese expat had been right: everything was available here, though I found not always easy to purchase. I saw a department store promoting a sale with balloons and enticing discounts. The invite ended inside the windowless void, there were more staff than customers, uniformed girls, shop assistants by name, but not a single shit was given by any one of them. Surely, a state-appointed position, some kind of how-to-avoid-work-experience, they were too lazy to lift an eye, too bored to bother. The store had all the apathy of a compulsory school disco, the enthusiasm of a wet playtime. Still, three of them left their stupor to take money, fold and bag my long underwear and Smartwool socks. It was a painful purchase, not for the usual financial reasons but for the effort involved in stirring the long-term listless to life. However, now stocked up, perhaps finding the power to revive was good practice for the cold mountain miles to come.

I'd had more than enough new experiences for the day, and returned to the pizza place for dinner, for familiarity, for pizza. The previous night, as I had dined I had formed a plan and tonight I formed a new philosophy. I was asked what I would like to watch by the Dutch owner. At my request, he put on a live Pink Floyd DVD and I totally forgot where I was. I was at that gig ... now I was here ... what if, in the future, I was watching a DVD of southern China and I had to say, yeah I was there, but couldn't afford to see that sight …

Fuck the expense, I would not rough it, I would not be cold, I would not live on a budget below comfort. I still had some savings accumulating for the next trip, what about this trip? I was here now, and anything could happen to prevent me coming again. So I would enjoy China and all it had to offer, not depriving myself, I would live for now, the future was uncertain, especially considering the three road accidents I had seen today. I was 37, I'd earned this, and with that realisation another wave of excitement washed over me – or it might have been the beer, bugger drinking tea.

I hit the streets and find the posh hotel I've booked for tomorrow, it's nothing special, they probably say the same about me. And to think I paid extra for a rooftop swimming pool – ice rink, more like. I walk to the bazaar where I'm hassled constantly, it's hardcore, relentless, and I've tanned, not that you can see it beneath the filth of transit and I'm wearing most of my wardrobe. How will the pale newcomers fare if I get this much attention? The streets are dark, cold and noisy, I recall some of this area from six years ago, but don't see the high-density, drug-and-cockroach-rampant-roomed guest house where the surreal and erotic occurred. Probably pulled down and replaced by an internet café. There was no such thing then, only *poste restante*. Now there is demand, and a high-speed supply. It's cheap, fast, and subterranean, I've never seen so many computers, they generate a lot of heat and I stay there longer than my inbox requires. I'm fed but still hungry, warmed but still uncomfortable, arrived but can't shed my veil of transit. I have a place to stay but still feel homeless. The streets don't welcome nor do they encourage me to go back to that repugnant little room, although somehow those rancid four walls still incite a homing instinct. I brush my teeth for the first time in forty-eight hours. I haven't sat on a toilet in eighty hours what with having a dose before I left Goa, and I don't want to squat over this one either. No hot running water but I can order a bucket if I like. I'm unshaven, my hair is stiff and body wretched, I think a bucket of hot water is beyond the pale. I need a soaking, submerging, lucky Sofia isn't arriving tonight, I've got a lot of preparation to do. I'm fully clothed and under three blankets which undoubtedly were not washed after the last guest, perhaps not even the first. My head is covered, I shiver myself to sleep but the chill has me leaving my room for the place of communal contamination deemed a toilet, but only once, after that I use my water bottle until it's full. Completely and utterly filthy and woeful, there was more hygiene in the train toilet, more dignity in rail-side slums than this hovel of a hotel.

Turn the 'M' upside-down, 'Me' becomes 'We'

I generally associate cold with cleanliness, a fridge for freshness, freezer for solid preservation, snow is pure, crisp, white, pristine. The Arctic uncontaminated, unpopulated.

Heat on the other hand generates life, growth, culture, sweat, inflammation, parasitic germination, infection, festering pustular excretion.

So what I have here is the worst of both worlds. It's cold beyond comfort but there is no purity in this cryogenic chamber of contamination. The bottle is full, so is my bladder. I'm not going to request a bucket, I've now reached a comfortable phase of my degeneration, nothing now can rub off on me, I am the contaminator, contact will only lessen my load. Talking of which, after ninety hours it comes to pass. All I consumed on the train has finally departed, only to be delayed, stopped in its tracks on the frozen surface of the squat toilet, I depart.

I walk into the surreal, misty streets of the city. It's quiet – well, for India. The cold has hushed the hubbub, muted the audible onslaught. I want to photograph it all but it can't be captured, it's something in the atmosphere, not tangible. It can only be experienced in person, a passive ambience, and consequently I don't take a single picture. I feel like I'm drifting through, no physical contact with person or pavement, a voyeur in the vapour of a million shivering breaths. I'm looking for the other posh hotel, and catch myself in the ultimate vulnerable telltale pose of the backpacker. Standing at a crossroads conspicuously looking down at the *Lonely Planet* in my hand. Except I appear to be a parody; there is no backpack, no sign of susceptibility, no invitation to approach, at least not by the usual suspects. Not wishing to evaporate the haze of this extraordinary morning, a rickshaw driver glides to a halt by my side saying only, 'Hello, Indian helicopter?' Seems like the perfect way to increase the altitude of my levitation so I climb in. We fly round the corner and with a smile he tells me we've arrived. For the price of two cups of chai I disembark and float into the overrated reception of an overhyped guidebook hotel. The price is high but the standard isn't. I hear myself saying for the first time, 'Do you have a better room?' as opposed to my usual 'Do you have a cheaper one?' But they don't. The rickshaw driver is still hovering around outside, offering to take me even higher. 'You want joint, opium, something? I take you there.'

If ever there was a morning, if ever there was a situation, I think to myself.

If ever there was a client, he probably thought, *looking at high-end hotels dressed like a drifter.* But my squalid digs are no opium den, my demeanour doesn't go beneath my skin and, anyway, me bird arrives tonight. I gotta shake off this creeping torpor.

Chai warms me up and stodgy banana porridge brings me back down to earth. Gotta take control of this day. *We send everything anywhere* says a sign on a shutter. I think they mean *anything*, so how much to send a bicycle back to England? I enquire.

'How much you wait?'

'About six weeks, why?'

'No. Kilos.'

'Oh wait, you mean weight. Well, with bags …'

It turns out that for 800 cups of chai they can send it home. I think I'll weight.

I go back to my room and manage to carry everything in one go to my new, supposedly prestigious, accommodation. I dump it panting in the lobby where it is instantly taken from my sight, I'm not comfortable with this, not in the least. I spend every waking and most resting moments protecting my possessions, keeping them in sight of an open eye, in contact with a sleeping body, and under my own lock and key when we are apart. Now to watch it all being removed is unsettling, it is of course being taken to my room – well, *a* room. When I get to the landing I find my bags dumped outside a different door to the one I have the key for. I start to unpack and get a knock. For a tip? Room service? I didn't order this; I'm ordered to move … to an identical room. They don't explain and I don't ask, at this point it's moot anyway. There is no hot water. I'm told to wait.

'How long?'

'Oh, about three.'

'Kilos or grams?'

I really want to wash; this prolonged gratification has reached the point of germinating. They fuck around with the plumbing for three hours until there is no water at all. I'm considering the rooftop pool at this point. I go back to the streets, wandering on in socks and sandals, it's only one level above the local look this morning, of flip-flops and socks. Everyone is huddled in blankets and shawls, shrunken and shivering, under-insulated from this interminable cold. Which gives me the impression this low temperature is a rarity; everyone is as unprepared as I am with my Goan glow.

It seemed, with my new philosophy in place, and placed in adequate accommodation with a clear plan ahead, my worry-free awareness was ready to wander. Free from restraints, my mind left my sleeping body and went far, in fact it went home but left the bike here. I wasn't exactly sure where I was when I awoke; I had to look out of the window to confirm location and then physically touch my bike to make sure the dream was over. My mind was back in my body, my bike in my room, we were all in the same country. Reason recalibrated and after that confusion was cleared up I went and found more.

At the breakfast buffet, there were many unknowns. If it had been all-you-can-recognise as opposed to all-you-can-eat I would have been dining mainly on eggs. Through the window I saw the Dutch guy from yesterday and like a dream I let him get away. I kind of wanted the company, but that rarely ever comes on cue.

I decided to have a practice day and cycle to Dian Lake; I was no more going to cycle round it than I was around China. It had a circumference of over 160 kilometres. But, like the country, I knew I didn't have to do it all, I just wanted to see some sights. So with just one emergency pannier, looking like a day tripper I wheeled the bike outside. Having left most of my long-distance credibility in the room I immediately met a fully loaded Aussie couple on bicycles. They had left the UK two and a half years ago and were heading home. They knew the Dubliner I had met in Thailand, but not Ana and Stefan (from whom I had bought the bike) as they were going around the world in the other direction. I suppose the longer you're on the road the more people you meet and your expedition precedes you. Obviously, I knew nothing of this couple but they had quite a following, had a website and everything. 'What, like Yahoo? Wow.' They said there was nothing to see from Dali to here, and for me it would all be an uphill, truck-congested struggle, I'd be better off getting a bus to Lijiang, enabling a freewheeling return. They slept in truck stops, on squalid bunks, it sounded horrid, but I wanted more information and changed the subject to my immediate concerns, physical discomfort. They both had leather Brooks saddles, which had taken a few thousand miles to break in, apparently, but then had memory-foam comfort. I showed mine. If it had ever formed around an arse it was Ana's, lovely though it was, mine bore little resemblance. I mentioned my knee issues. They said it was all down to the seat height, and their website had a formula to work out the sweet spot. But ultimately they said my frame was too small, which wasn't easily rectified. So the length of a Chilean girl's legs and the size of her bum seemed to have been the problem, and with this advice from down under I felt I was abreast of what had been causing my discomfort. I could have stood there and milked them for information all morning but annoyingly they had somewhere to go … Australia probably. But they did recommend a Muslim-owned noodle restaurant and I reciprocated with my pizza parlour suggestion. I tried to appear cool, but inside I was begging for their company a little longer. They assured me all questions were answered on their website and we could even communicate that way. I felt like a bony, pleading finger poking the robust thigh of a hardened cyclist, and website communication was of little consolation as, other than emails, I was not what you'd call internet literate.

I headed south. Cycle lanes ended at the city limits and exhaust fumes hung in the warm, high-altitude air and stung my throat, I considered digging out my Bangkok mask. I was just beginning to doubt my direction when I saw the shore. That alone was an achievement, both yesterday and today I'd found all the places I wanted with my dodgy map. The lakeside catered for pedestrians, had large pavements and benches with viewpoints, with cheap plastic trinkets all made locally. I cycled beyond the tourists to fishing communities which then spread to more commercial premises of concrete and smokestacks. So I crossed a bridge and took a rising road towards the Magnolia Garden, but I seemed to have lost my uphill legs and instead opted for a city view from a comfortable elevation. The sun shone, and it was a pleasant excursion, nothing too thrilling or worth repeating but all the while I was familiarising myself with these surroundings, and that, I reminded myself, was the point of a practice run.

I took a motorway back to the city. It too had a cycle lane and I recognised a junction by description and found the noodle restaurant the Aussies had spoken of. If only they had been there. Sitting on my own at the tiny two-table terrace looking on to the street, I took a moment to zoom out and see beyond my bowl. The row of shopfronts the other side of this cobbled street meant little and attracted less attention. But above the commodities I noticed the construction, it was all wooden, intricate carving and Georgian-style windows. It was all so … I don't know, *authentic*, I suppose, and that was when I was hit by a sudden realisation. Every Chinese restaurant I'd eaten in, the Chinatowns I'd visited, from red lanterns, dumplings to turned-up rooftops, it'd all been replicated. But this was original, real, functioning. I watched native Chinese people pass before my eyes, on bicycle and foot against this backdrop which was genuine China to the bone. And there, in the foreground, on this back street, was my bike. Dream realised. Achievement accomplished. I was sitting eating noodles in China and I had ridden to this restaurant. Now that was a flavour to savour.

Fully fed, still feeling somewhat enamoured and cycling even slower to take in my new level of fulfilment and awareness, I spotted an outdoor clothing shop. I didn't need anything, but Mountain Hardware at down-to-earth prices was a tough temptation to turn my back on. I settled for making a mental note of the location. Back in the safety of the cycle lanes and now more familiar with protocol and orientation, I was able to observe

245

my fellow cyclists. My streamlined bike, forward posture and slick bar gear change had me feeling like a revving Ferrari as we congregated at the lights. It was not that all eyes were on me, a popular pastime for the lady cyclist while delayed at a junction is to pull knitting out of the wicker baskets on their bars and do a few rows as they wait for the lights to change. I was not in a hurry but I couldn't help but beat them to the next red light. Weaving through the network of knitters, I half-expected to be shouted at by uniformed authority. I assumed that when the little old ladies heard the words 'Pull over', they just showed the knitting in their baskets and said: 'No, it's a hat.'

I just couldn't keep their sedate pace. The streets were flat, the surfaces smooth and my cruising speed was simply faster than theirs. I would have felt like a stalker had I followed, so I just had to resign myself to being the arse-in-the-air, wheel-spinning wanker, the butt of their jokes who had them in stiches when they told their yarns.

The date meant little to me, an early night in my lovely room meant more. I had no intention of staying up to see the new year in, and anyway, I knew of nowhere worth doing it. So out of habit I had dinner at the pizza place. Now that I was a regular I was invited to a table with two Dutch, an American 'fugitive', his Chinese wife and an Aussie girl with a Chinese husband. Time passed, food was consumed, alcohol flowed and I was encouraged to go to a bar with them. It was ex-pat packed, absolutely the sort of place I did my hardest to avoid. Too loud to talk, too crowded to sit, too smoky to breathe, and as for prices, well, I was too drunk to notice. Soon enough, I was holding a drink with a sparkler in it and everyone was kissing each other, but missing me. I wouldn't be missed, I sloped off outside. The only other person on the streets was the pizza parlour owner coming in.

Unintentionally, I had made it to midnight, and with full intent I was in China as 2003 rolled in. As celebrations go, this one was more about making it here than seeing in the New Year. I walked back alone down cold, empty foreign streets, reflecting chronologically on previous New Years. Alone and overseas I may have been, but it was so much better than the most recent, when I had been trapped in a Denver basement and a dysfunctional relationship, harbouring resentment and promising myself a better life. Well, that resolution had become a reality. The year before that had also been spent in the US, when the country was compensating for missing the previous one, the big one, the new millennium. The nation had seemed too afraid to celebrate Y2K, but not me, I had been on Copacabana beach partying like it was 1999 as the digits changed to 2000.

The build-up to New Year's Eve, the pressure to do something significant as the clock strikes midnight and wistfully promising to continue to have cause, purpose and significance for the year to come is, regardless of levels of intoxication, really quite unlikely. Tonight's little foray into a bar on the outskirts of some foreign town came with no expectations, no build-up, so no let-down. As the chill sobered me up I realised that the whole of the previous year had been a build-up, filled with the inevitable expectations of getting to China. It was now up to me to make sure there would be no let-downs. It was an awareness worthy of a celebration, a doctrine to take into 2003.

I want champagne for tonight but find whiskey which will warm my innards. Now I've just got to redesign the exterior. The suite now proudly boasts lukewarm water, I can't wait any longer, this will have to do. It's warm enough to mist up the bathroom mirror but that's only because the room is so cold. It's not the steaming power shower I longed for, just warm and wet, like sweat but from an external source. I channel surf and shiver under the bedcover until I dry off. The waiting has escalated to full-blown impatience now. I book a taxi to the airport, I don't recall ever being so excited for a New Year's Eve, ever. Perhaps the millennium, but it's not midnight I'm counting down to, it's 6.30 p.m. and the end of a forty-two day wait. I have a few wee drams of whiskey, it's a necessity to keep me warm while watching Isle of Man TT races on TV. I'm in awe of the unfathomable high-speed road racing, reminding me that motorbikes are where my heart really is. The bicycle may never come back out of its bag. This Indian excursion hasn't done for me what China did. Perhaps I shouldn't have done the second one.

The going is somewhat slower on the streets of Delhi than on telly, a virtual standstill, in fact. There is no way I'll get to the airport on time. I'm reminded of Sofia's last words to me: 'If you're not at the airport to meet me consider yourself dumped.' To which I flippantly replied, 'If I'm not at the airport to meet you, consider *yourself* dumped.' I didn't anticipate this delay and when I get a text to say she's landed I make the ultimate chivalrous gesture, bite the bullet, pay the roaming fees and call her. Her relief comes through the receiver with a force that could puncture an eardrum. I can see the airport from this jam but nothing is moving, except, that is, the meter on the taxi, such a rarity to find one that actually works. A broken meter and no change are two prerequisites of being a taxi driver. The same lights go from red to green and our position stays the same, the streets are jammed, the pavements are thick with people, there is jubilation in the air but a plane on the ground and a passenger waiting alone.

An hour later than anticipated we pull up at arrivals and the fuckers want 50 rupees just to go inside the terminal. A Scot is looking for his lassie and won't cough up the entrance fee either. I see through the glass the only blond hair in the airport, she has her back to the door, damn it, I shout but she doesn't hear, I'm a face outside the window pane. *Here, take your damn entry fee.* I run in, approach from behind, lean over and kiss her, yep that's definitely her, phew.

Instantly, all doubt disappears. The parting had turned to longing, then loss, defeat progressed to acceptance, and that was bordering on indifference. The five stages of separation, my subcontinent coping strategy, brought about by phone calls with delays on the line, emails that didn't ease and texts that intensified the tension. One kiss, one single kiss and all insecurities, all time, all miles, all missed communication evaporates into the empty arrivals hall. And that will be our last public display of affection. I probably should have explained that to her, she expects me to take her by the hand as we head for the taxi, but her backpack is the only thing of hers I will hold in public. This reunification has been so premeditated, although it remains unscripted, and perhaps our emotions are not as expressive as our demonstrative expectations. It's so Bollywood, yet another movie with an unconvincing love scene, censored by protocol and respect for the culture, also the awkwardness of being a little unfamiliar with each other.

The taxi driver gushes apologies but his counting hasn't stopped, mine has though. The waiting is over, the solo journey has reached its destination. Her arrival has also dispelled the hardships of cold, she has brought my fleece, sleeping bag, warm clothes and trainers. Room temperature will not be such a concern, occupancy will be doubled and costs halved.

In other momentous news, this being the last page of my 2003 diary, she has brought me a bigger one. After fifteen years of A6 I've moved up to A5. I can do more with my days, or write about the dullness in greater detail. This is huge, this changes everything, not least the size of font with which I write. It's another step in the direction of becoming a writer, my daily ritual will be richer, less restricted, making for better recall when the time comes to recount. I'm making resolutions in my head, ambition and desire, like, apparently, my palm predicted: a single-minded achiever. Three-hundred and sixty-six empty A5 pages and a year to fill them, the possibilities are endless. If I take control of my days, lead life in my chosen direction, then I'm dictating what will be written, this ain't fiction, every page is a potential reality that's yet to be lived. Tomorrow will be the first day of the rest of my life.

Worryingly, she's not that impressed with the hotel. It's my belated Christmas gift to her. I'm not hurt she is underwhelmed but, *darling, you should see where I've come from, this is luxury and the downgrade begins tomorrow*. She's noticed the cold too; I decide not to mention the rooftop pool.

With three hours until 2004 we head out. The thoroughfares are dark, reverted back to this morning's phantastic misty mysticism. Now clean and insulated from the cold I'm seeing them fresh, and through her eyes. Cows barge through narrow streets with forceful authority, there is a different kind of noise, still the constant horns, two-stroke whingeing but the chatter has a vibrant tone, similar to the excitement of reaching the station of destination, or in this case the arrival of a new year. Regardless of what's instigating this atmosphere, it's in your face, in her face anyway, I may have stopped levitating but I can still rise above the bombardment, although I can see it's freaking her out. We duck into a café and I introduce her to chai, the first of many wonders I want to share. However, the rest can wait, she needs to rest, been transient for too long to count, homeless since before Christmas, living with her sister and young nephews. My last suggestion of the evening is we take a whiskey to the rooftop, not for a swim but to see the New Year in. There are fireworks dimmed by distance and dampness, and a parade of aimless drummers wandering backstreets; typically Indian, what they lack in composition and formation they make up for in enthusiasm and of course volume. But the strangest sight of all is looking down at affluent Indian men in expensive suits dancing aggressively, throwing themselves and money around, wads of notes clutched in their fists are freely but fiercely thrown. They are surrounded by the vagabond vultures who pick up the windfall. It's like a mosh pit of money surrounded by onlookers of insufficiency, all overlooked by us, incredulous and sleep-deprived. This time last year I was in China about to start cycling. I've come a long way, that'll do for this year, for today. On a night like this I can't help but be reflective and thoughtful. It's quite the climax, which begs the question: 'What next?' Will the thrill of desire be replaced with the drudgery of the journey? Six weeks apart followed by the shock treatment of being intensely in each other's company. Will this relationship that's been in suspended animation cool down and preserve, or heat up, burn out, fester and decompose?

End of Book 1

FOR PHOTOS AND A FREE INSTANT
AUDIO BOOK DOWNLOAD GO TO
grahamfield.co.uk

About the author

Photo by
Angelo Angelov @cobcamp

Graham Field was travelling to foreign lands before he was eligible to have his own passport, rode motorbikes before he was old enough to have a licence and has kept a daily diary for over thirty-five years. He was born to tell tales of travel; it just took him a long time to realise it. The first 20 years of his working life were spent behind the wheel of a truck, thinking and not fitting in, then under a sink, fitting kitchens.

One day he decided to ride his motorcycle to Mongolia then told his story. Now the author of six books, he has become a recognised name in certain niche circles and veers away from mainstream potential. His articles have appeared in publications around most of the English-speaking planet, and along with TV, column and podcast residencies, as well as presentations, his face, voice and words have reached the global receptive.

Often outspoken, always opinionated, but rarely offensive, his ridicule is disarmed with a cheeky smile and cogent observations come with a cutting wit. He dabbles in social media where he has a small, but loyal following, some might call him a cult, but not to his face.

In 2015 Graham gave up his native Essex, UK to live in Bulgaria, where he remains misunderstood but this is mainly due to his inadequate, but enthusiastic attempts at speaking the language. Bikes, travel and writing remain constants in his life, along with periods of solitude and introspection. He has an infectious way of sharing life learnt wisdom conceived inside the helmet, found on the road and gifted to him in those precious encounters that have always made travel harder to put down than a half-finished bottle.

A Heartfelt Thank You

This is my list of gratitude, a namecheck to my faithful readers who had the conviction to pre-order this book, based solely upon the content of my previous offerings, knowing nothing more about this one than the title.

This might just look like a list of names and although I may not recognise you in the street every name is familiar to me, from social media posts, from books I've signed, emails I've received, reviews you have written and, of course, website sales. To all of you listed below, don't see this as a shared, diluted and general word of thanks. This is genuine recognition, utter appreciation for your support, without you I would not be writing this.

And to all of you who wished to remain anonymous, your names are written between the lines.

David Prigel
Rob Tibbetts
Daniel Back
Graham Peach
Michael King
Stuart Marshall
Samuel Jameson
Colin Clarke
Christopher Ball
Nigel Grace
Andy Gray
Robert Campbell

Arthur Middleton
Keith Stovin
Craig Winter
Dan Towers
Graham Cotter
Marc Hudson
Mark Noel
Andrew Perhar
Steven Kirk
Jeffrey Westfall
Ryan Woolley
Mike Silvester

Paul Boother
Richard Underdown
James Wert
Damien Murray
Don Nelson
John O'Reilly
Scott Cunliffe
Ernest Lindgren
Mark and Heather Moscrop
Jochen Riehn
Simon Vancliff
Flip Morton
Jamie Shearer
Ian Proudfoot
Maria Schumacher
Angus Morrison
Kieron Roland
Lynne Ashcroft
Nick Alcock
Rick Hersee
Don Gillanders
Bob Godfrey
Michael Bateman
Damien Bove
Deborah Horne
Dan Korolyk
Chrissy Kerss
Andrew Morris
David Coffaro
Stephen Vancliff
Paul Tomkins
Pamela Nixon
Kaylen Richardson
Andy Sadler
Holiday Farmbus

Poppy-Bella Cahill
Tammy Wilson
Paul Ayers
Phil Stocker and Imogen
Stocker
Paul Evans
Daraius Master
Alan Quinby
Graham Pryke
Paul Whitehead
Louis Pace
Nick Lewis
Travis Tranfield
Jocke Selin
David Mason
Jay Knight
Simon Murray
David Pickering
Julie Pickering
Nicki Ratcliffe
David Jones
Nick Laskaris
Jon Havercroft
Paul Crowley
Deb Little
Mark Vilskersts
Dennis de Geus
Rhonda Rice
Ian Napier
Rob Murray
Malcolm Owers
Philip Barwick
Tim Archer
Chris Morgan-Cettler
Alistair McColl

Paul Markham
Paul Boardman
James and Rachel Hutchon
Neil Evans
Stephen McEwen
Chrissie Rudge
Bob Thompson
Rob Osborne
John O Sullivan
Michael Rhodes
David Gallagher
Colin Lindstrom
Kerstin Jesse

Seth Hoyt
Richard Carter
Bill Roughton
Roelof Veldhuis
Pauline Oldacres
Borut Svajker
Philip Doyle
Phil Owen
Simon Barnes
Martin Blizard
Adrian Cromey
Colin Baines

As long as you keep writing your honest reviews,
I'll keep telling my honest tales.
Cheers to you all
See you for part two.
Graham